Vera-Ellen:
The Magic and the Mystery

Vera-Ellen

The Magic
and the Mystery

by David Soren
with Meredith Banasiak and Bob Johnston

With Contributing Writers:
John Bailey, Michael Day, Russ Decker, Bill
Dennington, Terry Dennison, Clark Evans,
Caren Roberts-Frenzel, Rosarie Hartmeyer,
Fred, Mark, Mary and Toddy Maurer

Luminary Press
Baltimore, Maryland

Photo Credits
Guy Farris 8
Bill Dennington 10, 161, 179, 184
Fred Maurer 9, 15, 19, 21, 22, 23, 32, 62, 64, 65, 74, 111, 131, 135, 174, 176, 193, 210
Jo Alexander and Norwood City Schools 18, 20
Bob Johnston 40, 49, 52, 82, 213, 235
Michael Day 73, 74
Dale Stedman 64, 65
Photofest 25, 41, 76, 80, 85, 86, 87, 90, 91, 95, 96, 100, 104, 106, 114, 115, 117, 119, 123, 124, 127, 129, 132, 140, 145, 146, 147, 164, 165, 166, 170, 199, 202, 237
National Screen Service 49-57
20th Century Fox 58-70
Warner Bros./MGM 71-120
Warner Bros. Television 122-129
Allied Artists/A.B. Pathe 162-167
Caren Roberts-Frenze contributed 66 photographs to the book and additional personal memorabilia and stories for which we are most grateful.

ISBN 978-1887664813
Library of Congress Catalog Card Number 2007943780
Manufactured in the United States of America
First Printing by Luminary Press, an imprint of Midnight Marquee, Press, Inc. November 2003
First Paperback edition by Midnight Marquee Press, Inc., January 2008

*Dedicated to the memory of
Vera-Ellen, our favorite
dancing star, with the hope
that she will receive at last
the appreciation and recognition
she so richly deserves*

*She was a real accomplished dancer, that girl.
Ballet, tap dancing, anything you wanted to do.*
—Fred Astaire

Table of Contents

8 Acknowledgments

9 Foreword to the Second Edition

11 Introduction

13 Chapter One: The Kid from Norwood

22 Chapter Two: Growing Up

48 Chapter Three: Toward Hollywood Stardom

77 Chapter Four: MGM Heyday

108 Chapter Five: *The Belle of New York*

122 Chapter Six: Ups and Downs

142 Chapter Seven: Christmas Joy

169 Chapter Eight: The Machine Wears Out

192 Chapter Nine: Anorexia Nervosa

210 Chapter Ten: The Magic Lives On

219 Epilogue

223 Bibliography

227 Radio Credits

229 Television Credits

231 Vera-Ellen Recordings

233 Filmography

243 Vera-Ellen Websites on the Internet

245 About the Author

247 Index

Acknowledgments

This book would not have been possible without the help of many people. First and foremost is our crack research team of Meredith Banasiak and Bob Johnston. Meredith organized one-sixth of the material, conceived several chapters, wrote a preliminary text for them and made a trip to Norwood, Ohio to meet friends of Vera-Ellen and find additional resources. Bob tracked down Vera-Ellen's gravesite, many photos and much information ranging from her will to the locating of Donald O'Connor and her cousin, the late Fred Maurer. Additional assistance was provided by the keeper of one of the few Vera-Ellen websites on the Internet, Angela Boyko. Michael Day and Guy Farris provided information and visuals, and enthusiastic support for the project. On the Norwood home front we thank Jo Alexander of the Norwood City Schools for yearbook information and Katherine Ralstin Murphy for sharing some memories of her lifelong friendship with Vera-Ellen. For Vera-Ellen's Broadway years we thank Jim Schlader. The Margaret Herrick Library provided microfiches and stills.

We are grateful also for the chance to talk to her very close friends A.C. Lyles and Marie Windsor, and her cousin Fred Maurer and his wife Toddy who provided photographs and insight into Vera-Ellen's life. Betty Garrett, MGM star and co-star with Vera-Ellen in two films, and Nick Clooney of *American Movie Classics* also provided recollections. Val Guest, director, producer and screenwriter (he wrote *Happy Go Lovely*), also offered reminiscences. Thanks also to the National Film Information Service, Warner Bros. and agent Phil Gittelman for help with research and stills. Pamela and Rob Stackel, owners of Vera-Ellen and Alma Rohe's Studio City home and Reverend David Palmquist of St. Paul's First Lutheran Church provided additional information. Dr. Nancy Eldredge provided enormous help in studying anorexia and bulimia nervosa. We would also like to thank John Eidswick and the good folks at Casa Video in Tucson for their kind assistance.

Thanks to my wife Noelle whose constant support these 33 years has made my whole life worthwhile. Thanks to my miniature golden retriever Angel without whose constant "assistance" I would have finished this manuscript much more quickly. And finally thank you to Vera-Ellen, whose artistry and genius have inspired me for over 40 years. I am so sorry I couldn't have done this for you sooner.

A.C. Lyles and Vera-Ellen in 1953

Vera-Ellen:

Foreword to the Second Edition

In 1999 when I finished writing this manuscript nobody wanted to publish it. McGraw-Hill reluctantly took it on as an educational paperback and ran off approximately 1,500 copies. I was grateful that they did, even though they left out several small sections of text and wouldn't advertise the book or even list it as one of their stock. Photo permissions were incredibly hard to obtain with costs running enormously high, so that McGraw-Hill ended up losing about $1,000 on the project.

Information about my favorite dancing star had also been hard to come by. I worked for four years aided only by Bob Johnston and my student Meredith Banasiak in trying to track down everything we could find, which wasn't as much as we had hoped. In the first edition, I made a number of errors, mostly due to the fact that the personal recollections of Vera-Ellen's friends weren't always accurate, but sometimes the mistakes were due to my own carelessness.

However the response to the first edition was amazing. We had urged McGraw-Hill to do a bigger print run, but they had never heard of her and didn't want to invest in a marginal project any further. Nonetheless, in no time at all, the book sold out its brief run and started to become a cult work, sometimes selling for over $200 a copy on E-Bay.

And then an even more wonderful thing happened. Vera-philes (i.e., Vera-Ellen fans) began to appear from everywhere on the Internet to offer help once they heard that a book had come out about their favorite star. Vera-Ellen devotees are not ordinary people. They *love* her and they are outraged that the powers in Hollywood did not allow her to leave us a greater body of work. They are equally outraged that critics and film historians, who govern what we read regarding classic films, have almost entirely allowed her to be forgotten. In no time at all I was deluged with a huge amount of new material. It took three years to sort and evaluate the accuracy of all this information and integrate it into the text. The result is the new edition, graciously and lovingly taken on by the wonderful folks at Midnight Marquee Press, Gary and Susan Svehla, my friends for over 35 years.

Vera-Ellen admirer Terry Dennison of Hastings, Michigan has an enormous collection of Vera-Ellen memorabilia including a costume from *The Belle of New York*, wine and bar glasses, a tea set, her red crystal heart, a crystal candelabrum, brass trays and various examples of her film costumes. A fan since 1957, Terry has devoted a siz-

Tiny Vera-Ellen on the left at the Hesslers' Dance Studio in 1934

Vera-Ellen with Bill Dennington in 1966

able portion of his life to making sure that Vera-Ellen's artistic contributions will be appreciated for generations to come. Michael Day has maintained a website devoted to Vera-Ellen and has an extensive collection of paper memorabilia from her career, plus a detailed knowledge of her aviation and military connections which he has shared with us. Bill Dennington was not only a fan but also Vera-Ellen's close friend and confidante in the last years of her life and graciously shared his reminiscences and beautiful photographs for this book; Bill's vast knowledge of Vera-Ellen's private feelings can be found expressed throughout these pages. Russ Decker, another longtime fan, sent us stacks of photocopies covering Vera-Ellen's films. Clark Evans provided meticulous, detailed research of obscure performances and family genealogical details about which, until he unearthed them, we knew nothing. Caren Frenzel, a fan of Vera-Ellen since her teens, has collected memorabilia for years and corresponded intimately with many individuals who were important in Vera-Ellen's life.

Karine Philippot has provided information on Vera-Ellen's voice doubles in almost all of her films, while Dr. John Bailey and Rosarie Hartmeyer analyzed and commented on Vera-Ellen's medical and psychological condition in detail, offering much the same conclusion about her physical and mental health over the years. Jo Dennis, a neighbor of Vera-Ellen's, also received a substantial amount of memorabilia from her family and has been a consultant for the important Michael Day website.

New readers should realize that this is first and foremost a book for her legions of admirers, which was written by a fan with the loving help of her other fans. But we have also tried to tell her difficult life story as objectively and accurately as possible. It is not always a happy story but rather the tale of a complicated life and a legacy of unique artistic achievement.

Vera-Ellen's number one fan Terry Dennison with Vera's star on the Walk of Fame

Vera-Ellen:

Introduction

Vera-Ellen should have been one of Broadway and Hollywood's most enduring stars. She was a fine dramatic and light comedic actress, and was considered by a number of authorities to be the greatest all-around dancer of her generation. And for a brief moment in 1950, she was an American household name, as famous as Babe Ruth, Joe DiMaggio or General Douglas MacArthur. She could do tap, toe dancing, adagio, modern dance (formerly known as dramatic dancing), comic dancing, partnered dancing, prop dancing, Apache dancing and advanced acrobatics. She could also sing well enough to be featured on Broadway and television. Her obsessive perfectionism was legendary; nobody worked harder on a routine or accomplished it with greater attention to detail. Not only were each of her steps perfect but the transitions from step to step were flawless and remarkably beautiful to observe. Like Fred Astaire, who admired her, she had the ability to make each complex routine seem effortless, as if she were expressing herself spontaneously.

She excelled as a soloist but could also perform to perfection with various male partners. She achieved sublime and precise balletic duets with Astaire but also did jaunty tapping or athletic ballets with Gene Kelly, herky-jerky comic dancing with Ray Bolger and surprisingly romantic ballroom dancing with Donald O'Connor. She could handle dramatic roles or breezy musicals with equal ease. She was the girl next door,

the girl you wanted to bring home to mother, even after she received the Hollywood sex and glamour treatment at MGM. Her trademarks were a pencil thin waist (20 inches but at times even as small as 18), shapely legs, perfect posture, a turned-up nose and the sweetest smile in any Hollywood musical.

Most of Hollywood's famous musical film dancers and actresses couldn't equal the dancing talent of Vera-Ellen. Ann Miller was her match as a tap dancer but lacked her balletic grace and gymnastic and partnered dancing skills. Ginger Rogers was a fine partnered dancer but very limited as a solo dancer. Cyd Charisse was a graceful ballerina in solos or alluring and technically superb in jazzy partnered ballets with

A 1949 studio portrait

Astaire and Kelly but she was not a tapper or gymnastic dancer. Eleanor Powell, usually considered the greatest all-around female dancer of the screen, was the only performer whose skills in tap and gymnastics rivaled or, according to some, exceeded those of Vera-Ellen, but even she could not approach Vera-Ellen in balletic skills or overall grace of form. And Powell, a superb and highly individualistic artist, was not skilled as a partnered dancer.

In 1995 Joe Frazzella, in the only significant article to assess Vera-Ellen's work, wrote in *Films in Review*:

> She was unique in Hollywood during the movie musical's golden age. Vera-Ellen could do a precision tap routine as well as Ann Miller or Eleanor Powell; execute *grand jetés* and *tours en l'air* with all the beauty and finesse of Cyd Charisse or Leslie Caron; rip into an intricate jazz combination, conveying a sexuality to rival Gwen Verdon or Mitzi Gaynor; and like Ginger Rogers, discover all the graceful stylistic nuances in the eclecticism of partner dancing. Yes, she could do it all.

Vera-Ellen in a 1954 glamour pose

This then was the magic of Vera-Ellen. And yet, with all her talent, it is astonishing that there is no grand summation of her work and no written biography. This is way past due. It is a shame that she didn't live to see this book and even sadder that her life, which began with so much promise and reached such dazzling heights, was filled with heartbreak and misfortune not of her own making. Much of her story has been a mystery for decades and some of the things disclosed in this book will be a revelation to her family and friends and much may have surprised even her. Many questions about her life cannot be answered and may never be. But the fact that she is one of the unsung geniuses of her profession is incontestable. And her fine character—the fact that she was one of the kindest, sweetest, most considerate, devoutly religious, ethical and moral human beings who ever lived—is revealed in this close look at her life. Toddy Maurer, wife of Vera-Ellen's cousin Fred, recalled the first time she met her:

> Sometimes when you meet someone for the first time you just know instantly that this is a good, kind, wonderful person. That's how she was. She just radiated kindness and it was real.

Vera-Ellen:

Chapter One
The Kid from Norwood

In 1858 Herman Rohe was born in the tiny town of Crete, Illinois just a few miles south of the quickly growing city of Chicago. He lived his uneventful boyhood there, grew up and married his sweetheart Mary, who was one year his junior, and became the local harness maker. Both of their parents were German immigrants. They had three children, the eldest of whom was good-natured and musically inclined Martin Rohe, born October 15, 1882. By the age of 17 the quiet and shy Martin was already employed as a piano tuner and had a younger brother Walther and a sister, 7-year-old Julia.

Julia grew up and married Fred Maurer, then promptly moved to a small town in Minnesota, but the family remained in touch through the years via letters and postcards. Martin stayed for a time in Crete, then suddenly set off on a great adventure. It is not clear what prompted young Martin in his early 20s to leave Crete and the booming Chicago area around 1905 and travel 300 miles away to Cincinnati, but he did. In 1906 Martin became a piano tuner at the Smith and Nixon Piano Manufacturing Company in downtown Cincinnati. There had been a branch of Smith and Nixon's in Chicago, and he might have wanted a change of pace and gotten himself transferred to their Cincinnati factory, but even there he didn't last long.

In 1910 Martin left the firm for unknown reasons and began to work independently as a piano tuner. He married Alma Catherine Westmeier on January 31, 1914 at the First Lutheran Church in Cincinnati. One can only surmise that they might have met when the Westmeiers needed a piano in their parlor tuned. Alma had worked for several years as a stenographer and was living with her widowed mother Elizabeth, who was known as Lizzie. Alma was a tiny woman and Lizzie was even smaller.

If Martin's family background was ordinary, Alma's was equally lower-class but a bit rowdier. Alma was born on November 23, 1890 to Henry and Elizabeth "Lizzie" Westmeier of Cincinnati. Lizzie's maiden name was Kasselmann and she had been born in Hanover, Germany in 1866, migrating to America in 1885 and finally becoming an American citizen in 1895. On her arrival in America Lizzie quickly found work as a dressmaker and took up residence with another German immigrant couple named John and Agnes Westmeier, who most likely had connections to her family in Germany. The residence contained a saloon at which young Lizzie practiced her craft.

John and Agnes Westmeier, the saloon owners, raised six children. The eldest, Henry, dropped out of school by the time he was 12 and soon was helping to run the saloon for his father. Just 5-feet 4-inches tall when fully grown, Henry apparently fell in love with the even more diminutive Lizzie Kasselmann while Lizzie was living with his family, no doubt in a rented room. Henry and Lizzie married when they were in their early 20s, sometime in the later 1880s, and Henry finally found employment as a house painter. Later, Henry, despite having a wife and child to support, enlisted as a private in the Spanish-American War in 1898. The reasons for this are murky, for he was a poor soldier who was found guilty of being "insolent to his commanding officers," "lying out of quarters" (going A.W.O.L), and exhibiting "drunk and disorderly conduct." Perhaps the marriage of Henry and Lizzie had failed and Henry abandoned

Martin Rohe (left) tuning a piano in 1915

his family, but this is mere speculation. In any event, in 1906 he was residing at a boarding house, not with the family. Alma was apparently an only child and the marriage endured at least in name for about 20 years, and Henry died before his 40th birthday—never rising above the bottom rung of the economic ladder. Lizzie's daughter Alma did not have an easy life, and tried hard to make ends meet as a stenographer at age 17. She was no doubt hoping for a better life when she married Martin Rohe. She also needed a place for Lizzie, who stayed with them until her death, the date of which is not precisely known but was after 1934. Her photo album, marked "Lizzie," was one of the prized family keepsakes until the early 1980s.

Martin and Alma Rohe had only one child: Vera-Ellen Westmeier Rohe (it rhymes with go, but was originally pronounced Roy). She was born near, but not quite in, Norwood, Ohio—a small, self-contained old German suburb of Cincinnati that had originally been about seven miles outside the heart of the city. The modest bungalow where she first lived was on 2744 Markbreit Avenue, and it is still standing. In 1924 the family moved to 5715 Carthage Avenue and stayed two years before moving to 2780 Minot Avenue in 1926. It was only one block away from their first home. The Markbreit and Minot homes were just over the border and within the Cincinnati city limits. Although Vera-Ellen always said she was from Norwood, technically she was a native Cincinnatian by about half a block. In 1926 the Rohe family moved once again, this time to 2218 Cathedral Avenue, which Vera-Ellen considered to be her childhood home. She once recalled that Norwood was a place where almost everyone spoke with a Teutonic accent, which was so thick she felt as though she was "as close as you can come to being foreign-born in the United States."

Vera-Ellen:

Though her birth date is usually given as February 16, 1926, Vera-Ellen was actually born on February 16, 1921. When she went to Hollywood at 23, she and her mother decided to shave five years off her age to make her appear a precocious teenage sensation. During her days of Hollywood stardom she always would tell close friends, "My age depends on whoever is talking to me at the time."

Childhood friends attest to the earlier birth year and it is further confirmed by her Norwood High School yearbooks where she (then called Vera Ellen Rohe without the hyphen) is pictured in the ninth and tenth grades in the years 1935 and 1936. This innocent subterfuge was not unusual in Hollywood where ingenues often lied about their age, usually shaving off a year or two so that they could extend their careers as leading ladies. Actress Constance Bennett subtracted a year every few years until she ended up miraculously younger than her little sister Joan.

Vera Ellen Westmeier Rohe, a big name for a tiny girl

Certainly Vera-Ellen could not have been a 10-year-old high school sophomore. Yet her diminutive stature suggests otherwise, for Vera-Ellen did look like a 10-year-old in 1936. It was precisely this quality, her petite and undeveloped frame, that led her to dancing, and which may have ultimately contributed to the serious problems with self-image that she would have as an adult.

Martin and Alma Rohe worried about their frail child, who was a full head shorter than most of her fellow students. They were concerned that she was spending too much of her free time in sedentary pursuits reclusively buried in books. It was felt that she needed exercise to improve her health and change her life, so they proposed a goat's milk diet and dancing lessons to strengthen the tiny nine-year-old. Years later she remembered:

> I was called a bookish child. Mother sent me to a ballet teacher in Cincinnati when I was nine years old. I guess I was an awkward child and the family wanted me to be graceful. When I found out I liked to dance and people seemed to like to watch me, I was determined to go places.

The Magic and the Mystery

15

Vera in 1924

Martin's career, based as it was on the unnecessary luxury of a piano in the house, was hit hard by the Depression and he also had the added support of his mother-in-law Lizzie, who lived with them in the family home. Initially, he paid for his daughter's dance lessons at Eleanor and Harry H. Hessler's Mount Adams Dance Studio at St. Paul's Place by tuning the studio's piano. He was known for being soft spoken and having a particularly sweet smile, which little Vera-Ellen inherited.

As she became more proficient as a dancer, Vera-Ellen became a major provider for her struggling family by dancing before many of the fraternal, charitable and service organizations in Ohio and Kentucky. During an interview later in her life, she recalled her days as the Hesslers' star pupil, but was unable to explain the reasons for her early dancing success:

> I don't remember whether I liked it because I was good at it, or if I was good at it because I liked it. Maybe a little of both. I guess it was being a drum majorette at our Norwood High School football games that really started me dancing.

Her enthusiasm for dance and the attention and praise it earned her spilled over onto those surrounding her. Vera-Ellen was so driven and manic about it that she persuaded her neighbor, Mrs. Cole, to enroll her son Douglas in Vera's ballroom dance class, much to the young boy's dismay, along with another local girl, Doris Kapelhoff, This local girl, who grew up to be Doris Day, the actress, lived in a nearby town. The three youngsters carpooled together to the dance studio. Doris and Vera-Ellen were never particularly close because of their youthful rivalry. They did not keep in touch over the years, despite having so much in common. However, they did remain cordial after each became a success. Doris Day was on her way to becoming a fine dancer but very early in her professional career (a few years after her Hessler Dance Studio days) she was touring in Ohio and her troupe's automobile was struck by a train near Hamilton and dragged down the tacks. She broke her right leg in two places and was incapacitated for 14 months. As her career progressed she did little vigorous dancing until she was called upon to do steps in the 1950 movie *Tea for Two* and then caused a furor with her fine athletic dancing a few years later in *Calamity Jane.*

Vera-Ellen:

As a little girl Vera-Ellen's nickname was Bunny—because she liked to eat lettuce for dinner. Her passion for dance was matched by her pursuit of the highest honors in school. Hessler classmate Douglas Cole later remembered:

> We went through Norwood View Elementary School together. She was the smartest kid in the class. She was the smartest and most talented person who ever attended Norwood View.

Strong ambition and obsessive perfection were Vera-Ellen's character traits right from childhood. She even wrote an autobiography at age 12 revealing her desire for superstardom. The young author did have a problem with her spelling, which she worked hard to improve. She also developed a remarkable flowing and calligraphic handwriting style that is beautiful in its clarity and deliberate precision and its lovely, graceful transitions from letter to letter. This same clarity and attention to graceful transitions would later be evident in her dancing style. Her credo in all things was that if something, anything, was worth doing, it was worth taking the care to do it carefully and right.

Her elementary school music instructor Pearl Ewing recalled Vera-Ellen at age seven:

> As a first grader, she danced up to me and said: "I can do everything the other kids can—and more." The first time I saw her she told me she loved to dance and sing. She was so tiny we had to put her on a special stool.

Before she was out of elementary school she had become the chief majorette of the school band even though she looked more like six than 12. She was a bit pudgy, puffy faced and tiny and her mother put her on a strict dietary regimen to lose weight, one of a seemingly endless number of special diets Alma Rohe adopted for her daughter from the time she was born. These rigid diets would leave Vera-Ellen extremely particular and finicky about food her entire life. Her mother was especially fond of diets such as Dr. J.D. Levine's Iriological Diet and Health Plan as outlined in his 1928 newsletter *The Health Messenger*. The diet called for the strict avoidance of salt, bread, cereals, pasta, grapefruit, lemon and many other items now recognized as quite valuable for good health. Items that could be eaten were generally not very appealing, such as apple cider mixed with honey and cold water, stewed fruit, lima beans

"Bunny" in 1931

cooked until dry and sour milk. Neighbors and friends knew to avoid bringing up the question of health foods or dieting in Alma's presence because she would give frequent unsolicited lectures on her opinions of proper diet and subjects like vegetarianism or the merits of alfalfa tea. Alma was also a stickler for good posture, so it is not surprising that Vera-Ellen's excellent posture became one of her trademarks.

Alma was an extremely slight but seemingly sweet woman who was well liked in the community and generally quiet and soft spoken unless discussing her favorite topic. She was obsessively neat and had a peculiar walk. Pamela Stackel, a California neighbor of Alma's later in her life, described her hurried gait that made her appear as if—

> ...she were wearing roller skates and kind of scooting along even though she wasn't; I never saw anything quite like it... and she was fastidious and neat and seemed to be really regimented about everything she did.

A youthful majorette leads the band at Norwood View elementary circa 1933.

She believed that whenever she did not feel well she should scrub the kitchen floor, but just what the reasoning was behind this nobody was sure.

Alma also had a strong desire to make her own life amount to something and she was becoming increasingly dissatisfied with her husband's lack of ambition, creative energy and success. She therefore began focusing on developing her daughter into someone special.

In high school Vera-Ellen sang in the Choral Club and was featured in the school's popular annual Minstrel Show when she was in the 10th grade. By this time she had slimmed down to an almost emaciated state and, although short, she was adorably cute. She had a turned-up button nose and a sweet smile that melted hearts, especially when she performed. She excelled at the Hesslers' Dance Studio, but soon the Hesslers realized that the dance classes, however wonderful and encouraging, were not enough to sufficiently challenge her. She supplemented her dancing classes by becoming leader and ace baton twirler for her elementary school rhythm band at Norwood View Grammar School on Carthage Ave. Later she became drum majorette for the Norwood View High School 88-piece band and she also took additional dance classes there. Dr. H.J. Bingham, who was a classmate of Vera's, remembers her tap dancing while two male students would dance around her during the half-time show at the

In 1934 Vera is on the right while performing for Hesslers' Dance Studio.

football games of the Norwood Indians. He also remembers a classmate telling him the rumor that Vera's mother wanted to keep her small so she deliberately fed her pink bananas. This story suggests that even at this early date the students realized that there was something strange about Vera-Ellen's relationship with her mother and her diet.

While at Norwood View High School, an admiring classmate gave her a heart-shaped locket that immediately triggered her lifelong fascination with collecting hearts. She had heart bracelets, earrings and necklaces. Hearts were embroidered on her panties, bras, nighties, dresses, gloves and shoes, and they outlined the window frames of her bedroom. So it is not surprising that in her very first screen solo performance, in *Wonder Man* (1945), she wears an outfit decorated with little hearts for good luck as she dances to "So In Love." And by the 1950s she was known for her possessions decorated with little hearts: jewelry, gloves, shoes, dresses and even a heart-shaped mirror in her dressing room.

By the time she reached her early teens she was offered a position as a dancing teacher at Hesslers and years later she recalled how much dance meant to her at the time:

> I'd like to recommend dance training for almost every girl, because I know how beneficial it can be. And I don't mean training for a professional career, of necessity, but just developing the muscle tone and body poise that proper study can bring. I always like to point to myself as an example. The only reason I decided to take up dancing, to begin with, was the fact that I was sort of a puny child. I decided that I owed my body something, since I would have to live with it

The Magic and the Mystery

Vera (right, first row) in 1935 in ninth grade at age 14 is a head shorter than her classmates.

more or less the rest of my life, and I wanted it to be as sound a body
as I could bring about.

For her, dancing became a way of life that was both healthy and essential for developing one's character and she set out to devote her life to its study:

When you first study dancing you discover that you have muscles
and tendons of which you never before were aware. You immediately become conscious of your body and what a beautiful thing it
can be if given the proper attention. For example, walking seems like
an extremely simple art which anyone can master with utter ease.
This is true up to a point. Not all walking is the same. You can stroll
down the street like a sluggard, with one foot just dragging after the
other, or you can make high adventure of it, with the movements of
your leg and the balance of your body as you move becoming a sort
of dance step of its own, indicative of the nature of the person. Dancing brings out the best in a person because it helps develop a healthy
body.

But her interests were not confined to dance. An Honors student in high school, Vera-Ellen earned an award for accomplishments in Latin and averaged a grade of 98% in all her other subjects during the three years she spent there. She overcame her spell-ing difficulties by working hard to memorize words for her spelling tests and looking up words for her writing exercises. She was a self-proclaimed obsessive—a "victim of the desire for perfection in whatever I undertook." She was the ultimate perfectionist.

Oddly, the one subject she struggled with and did not enjoy was physical educa-tion, where she only earned a grade of 89%. In later years, she would spend much time

Vera performing at Hesslers' Dance Studio in 1936

and money on sports lessons for tennis, golf and swimming, perhaps in an attempt to conquer this one last obstacle separating her from perfection and to make amends for that high school grade.

In 1936, when she was in the 10th grade, Vera Ellen appears for the last time in the yearbooks of Norwood High School. It was during this year that she began her advanced dancing studies and set a personal goal to someday dance on Broadway. Seeing her tiny frame in the 1936 *Silhouette*, the Norwood High Yearbook, it is unimaginable to think that this frail creature would have the drive to quit school and become a dancing phenomenon in New York City, but somehow she did.

The Magic and the Mystery

Chapter Two
Growing Up

In 1936 Vera-Ellen was just 15 but already teaching at the Hessler Dance Studio. This was the year that the Hesslers encouraged all their dance teachers to attend the Dancing Teachers of America Normal School and Convention in New York City, but Vera-Ellen was the only delegate from their studio interested in going. Her father was concerned about his young daughter going to the notorious big city, but her mother solved the problem by joining her daughter and the Hesslers for the trip. Vera-Ellen was quite naive, and very devoted and respectful toward her parents, whom she wrote about to friends—always using capital letters for Mother and Father.

At the convention she learned new techniques and routines to teach her students in Ohio and it was an unforgettable experience:

> This trip fascinated me and after I got back home I could not get New York off my mind and I pleaded with my folks to let me go back to finish my studies there and also continue with professional dancing, etc. So about two months later while in high school, with Dad's consent, Mother took me to New York.

Her father had reluctantly allowed the trip, provided that Vera-Ellen agreed not to take any engagements where liquor was sold until she was 18. It seems extraordinary to

Vera leads the troupe of young dancers at Hesslers' Dance Studio in 1936.

Vera-Ellen:

think of Alma Rohe, in the heart of the Great Depression, setting off for the big city in the hopes of developing a dancing career for her daughter—removing Vera from school and leaving her barely employed husband to fend for himself. There may have been a rift or sense of crisis or desperation on the home front, but these details remain unknown.

Yet it is certain that Alma Rohe believed in her daughter's talent. At this time Shirley Temple ruled Hollywood as a mini-megastar and mothers all over America, who thought their little moppets were every bit as talented, enrolled them in dancing and singing schools in the hopes of striking it rich in Hollywood or New York. Vera-Ellen was tiny for her age, cute and blonde and she could sing and dance. If she was popular locally in Ohio and Kentucky, why couldn't she conquer the whole country? To Alma Rohe, it seemed predestined. All that was

Vera poses for a 1936 portrait.

needed was a break—a chance to get an audition for "Cincinnati Night" and win the prize on Major Bowes' famous amateur show, one of the most popular radio and touring shows of the day. Vera's family did not have much money at this point but Pearl Ewing, a teacher and counselor at Norwood High, quietly helped Vera by giving her money and paying for some clothes and shoes for her and her mother to make the trip. Vera remembered the episode in 1952:

> I remember once when our family fortunes were especially low, my mother's shoes were worn out and we had no money to buy new ones. She prayed. Within a day, a friend said to Mother, "I've bought six pairs of new shoes, and now I find that they don't quite fit me. You wear almost the same size as I do. Won't you try them on and accept them as a present from me if you like them?" They fitted perfectly.
>
> Nobody can tell me that my mother's prayers didn't get results! Just the memory of those childhood lessons has helped me many times. Whenever I pray, I know that God is listening and will watch over me.

The Magic and the Mystery

The colorful Major Bowes, who had been in military intelligence, was a civic reformer against the Tongs in San Francisco at the beginning of the century. He had made and lost several fortunes in real estate thoughout the years. The Major was particularly interested in the entertainment field and was one of the developers (and general manager) of the famed Capitol Theater in New York. He booked vaudeville acts for the Loews theater chain and started his popular amateur contests that soon made him a household word. He held regular auditions for his show, often focusing on a specific region of the United States. Those lucky acts selected to participate would gain radio and touring exposure and maybe even get a real break in show business. Such acts were well regarded in the entertainment field because they were truly talented and many of the youngsters had major careers, like leather-lunged singer Teresa Brewer, the famed black tap dancers known as the Step Brothers and even Frank Sinatra.

Irresistibly cute and remarkably talented Vera-Ellen became a hit almost as soon as she hit New York City in October 1936. She and her mother rented a second floor apartment at 37 West 88th Street. Together they set out to make a name for the little girl in the big city. By early January 1937 she finally won a spot on Major Bowes' Cincinnati Night and appeared on the show on January 21. She tap-danced and sang "When You're Smiling" with sensational results:

> My first try-out while in New York was on *Major Bowes' Amateur Hour*. This was on Cincinnati night, and shortly after my number I was informed that I had won and was told to prepare immediately to leave with his "All Girl Unit" that night for Cincinnati and that the train would leave in about an hour. Not expecting anything like this, naturally I was not prepared to leave on such short notice. I was never so excited in all my life. The thought of performing at one of the theaters in my own home town where all my friends could see me was really thrilling.
>
> We left Major Bowes' Program after my number and rushed to our little apartment on 88th street near Central Park West, and in just a few seconds the news had spread through the entire building and before we knew it, everyone was involved in our departure. Mother and I were so excited we couldn't find anything. Everyone was trying to help us pack. We finally told them to just put everything in the suitcases they saw around, which they really did and you can imagine the result. Many things that we would never need were packed up and the other belongings that we actually needed were omitted, and we had to buy things as we went along. After all, you see we only had an hour to pack and get down to the depot. At any rate, we made the train but we surely were mentally exhausted.

The show's "All Girl Unit" appeared in movie theaters of major cities across the country (including St. Louis, Pittsburgh, Washington, Baltimore, Philadelphia and Boston) and the girls earned $50 per week. The planned grand return to Cincinnati, however, did not go as scheduled:

Vera with Major Bowes

We arrived in Cincinnati during a blinding snowstorm. The trains did not run into the city proper owing to the heavy snowfall and we were left stranded miles out in some little town. We finally reached my Dad by phone after several hours and he managed to call for us and drove us into town. Then too, just at this time, Cincinnati was having one of their awful floods. The old Ohio River was on a rampage. Well, at any rate, we opened at the Schubert Theater that night but on account of the weather, many of our friends could not get down. The following day was even worse, the electricity was cut off

The Magic and the Mystery   25

and also the water and gas in many places, which meant no show that night and from all indications we would not be able to open for four or five days.

Under the circumstances, word came from the New York office to take us right on to St. Louis, where we played for several weeks. You can just imagine—my first big chance in my own home town and then all this. Well, it could only happen once in a lifetime and to say my heart was heavy would be putting it mild. From St. Louis we went to Indianapolis. We had many interesting experiences while on the road with the Unit, all of course, new to me.

There was one in particular that I shall never forget. Most of the others in the company were regular troopers [sic] and had road experience. One night while the group were having quite some party at the hotel in Indianapolis, things got so noisy that the hotel management stepped into the picture. You see in the first place I was considered too young and inexperienced to attend these parties, so Mother tucked me nicely into bed. All was well until suddenly the phone rang and Mother very quietly and politely answered, when the manager informed her that the noise in our room would have to cease as there were complaints from the guests. Well, Mother almost fainted, never having had anything like this happen to her before (you could understand if you knew her); she was so shocked she couldn't even talk back.

However, she soon collected herself and went right down and notified the management of their *very grave* mistake and told them that her young daughter was sound asleep at the time and that anyone could have heard a pin drop in our room. It was all very funny at the time but to appreciate it one would have had to have been there.

After several months on the road with this "All Girl Unit," we came back to New York where I took up my studies again. We still had our little second floor, everything was wonderful and we were quite happy until the owners who lived beneath us complained that their chandelier would do the dipsy-doodle whenever I was at home. Of course I had to practice my dancing and they soon got used to it and said they missed it when I was not around.

It has been widely rumored that Vera-Ellen made a short film with Major Bowes entitled *Major Bowes' Amateur Theater of the Air* but no print of the film has been found to confirm the actual existence of this film. There was a CBS radio broadcast on January 21, 1937 in which she performed her first prize-winning tap dance to "When You're Smiling." A recording of most of the "Cincinnati Night" show still exists at the Library of Congress, including portions with Major Bowes announcing Vera-Ellen's leading vote totals and her inclusion into his "All Girls' Unit" but her tap dance number is unfortunately missing.

Following the tour, Vera-Ellen returned to dance classes at the Sonia Serova School of Dancing in Steinway Hall on 57th Street in New York City. Her mother worked there as a secretary to pay for the lessons in tap, ballet and body conditioning. Alma Rohe was extremely supportive of her daughter's extraordinary talent, accompanying her on numerous auditions, certain that Vera-Ellen had talent and was going to make it to the top of the entertainment profession.

But at age 16, Vera-Ellen was just four feet six inches tall and weighed 76 pounds—she

Vera Ellen's first marquee appearance with Ted Lewis in 1937.

had not grown one inch in two years. At Norwood High School, she had worn high heels to try to be nearer the height of her girlfriends. No matter how much dancing talent she possessed, her inadequate height impeded her career. As one producer noted following her audition for a Broadway play while she was in New York:

> Your dancing and reading are terrific but you'd look like a midget beside the others. I'm sorry.

But this traumatic rejection literally inspired her to new heights. She devised a series of exercises modeled after various dance styles. She said:

> I'm either going to stretch myself out or kill myself trying!

She first built herself up by performing the exercises for a few minutes each day and then worked up to one-half hour. They included hanging by the fingertips from doorways, doing dozens of high kicks, and stretching out as far as possible on the floor. Insecure and blaming herself for her appearance, she was determined to change her height because "I goofed many jobs because I was too short."

Whether it was from the constant stretching, prayers and wishful thinking, or, as seems likely, an overdue growth spurt, Vera-Ellen reached the height of five feet four and one-half inches by the time she was 21. The association of this spurt with her devotion to stretching exercises and fervent prayer led to her belief that she could change the shape of her body by the force of her will, special exercises and diet. As late as 1954 she still claimed to be able to stretch her body upwards an additional half inch per year.

Vera-Ellen's dancing studies in New York went well, but she was constantly on the lookout for any opportunity to get ahead in her profession, especially since work during the Great Depression was not easy to find. By chance one day she found herself face to face with bandleader Ted Lewis, who during the 1930s represented big-time show business and flashy showmanship. He had come out of vaudeville and was popular with the older set, having had over 100 popular song hits between 1920 and 1933.

Although his shows were considered corny and old-fashioned, Lewis was still a force and a young dancer working with him would have a golden opportunity:

> While at dancing school one day, I was asked to deliver a message to my tap teacher who was several floors below on business. When I opened the door to deliver the message, who should I see but Ted Lewis auditioning people for his next road show? I immediately stepped back and started to close the door, when he called and asked me to come in. Before I had a chance to tell him what I came for, he asked me if I could dance and of course I said YES. So he told me to put on my tap shoes and show him what I could do. I didn't have any tap shoes with me but I assured him I would be back with my shoes in a minute and believe me, I was.
>
> I don't think I ever ran up or down any stairs as fast in my life. I even forgot that there was an elevator in the building. Well, after my audition he signed me up immediately for his next road show. I was given a wonderful tap specialty and he also built up a very beautiful and effective toe number for me to the lovely tune of "Estrellita" which thrilled me no end, knowing that Estrellita meant "Little Star." I was really living in a little world all my own every time I did this number and I loved every minute of it.
>
> The only bad feature of this incident was that I later learned that my tap teacher had taken one of his other advanced pupils down to audition for Ted Lewis that day hoping he would get the job, but by accident I came in to deliver a message and was signed up. We left New York shortly after that and played in a number of large cities.
>
> Here again, I had hopes of getting to my home town but it seemed the cards just wouldn't fall that way. We did however get to the Beverly Hills Country Club in Kentucky which is just across the river from Cincinnati and many of my friends came over to the Club to see our show....After several months on the road with Ted Lewis and his Band we again returned to New York and once more I took up my studies.

Vera was still training at the Serova School of Dancing in 1938 where her acrobatics instructor was Jack Dayton, who always called her "Tootsie." Another student at the time, Eleanor Stoetzel Luedice, remembers her as "really sweet and quiet."

One day after her 18th birthday, Vera had gained enough height and self-confidence to answer a casting call from the famed showman Billy Rose for "line girls," dancers and singers for his famous Casa Manana nightclub on Broadway and his New York World's Fair Aquacade. Having at last outgrown her father's anti-liquor establishment rule (which in typical Vera-Ellen obsessive fashion she obeyed to the day), she found herself among hundreds of hopefuls at the Hippodrome Theater:

> It seemed there were thousands at the theater when I got there and my first thought was to turn right around and leave. I couldn't see where I would have a chance with all this talent. However, I finally

decided to stay. Being very young and quite small for my age, I had made it my business to wear especially high heeled shoes and a hat that really made me look a lot taller, so I thought I was all set.

Vera in 1938

Well, you can imagine the disappointment when the first thing they had us do was to remove our hats and take off our shoes. I felt this was the end of me but I stayed right on. I noticed that the other girls ahead of me had all auditioned for chorus work and I wasn't at all impressed with this. Finally when my turn came, Billy Rose looked me over rather skeptically and then asked me to do a few time steps. I told him I wasn't interested in chorus work.

Well, he really gasped and said: "Well, if we want specialty dancers we could call on Eleanor Powell and Fred Astaire, but if you think you are as good as they are, well then just have a seat over there please." Of course, I am sure he thought I would leave but I went over and sat down; I felt I had nothing to lose. Well, I waited and waited for what seemed to be ages. I thought he had forgotten all about me but finally he called and gave me my chance, although I doubt if he was serious about it at the time. He probably just wanted to see what I could do under the circumstances. At any rate I auditioned and got the specialty "Little Nellie Kelly." I do believe Mr. Rose was a bit irked at me, but he gave me a tryout just the same. Three weeks later I was doing a specialty in his Casa Manana nightclub.

At the audition, Vera-Ellen had done her amazing toe dancing/tap/acrobatics rendition of this old George M. Cohan song. With her dance feature in Rose's Casa Manana show came a considerable salary.

The renowned production director of that show, John Murray Anderson, noted for his innovative theatrical shows and his blockbuster movie musical *King of Jazz*, nicknamed Vera-Ellen "Seabiscuit" because she was, he felt, going to be a blue ribbon winner:

Although he may not know it, I have always remembered this and it has been an incentive to work hard and always give the best that is in me.

The Magic and the Mystery   **29**

Vera and her mother at Grant's Tomb in 1939

Vera-Ellen always remained true to this ideal. No matter how bad the material she had to work with in the movies or on television, she never gave less than 100%.

The dance director at Casa Manana was Robert Alton who went on to a distinguished stage and Hollywood career. He would work many times in the future on both stage and screen with Vera-Ellen. It was Alton who worked with Gene Kelly on the direction and choreography of the glorious "Slaughter on Tenth Avenue" sequence in *Words and Music* featuring Kelly and Vera-Ellen. She would do some of her best film work over the years, including *Call Me Madam* and *White Christmas* with Robert Alton. During the Casa Manana days, Alton had already acquired a reputation as a superb choreographer with an excellent eye for talent.

Vera-Ellen still felt unprepared for the Broadway stage and hoped to gain more experience as a working dancer in clubs first. After the Casa Manana closed, she worked for a few weeks at the International Casino on Broadway, then moved on briefly to the Paradise Restaurant where she did a specialty number to the tune of "Nola" while wearing a little white frilly dress covered with daisies:

> I found the club work quite interesting and a real lesson in sex education as I had this on all sides. I can well remember coming home one night and telling Mother about a very nice gentleman who wanted to take me out and was going to buy me a fur coat. Well, that was the beginning of the end of club work for me. Confidentially, I got my first fur coat but Mother bought it. I am sure it wasn't the kind the nice gentleman would have bought me, but I was very happy with it. Well, from here on Mother watched the daily papers for the opening of new shows and a week or so later I was auditioning for the (famous Broadway producer) Vinton Freedley show *Leave it to Me*. I already had the blank contract in my possession when it was decided that I did not have quite enough sex appeal for the part, so it was out.

I wonder what Freedley would say now if he saw "Slaughter on Tenth Avenue"?

Nonetheless, the show, even without Vera-Ellen, became a thunderous hit. The big sex appeal number in the show went to an unknown and unsuccessful nightclub entertainer named Mary Martin who made the most of her small part and instantly became one of the superstars of the American stage. Her showstopping song was "My Heart Belongs to Daddy."

Vera-Ellen's dancing in these clubs and restaurants brought her some money and endless lonely trips home on the New York subway at 3 a.m. Anxious to move onward and upward and still just 18, she auditioned again for Broadway in 1939. She won a part in the chorus in the Jerome Kern and Oscar Hammerstein II musical *Very Warm for May*, which opened at the Alvin Theater on November 17, 1939 and closed before the year was out. She appeared in a dance ensemble with June Allyson, whose warm stage presence and all-American-girl good looks would later propel her to become one of MGM's most enduring comedic, dramatic and musical stars, even though she couldn't sing or dance very well. Vera-Ellen's one line in this Vincente Minnelli co-directed production was spoken during a blackout: "There it is!"

In that same show was the now president of the American Theater Roundtable (located in Cheboygan, Michigan), Frank Egan, who recalled young Vera-Ellen at the early stages of her stage career:

> She was indeed a charming, highly professional and talented dancer. Her acting was fresh and natural, and she was very pretty. In person, she was perky and very friendly, just as she appears on the screen. I know this first hand.
>
> I spent five months with her in ...*Very Warm for May*.... "Darling Bangs" was what we affectionately called Vera-Ellen for her cute hairdo.

The show is better remembered for introducing the beautiful song "All the Things You Are" and for being Jerome Kern's last Broadway score before he went to Hollywood and specialized in writing music for movies until his death in 1945. The show received mixed reviews and lasted only two months, after being clobbered by *The New York Times*. The title character May Graham (Eve Arden) was supposed to be a ditzy society girl who was running away from gangsters, ending up in a summer stock troupe in Connecticut. However, the book was altered at the last minute, removing the gangster sub-plot and making the title senseless. Faced with stiff competition on Broadway from Cole Porter's *Du Barry Was a Lady*, *The George White Scandals* and Rodgers and Hart's *Too Many Girls*, the show folded and Vera-Ellen was out of work.

But she kept trying and gradually won a specialty dancing role in *Higher and Higher*, which opened April 4, 1940. Here she attracted the attention of famed composer Richard Rodgers, who promised her a major part in one of his forthcoming shows. But *Higher and Higher* sank lower and lower as the days dragged on, lasting only four months, despite a Rodgers and Hart score. Despite following Rodgers and Hart's Broadway hits *I Married an Angel*, *The Boys from Syracuse* and *Too Many Girls*, *Higher and*

The Magic and the Mystery   31

Vera fixes her mother's hair in this photo taken in 1940.

Higher was a flop. It was originally written for the legendary dancer Vera Zorina, who was unable to do it because of her blossoming film career. The second choice for the lead, a Hungarian actress named Marta Eggert, was not a dancer at all and found the show an uncomfortable fit. Lee Dixon, a brilliant but volatile young tap dancer who had starred with Ruby Keeler in the movies in the 1930s, was also in the show. His performance shined, but he was not easy to work with due to alcohol problems. Later he would make a comeback in Rodgers and Hammerstein's *Oklahoma!*, but his drinking eventually drove him off Broadway.

Although the play was not a hit with the public, Vera-Ellen did score a big hit with the production stagehands who became infatuated with the little dynamo. At the close of the production they gave her a sugar cube with an attached message reading "Stay as sweet as you are."

Higher and Higher closed for a month in the summer of 1940. During that period Vera-Ellen was offered what she described as "a somewhat sexy dance number" during "Mirror Day" festivities at the New York World's Fair, but because she was so young, her mother could not be convinced to permit it. Then she got another chance to dance in a more conventional manner at the Fair:

> ...I was delighted to think I would be dancing at the New York World's Fair, but more than that happened. Who should be billed ahead of me on the program but Bill (Bojangles) Robinson [legendary tap dancer and Shirley Temple movie co-star] and this really frightened me. Imagine me doing a tap number after he had been on ahead of me. Well my heart really sank. But wait until you hear what happened; it must have been Providence.
>
> Robinson was late and they were stalling and holding up the program, but after waiting quite some time, they decided to go on without him, when suddenly in he rushed. I was standing right there just ready to go on. Well, to my surprise he stepped out on the stage ahead of me and announced that something very unexpected and im-

portant had come up and that he would be unable to perform and would have to rush away immediately, *but* said he: "I have a little protégé of mine here with me who will dance for you in my place" and then he went on to tell what a wonderful little dancer I was.

Well, everything turned black for just a second when he beckoned me to come out. I had never seen him before (except for on the stage) and I don't think he knew me from Adam, and he was introducing me as his protégé. Just about that time, something within me seemed to say "you don't have a chance like this every day so take advantage of it and give it all you've got" and believe me I did.

Vera's father had just gotten into town and was amazed to see the great black entertainer introducing his "protégé," but thanks to that odd boost she was an enormous hit at the Fair.

Vera-Ellen next was invited to join Russell Markett and his *Rockettes* at Samuel "Roxy" Rothafel's Radio City Music Hall. Markett was famous for his amazingly crisp unified drilling of his chorus girls as exemplified in the 1930 musical film *King of Jazz* in which he had worked for John Murray Anderson. Vera-Ellen's father was a big fan of these chorus line girls, but she only lasted two weeks for she displayed far too much originality and individuality onstage to fit in as a chorus clone. Her need to seek individual perfection in each routine was at odds with simple assembly-line kicking night after night. She couldn't stand it:

I never thought of it as anything more than a good job with lots of drilling and hard work. The show would last about 40 minutes and the film came on for about 90. That was the whole thing: show, film, show, film. I never left the theater until late at night. My mother joined me in New York and that was a great help. There's little chance for individual recognition as a soloist, but it was and I imagine still is a good way to learn ensemble discipline and professionalism. My grandfather, who saw me as a high school drum majorette, thought Radio City was the greatest. After Radio City what next?

...I invariably kicked higher than anyone in line and of course that would never do in this routine and precision work. However, I preferred not being limited in my work and although Russell Markett (director of the Rockettes) was quite anxious to have me remain and told me I would be doing solo numbers occasionally I nevertheless decided to go back to *Higher and Higher* when it reopened.

While waiting and hoping for her own Rodgers and Hart opportunity, Vera-Ellen was again supported by choreographer Robert Alton and won a lead dancing part in the stage production of *Panama Hattie* with Ethel Merman, which opened October 30, 1940. Thirteen years later, she would work again with Merman in *Call Me Madam*. It was during this run of *Panama Hattie* that she married her first husband, featured dancer Robert (Bob) Hightower, whom she had met during *Higher and Higher* when he was 23 and she was 19. At the wedding she wore a wedding dress with a heart-shaped neck

The Magic and the Mystery

Robert Hightower and Vera-Ellen pose for their wedding photo.

and hearts on the sleeves and the vest, and there was even a tiered wedding cake decorated with hearts. As one can imagine this wedding did not sit well with Alma Rohe. The Hightowers moved into an apartment at 326 West 55th Street. Coincidentally, his nickname was "Bunny," the same one Vera-Ellen had as a child. Hightower was lanky, handsome and muscular and was very attractive to the ladies, if a bit rough around the edges. Film director George Sidney remembered him at the time:

Vera poses with dancing team Lewis and Robert Hightower.

Robert and his brother Lewis were acrobatic dancers. Robert was off the deep end, a jokester. His idea of fun was to put a snake in a basket, so to speak. He was also very macho and very unpredictable, tending to the strange side. He never hit her or anything like that but Vera-Ellen deserved better. Robert wasn't cruel but he was rough, and seemed like he might hit or slap someone on the back so hard he would collapse. He was sort of a big, strong oaf.

The Magic and the Mystery

Vera-Ellen is second from the left in this photo from *Panama Hattie* in 1941.

Vera-Ellen had little opportunity to do much in the 500-plus smash run of *Panama Hattie* on Broadway, but when the show hit the road she was given four specialty dance numbers. She began to attract considerable attention as did Hightower and his brother Lewis who were also in the production. The show ran for a year and four months in New York and four months more on the road.

Panama Hattie also produced another stroke of luck for Vera-Ellen, for also in the cast were a number of chorus girls who would go on to become well-known actresses, including Lucille Bremer (who went on to dance with Fred Astaire in 1946 in one of Astaire's lesser vehicles, *Yolanda and the Thief*, which was largely ignored by the public but has recently gained acclaim for its artistic brilliance) and Janis Carter. Vera-Ellen grew to be friends with another chorine named Betsy Blair who at the time was dating a rising young dancer named Gene Kelly. Blair and Kelly would later marry. Luck was on Vera-Ellen's side during those days when Kelly watched the extraordinary dancing ability of Vera-Ellen and would remember it years later when he was looking for a dancing partner for his role in *Words and Music* for MGM. But that was in the future—for now, Vera-Ellen was again looking for work.

In 1942 she was finally given a big chance in a Rodgers and Hart show when she opened on June 3 in a featured, but not starring, role as the goddess Minerva dancing opposite Ray Bolger in the Broadway production of *By Jupiter*. This was the musical version of the 1921 one-act play, *The Warrior's Husband* by Julian F. Thompson, which had been revised into a three-act comedy, which had made a star of Katharine Hepburn

Dancing in *By Jupiter* in 1942

on Broadway in 1932. The production, which opened at Broadway's Shubert Theater, was full of *double-entendres* and sex jokes, and was considered pretty racy for the time. The story was set in Pontus, Asia Minor (what is now Turkey) near the Black Sea. Here the Amazon warrior women were in charge, led by their queen Hippolyta (Benay Venuta). As long as she wore the girdle of the goddess Diana, the men were subjugated, meek stay-at-homes forced to run the house. Hippolyta's husband Sapiens (Ray Bolger) was the most timid of the males. However, the Greeks led by the demigod Hercules (Ralph Dumke) and the Athenian hero Theseus (Ronald Graham) showed up to liberate the males, make Sapiens the king and tame the women. Lovely Constance Moore was the female lead as Antiope, Hippolyta's sister, but she left to return to her Hollywood film career (with very modest success). She was replaced by a newcomer, singer Nanette Fabray, who latter appeared in *The Band Wagon* (1953) with Fred Astaire and Oscar Levant and went on to great television success in the '50s as a comedienne, most notably as Sid Caesar's wife on the old *Caesar's Hour* (1954-1957).

During the run of *By Jupiter*, dancer Miriam Nelson worked with Vera-Ellen and had also been her friend during their time together in the Casa Manana:

> Vera would always make fudge for everyone. She was very enthusiastic and full of fun. She was a terrific gal—very outgoing, straightforward and ambitious. She liked to roller skate to work and was fond of wearing orchids. She was never moody—she was a very normal girl who loved to dance. All the girls liked to play word games in their dressing rooms and Vera did this and liked to kid and tease.

By Jupiter was a sensation and had the longest run of any Rodgers and Hart show except for the revival of *Pal Joey*. But the show closed when Bolger left Broadway to

The Magic and the Mystery   **37**

In 1942 the Hightower Brothers, Robert (center) and Lewis, posed for this publicity still with Vera-Ellen.

entertain American troops in the Far East. If not for this, *By Jupiter* would have been the number one Rodgers and Hart Broadway blockbuster of all time. Bolger was the big draw and when he left, the show was forced to close, ending Vera's stint as the leading dancer.

Reviews of *By Jupiter* on June 4, 1942 indicate that the show was a big hit with the critics. The Hightowers made a big splash too, *The New York World Telegraph* wrote:

> The neatest trick of the week...is a petite dancing doll named Vera-Ellen, who stole her way into Broadway's heart last evening. She's a

Vera-Ellen:

gem. One of the Hightower boys—Bunny—thinks so, too. That's why he plucked her out of the chorus in Dwight Wiman's *Higher and Higher* a couple of seasons back and married her. As for the Hightowers and their dance creations on the intricate stage settings of this production—magnificent!

The New York Journal-American especially admired the virtuosity of the Hightowers:

> Robert and Lewis Hightower do some spectacular and muscular dancing, and the whole show has the speed, gaiety and sophistication of Broadway's finest showmanship.

Other reviews were equally supportive. *PM* (a New York newspaper) observed that "...Flower Hujer and Robert and Lewis Hightower are a very good dancing trio..." and the *Daily News* agreed: "The Hightower boys, Robert and Lewis, Flower Hujer and a couple of other dancers, Vera-Ellen one of them, I suspect, ably point up the ensembles." *The Herald Tribune* raved too and called attention to Vera-Ellen's name, here hyphenated for the first time, but was more interested in 60-year-old Bertha Belmore's antics with Ray Bolger and a tune called "Life With Father":

> The veteran Miss Bertha Belmore stopped the show at one point with her surprising gift for modern dancing and, although the program does not make me certain on the point, I think the young blonde dancer who is of such dynamic and pictorial help is cryptically named Vera-Ellen.

A most important favorable review of the show came from Walter Winchell, the capricious and often vicious gossip columnist and reviewer, in the *New York Daily Mirror* for June 5, 1942:

> It is the cast, then, that provides the fun and the fooling, with Mr. Bolger promoting much of its corny merriment, and Robert Alton supplying his abundance of eye filling footwork. And it is a good dancing show; particularly able are Robert and Lewis Hightower, Flower Hujer, and Vera-Ellen, Dance Stylists.

The fine review prompted a hand-written thank you note to Winchell from Vera-Ellen that survives in a private collection.

John Martin, another reviewer, commented:

> There is also Robert Hightower, doing the same stunning acrobatics he did in *Panama Hattie*, with his brother William this time, instead of his brother Lewis as his partner and with Vera-Ellen being tossed about instead of Nadine Gae.

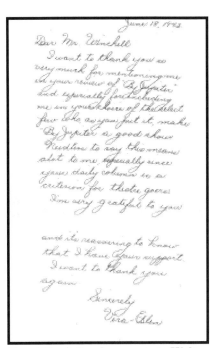
Vera-Ellen's thank you note to Walter Winchell

Though she kept her focus on Broadway, Vera occasionally took on club work. The Hightowers (Bob, brothers Lewis and William and Vera-Ellen, as she now called herself) became a dancing team performing from 1940 to early in 1942. Dancers Flower Hujer and Nadine Gae often appeared with them instead of Vera-Ellen or sometimes danced with her in this troupe, which occasionally included as many as six dancers. In the later 1930s Lewis Hightower had been the dancing partner of beautiful Margery Belcher Babbit whose husband Art was a noted Disney animator. It was for this reason Lewis' movements had been used as the model for Prince Charming in Disney's 1937 cartoon feature *Snow White and the Seven Dwarfs*, and Margery became the model for Snow White. Later Margery divorced Lewis Hightower and married dancer Gower Champion, becoming a star of stage and screen as Marge Champion in the later 1940s. Billed as Marge and Gower Champion, they appeared with Howard Keel and Kathryn Grayson in both *Show Boat* (1951) and *Lovely to Look At* (1952).

Little is known of the routine employed by Robert and Lewis Hightower and their group in nightclubs, but eyewitness reports claim that Bob played Svengali to Vera-Ellen's Trilby and that the two brothers would toss her about like a rag doll in a trance onstage during their adagio dance. Some of the routines stunned audiences with their degree of difficulty and danger. The act was known for doing dangerous throws that other teams would not attempt. During one of these performances Vera-Ellen injured her back, a problem that did not impair her dancing future but which plagued her in varying degrees for the rest of her life. A glimpse of the Hightowers' influence may perhaps be seen in the acrobatic sequences of Vera-Ellen's "You Make Me Feel So Young" number in the film *Three Little Girls in Blue*, made just four years later. The Hightowers' act would soon end when Lewis Hightower enlisted in the service and during World War II was killed at the Battle of Normandy.

In 1943, during the heart of World War II, Vera-Ellen again appeared on Broadway in a Richard Rodgers production, the revival of *The Connecticut Yankee*. The story was based on Mark Twain's novel about the adventures of the title character who is catapulted from the modern day back to sixth-century Camelot. It was Vera-Ellen's fifth Broadway show and became her springboard to stardom and to Hollywood. Performing the featured role of Camelot lady-in-waiting Evelyn La Rondelle, she exuded a style and vivacity that captured rave reviews. Actress/dancer/singer Betty Garrett went to the original show and reflected on it in July 1998:

Vera-Ellen in *A Connecticut Yankee*

I thought she was so adorable, this bouncy and joyous and slightly plump little person. She wasn't so pencil thin as she got later on. She was wonderful in that show. And I remember she had the most extraordinarily beautiful feet for a dancer.

Possessed of a Rodgers and Hart score that included such standards as "My Heart Stood Still" and the delightful "Thou Swell," the show was perfect wartime escapism—even though it had originally debuted in 1927 and had been Rodgers and Hart's

Vera-Ellen and Robert Hightower in 1943

most successful show of the 1920s. The new version was to be a vehicle for Lorenz Hart's friend, veteran actress Vivienne Segal, who played the crucial role of Morgan LeFay. It had some new songs and dialogue and a more contemporary prologue about the Navy. It also marked the last hurrah of Hart who, upon the show's successful opening November 17, 1943, promptly went on a drinking binge that killed him. This episode was later loosely dramatized in the movie *Words and Music* with Vera-Ellen, ironically, playing herself, and watching Hart played by Mickey Rooney collapse in her presence. In this period, Rodgers also took time to give young Vera-Ellen advice

Vera-Ellen:

concerning her selection of future Broadway vehicles to showcase her talent: "Don't do it unless the script's the best you ever saw in your life."

Vera-Ellen's singing talents were never considered stellar but she did record two duets with Charles Stratton on the cast album for the show by Decca Records which includes a number of photos of her on- and offstage. She could carry a tune and hit all the notes clearly but didn't project her voice and had little timbre or resonance. For that reason she never sang in the movies but was considered adequate for television. It was her dancing and vivacity that really scored with the public. She had grown to five feet four and a half inches but was still petite, wearing a size 10 dress (which today would be a size 4 or even a 2) and 4 1/2 D shoes. She had a cute, refreshing girl-next-door quality and a magical personality and energy onstage with flashing eyes and stunning smile that suggested she was enjoying every minute of the limelight. Even while *A Connecticut Yankee* was still on the road in Philadelphia, talent scouts repeatedly approached her with contracts for the movies but she refused all of them, holding out for what she thought would be the best offer:

> If I had accepted a Hollywood offer then, they could have gotten me too cheaply. I decided to wait until we opened in New York. You're always worth more when you're a hit on Broadway.

On opening night of her big new show, Vera-Ellen was a smash and her reviews were terrific. *PM* raved:

> With Vera-Ellen—the brightest and cutest young thing that the season has so far popped into a musical—to sing and dance them along with Chester [sic] Stratton and Jere McMahon, both "On a Desert Island and "I Feel at Home with You" sound as fresh as when they were written.

Reviewer Lewis Nichols added:

> The young lady who, last evening at least, put the most life into the musical was Vera-Ellen, not the greatest singer in the world but certainly one of the world's most engaging performers as a dancer or minor comedienne.

One of the most important reviews of the show was given by famed critic Jean Nathan, normally quite hard to please. He said that Vera-Ellen was

> ...as beguiling a package of beguilement as has beguiled the beguilable in what the poets describe as many moons.

On February 3, 1944 *Look Magazine* announced its four new girls who were their Broadway show-stoppers of a season that, despite World War II, was bustling and vibrant. Chosen were Joan McCracken of *Oklahoma!*, Sono Osato in *One Touch of Venus*, Betty Garrett in *Jackpot* and Vera-Ellen for *A Connecticut Yankee*. Vera-Ellen was

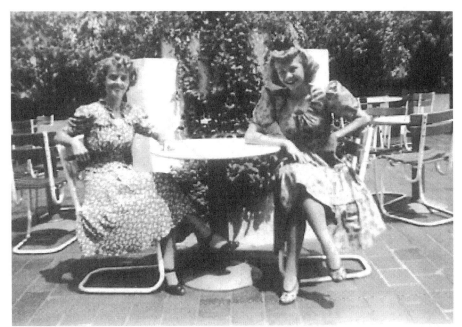
Vera-Ellen and her mother in 1945

cited as a "rubber-boned dancer-comedienne" who "has that electric X-quality which enables her to project herself over the footlights–and *blaze!*" *Look* couldn't stop raving about her:

> Baby-faced Vera-Ellen is the sauciest thing on Broadway.... Fresh as new-sprung soda, blue-eyed and golden-haired, Vera-Ellen is what makes the box-office cash register sing a golden tune.... And to bubbling, blonde Vera-Ellen go marigolds for not only stopping the show, but for being one of the major reasons why *Connecticut Yankee* is a hit. Vera is essentially a dancer with a strong sense of comedy. But in *Connecticut Yankee* she sings and acts; what she lacks in professional experience she makes up for in pert charm.

Look compared her to Betty Hutton but found her "less overpowering than Betty" and "more flirtatious."

In this period she found herself strongly influenced by the comedic dancing style of Ray Bolger and brought this to her role. She soon won the prestigious Donaldson Award as Best Supporting Actress in a Broadway production and attracted the attention of film impresario Samuel Goldwyn, who offered her a contract, but didn't offer as much money as two other studios. Instead of jumping at his offer, she held out for three terms: decent pay ($1,000 per week), large roles and no screen test.

On September 2, 1945 while rehearsing her dances for her second film, *The Kid from Brooklyn* she commented on her good fortune and tactics in dealing with the Goldwyn organization:

Vera-Ellen:

I told the studio scouts they had seen what I could do and if they wanted me to sign for pictures they'd have to forget that "test" business. Well, here I am, at Mr. Goldwyn's studio. His representative said: "Mr. Goldwyn doesn't make tests—he makes stars."

Goldwyn wanted her to leave the show immediately and head for Hollywood, but she was under contract until the following June. Goldwyn arranged for her to leave for Hollywood right after her last day with the road show in Chicago. The show closed just two weeks after she left. Her departure for Hollywood occasioned quite a sendoff from the show's cast—almost something out of a Hollywood musical:

> The six boys who danced with me in this show escorted me to the depot and their farewell wish was to remember me dancing, so right there on the station platform we went into our routine as best we could under the circumstances. Naturally we attracted quite a crowd and we got so involved in our dancing, I almost missed the train but the boys managed to get me on just as the train pulled out.

It all seemed so exciting and magical, like a movie come to life, and it was great fun at first. But Sam Goldwyn (real name Schmuel Gelbfisz) was not a man to be trusted, as Vera-Ellen would ultimately find out.

By using only her first name in *By Jupiter* and *A Connecticut Yankee*, Vera-Ellen stood out from the other players in public name recognition and was clearly emulating another Vera—Vera Zorina! Zorina was a strikingly elegant and beautiful Norwegian/German star of the *Ballet Russe*. She had starred in *On Your Toes* on the London stage and was brought to Broadway in 1938 by Rodgers and Hart to star as an angel married to a mortal (opera and operetta star Dennis King) in *I Married an Angel*. The charming plot line developed the idea that someone can be too angelic and therefore lack diplomacy, thereby ruining a marriage by being excessively honest. Choreographer George Balanchine worked on the show, fell in love with the star and married her. Zorina was a sensation and, when Samuel Goldwyn saw her in *On Your Toes*, he signed her to appear in his 1938 movie *The Goldwyn Follies*. To the young, driven Vera-Ellen the life of Zorina was *the* role model for success that she hoped to follow to the letter.

In fact Zorina had almost starred in a show that featured Vera-Ellen, *Higher and Higher*, which, as mentioned, was written with Zorina in mind. Richard Rodgers swore years later that if Zorina had starred in his show it would have been a big hit. Vera-Ellen had seen her on Broadway captivate audiences with her dancing. Zorina in the late '30s and early '40s was at the height of her fame and was starring in popular American comedy, adventure and drama films such as *On Your Toes* (1939), *I Was an Adventuress* (1940), *Louisiana Purchase* (1941) and *Star Spangled Rhythm* (1942). The ads for *On Your Toes* proclaimed:

> Zorina—she's heavenly! She's the gal who put romance into dance—direct from the role in *I Married an Angel* that made her the toast of the stage! It's zensational; it's zintillating; it's zuperb; it's Zorina.

Vera-Ellen and Robert Hightower, wearing his aviator uniform, in 1944.

Zorina's ability to do everything from Broadway musical comedy to the Metropolitan Opera to the *Ballet Russe* to tap dancing to films of all types opened doors of endless career possibilities for Vera-Ellen. She was determined to pirouette through those doors to stardom. And she felt she could be even better than Zorina, for the star had three flaws that hampered her film career: she was a foreigner with a rather heavy accent, she was not a very good actress, and her beauty while fine for the distance of the Broadway stage paled under the close scrutiny of the motion picture camera due to her slightly less-than-perfect mouth.

Vera-Ellen's mother shared her daughter's vision and fed it. She claimed to reporters that before her daughter was born her hyphenated name appeared to her in a dream, in giant marquee lights!

That story is almost certainly false, made up Hollywood fluff, because Vera-Ellen never used a hyphenated single name before *By Jupiter*. But her mother was fond of repeating the story to make it seem as if destiny itself or even God had a hand in creating a special magic for her daughter's career. In truth, Vera-Ellen and her mother were looking for something different to make the young dancer's name stand out like that of Zorina and so the hyphenated single name was invented. Vera-Ellen became the only one-name hyphenated star of the Broadway stage and Hollywood. Critics in Los Angeles, used to calling movie stars "The Face," "The Voice" and "The Body," now could celebrate "The Hyphen" although she often joked that she would rather be known as "The Dash."

In 1944 the Hightowers were still living in the nice apartment on 55th Street in New York next door to pianist Jose Meles, later famous as the combo conductor for television's *The Jack Paar Show*. Across the way lived a young stage performer named Jim Schlader who went on to appear in such Broadway productions as *Blossom Time*, *Lady in the Dark* and the original *On the Town*. At the age of 84 in 1998, Schlader still remembered the Hightowers. He often ran into the rising young Broadway star Vera-Ellen in the hallway as she was dashing about. He and Bob also built a sun-deck to-

Vera-Ellen:

gether for their shared use, which opened off from the Hightowers' apartment. To Schlader, Hightower seemed very tall, gawky and lanky, and didn't seem to have the build of a dancer, but Vera-Ellen was very beautiful. Most dancers he knew and saw were thin and bony but at this time Vera-Ellen was

> …rounded out and very feminine, a really stunning woman with a fresh, beautiful look. She seemed to always be enthusiastic and when she talked her eyes would sparkle and her manner was very animated.

Schlader had seen her dance in *By Jupiter* and *The Connecticut Yankee* and thought "she really stood out. I don't why she didn't go further than she did."

During this time Vera-Ellen was free from the strong dietary restraints of her mother and was eating well. She was keeping her weight on and building up extremely muscular legs, shoulders and a strong back. She was so healthy and in such extraordinary shape that she resembled a female bodybuilder rather than the "thin and bony" dancers Jim Schlader saw regularly.

The Hightowers were living in a comfy one-bedroom apartment in a nice complex, earning a decent living. They were unremarkable as neighbors—no parties, no screaming, no loud fighting—and the young couple were friendly and courteous to others, although Bob was said to be a bit unrefined. Their union seemed happy, cheerful and amicable. However, other members of Vera-Ellen's family, especially her mother, did not like Bob Hightower, and they were out to undermine him. Alma believed that he was trying to use her daughter as a stepping stone to further his own career and that he didn't have talent to match Vera-Ellen's. Other family members felt that he was domineering and tried to squelch her personality. But the marriage continued. Bob talked a lot about airplanes and flying and Vera-Ellen became increasingly interested in the subject. She wanted to learn to fly, but she could not because wartime regulations precluded training for other than war-related or civil defense pilots.

Bob became an aviation cadet stationed at Fort Dix, New Jersey and eventually gave up dancing. His love of flying led him to pursue a post-war career in aviation after his brother died and dancing opportunities had dried up. Vera-Ellen became the breadwinner of the family. When this happened the marriage began to show signs of strain. As Jim Schlader put it:

> I'm not surprised about their divorce. Theatrical marriages work well in the beginning when both are struggling but when one makes it big it puts a strain on the relationship and divorce is common.

One big problem for the marriage was Robert Hightower's jealousy, combined with a violent temper. Their relationship reached such proportions that Vera-Ellen fled to her mother in fear, then prepared to file for divorce. Vera-Ellen later told family that she feared he might kill her for leaving him.

After the breakup of her daughter's marriage Alma once again played a strong role in Vera-Ellen's life and became the shoulder for her to lean on. She was deservedly proud of her remarkable daughter and wanted badly to be part of the big move to Hollywood and Vera-Ellen's quest for superstardom.

Chapter Three
Toward Hollywood Stardom

A wide-eyed Vera-Ellen arrived in Hollywood hoping to embark on a career with Goldwyn in the footsteps of her inspiration Zorina. She and her mother set up shop in Los Angeles in a two-room apartment and bought a car, then waited to see how she would be presented to the public. The Hollywood reality wasn't like anything she had imagined. Samuel Goldwyn initially intended to use her as a foil to enhance the apparent dancing ability of Danny Kaye, his prize discovery. Kaye was untrained as a dancer but had a certain natural grace and could fake dancing fairly effectively—when surrounded by real dancers, he appeared to be dancing. He was known as an unsubtle, in-your-face comedian who relied on quick patter routines with tongue-twisting, impossible-to-memorize streams of dialogue. He had a mediocre singing voice and used contorted expressions, silly sounds and flashy showmanship to get by. Yet Kaye was also a capable and charismatic actor when given good material. His routines were described as zany, wild-eyed and frenetic—a style of comedy popularized in the later '30s and the '40s by acts such as the Ritz Brothers, Judy Canova and Martha Raye. This type of comedy continued to be popular into the 1950s with Milton Berle on television.

Goldwyn was obsessed with Kaye, and pursued him for two years before the comedian finally signed a contract. He loved Kaye's radio comedy and stage performances and believed he would be a successor to Goldwyn star Eddie Cantor.

Danny Kaye's first Goldwyn vehicle was made in the middle of World War II. *Up in Arms* (1944) starring Kaye and singer Dinah Shore became a huge hit and offered perfect zany wartime escapism—and helped make Danny Kaye a star. Goldwyn then decided that two Kayes were better than one and cast him as identical twins in his next film *Wonder Man* (1945). Goldwyn lovingly produced this effort, which featured Kaye in almost every scene. Unfortunately Vera-Ellen was little more than a specialty dancer in the cast. Goldwyn did have some initial praise for Vera-Ellen:

> She's radiant, buoyant, wholesome, energetic, and ambitious, and all of those qualities come out to you as you watch her on the screen.

Vera-Ellen became Kaye's dancing partner in *Wonder Man*, but it was Virginia Mayo who received co-star billing. This could have caused a rivalry but that never occurred—they became good friends, even vacationing together at Lake Arrowhead after the filming ended. Both women, however, were overlooked by critics driven to hyperbole by Kaye-mania. Danny Kaye became the darling of the New York critical establishment. But there was a silver lining for Vera-Ellen—she was a hit with the film-going public. Unfortunately, Goldwyn didn't recognize her star quality. Vera-Ellen received more fan mail than either of the two featured stars and for her next film, she was selected to co-star with Kaye in *The Kid from Brooklyn* (1946).

During this part of her career Vera-Ellen was pegged by reviewers as a ball of energy, an "ethereal little blonde" who was "appealing as a kitten, feminine as perfume

All grown up at 24, but looking like the 19 she claimed to be, in this portrait for *Wonder Man.*

and as gentle as a spring breeze, a girl who obviously wouldn't say boo to a mosquito." She was considered "a sort of combination Betty Grable, Eleanor Powell and Zorina" and was called "pert" and "chic" by *The New York Times* on June 9, 1945 when *Wonder Man* debuted. They added that she "dances with captivating rhythm." During a preview of the film on April 25, 1945 *Variety* praised her: "A fine young hoofer who can handle lines as well." In her first film, despite playing third fiddle, she garnered great praise among critics who delighted in the fact that she was still "unsophisticated" in the midst of Hollywood. Not content with this praise, she was openly longing to do meatier dramatic parts with more dialogue, hoping not to be confined to roles as a specialty dancer or ingenue. She wanted to escape being typecast as "the pretty hoof-and-mouthing of the flea-sized, dainty screen newcomer, Vera-Ellen..." as *Time* magazine referred to her.

The Magic and the Mystery

In this dance number from *Wonder Man*, Vera-Ellen seems to float off the ground.

Wonder Man marked Vera-Ellen's first screen appearance, first real acting role (although it was quite small) and first screen solo specialty dance (to David Rose and Leo Robin's Academy Award–nominated "So In Love"). Her solo was designed to showcase her boundless energy and stunning dancing ability. Although her singing was dubbed by June Hutton (wife of Frank Sinatra's legendary conductor/arranger of the 1940s, Axel Stordahl), her dancing was uniquely her own.

In the later '30s and early '40s Eleanor Powell had combined tap with acrobatics, prop dancing, meticulously detailed routines and occasional ballet to open up new avenues for women in motion picture dancing. Powell was following a tradition of combining various styles of dancing begun in the early 1930s by Fred Astaire.

Now, in *Wonder Man* Vera-Ellen took the Powell/Astaire dance style to dazzling new heights, thanks to choreography by John Wray. The choreographer makes full use of her talents even though nothing else Wray did before or after approached this degree of excitement. Vera-Ellen uses splits, acrobatics, high kicking, prop dancing, male dance partners and stunning spins to create a fusion of tap and ballet that is today still breathtaking. Her dancing shoes were specially constructed with padded fronts so that she could dance on them like a toe dancer while the rest of the shoe was designed as a conventional tap shoe. This allowed her to switch at will in mid-routine from tap to toe, infusing the entire number with dynamic movements, each fully articulated and perfectly executed. Her transitions from step to step are equally fascinating to watch as every movement, without exception, is fluid and linked effortlessly to the movement preceding and following. This characteristic and the interweaving of toe and tap routines set her apart and above the legendary Eleanor Powell as a total dancer. Vera-Ellen was already so adept at *all* types of dancing that of all the great female dancers she was

In the finale of her specialty dance in *Wonder Man*, Vera-Ellen literally steps up the backs of her male dancers.

the only one who was never known for any one particular kind of dancing form or style.

Another Vera-Ellen trademark was the execution of steps and transitions with an effortless grace that made her seem to float above the ground. In her early films she would simply smile winningly and shake her head and body back and forth nonchalantly while executing a difficult step. The overall impression is that of a young girl of seemingly boundless talent and grace deeply in love with dancing and inviting the viewer to share and appreciate her enjoyment. She made it seem so easy that critics often missed the fact that her routines were difficult and challenging and that they were viewing a unique young artist. In the finale of her specialty dance in *Wonder Man*, she literally steps up the backs of her male dancers as if she is walking on air.

She was also having a ball living in Hollywood too, and it seemed that she now had the opportunity to be the superwoman she had dreamed of becoming. Her apprehensions about starring on the Broadway stage and her excessive practicing had caused her to grow thin once Bob Hightower left her for the Service, but now she was once again enjoying the high life:

> I was so thin in New York, about 95 pounds. Since coming to Hollywood I have gained to the point where I have to be on the careful side. Picture work is easier on the nerves I guess than the stage. I really feel like a native now after getting my first speeding ticket the other day. I have learned to fly, too, although the studio won't let me solo. And the other night I went ice-skating—with a partner to hold me up. That's really fun.

The Magic and the Mystery

Vera-Ellen does the wild "Bali Boogie" with Danny Kaye in *Wonder Man*.

The opening number of *Wonder Man*, a typically goofy 1940s combination of Balinese dancing and boogie-woogie entitled *Bali Boogie*, paired Vera-Ellen on equal footing with the film's star Danny Kaye. Her main function was to give him the aura of a thoroughly trained and talented dancer. It was written by Sylvia Fine, Kaye's wife, and combined popular jive talk of the time with a Balinesian theme. The routine is delightfully nutty with Vera-Ellen matching Kaye's comic dancing and creating some humorous stylized postures of her own (angled movements, jutting rear end and funny walk) to go with his hamming. In one sequence she does a bounce split, which can be quite painful, stares out at the audience and oohs playfully as she bounces up and down, as if she has surprised even herself. Then Kaye pulls her back up to her full height by her hair.

Vera-Ellen had made an auspicious debut and was full of enthusiasm and hope. She thought she had solved Hollywood:

> I was a little scared when I came to Hollywood because it had been misrepresented to me. Around New York you hear so many strange stories from people who've been out there, I thought it would be an awful place. I know now that what they told me was mixed up with a few sour grapes. Movies have been wonderful to me.

This was the first of many statements she would make that would later prove to be sadly ironic.

It was during this period that she first met A.C. Lyles, who had worked his way up from mailboy at Paramount in the '20s to a major position in the publicity department. By the '40s he had risen to associate producer and eventually became a producer specializing in Westerns. The handsome, dapper 33-year-old Lyles found the 24-year-old Vera-Ellen unique and irresistible and they formed a close and special friendship that lasted for 36 years:

> I met her right after she came here and we became good friends and saw each other an awful lot. I came onto the Goldwyn lot to see a friend of mine and she was doing her first picture....I met her at that time and we would talk and see each other from time to time. I remember that I was going down Melrose one time and I stopped for a red light and she came up beside me and we yelled and screamed hello and how are you. And I said "What are you doing Friday night?" and she said "I'm going anywhere I can go and get dinner" and I said: "Okay. Call me and tell me where you are and I'll be there at seven o'clock." From then we were together an awful lot.

This was a happy time for Vera-Ellen. She and her mother had purchased a house at 2028 North Argyle Avenue in Los Angeles which she referred to as her San Fernando Valley home. Her former schoolmate in Norwood, Paul Murphy, came to visit her sometimes on weekends along with his Navy buddies. He was engaged to Katherine Murphy, one of her former dancing mates who was waiting back home. Vera-Ellen would write to her old friends in Ohio, reassuring them: "Please don't think I've changed. I still love you...." She maintained her friendship with the Murphys right up to the mid-1970s when Paul had a severe stroke and she and Katherine Murphy gradually lost touch.

In 1945, Vera-Ellen was noted for having a ravenous appetite for roast beef and steak and frequently startled those watching the petite blonde eat at the Goldwyn studio restaurant as she put away double orders of beef, baked potatoes and deep dish apple pie with ice cream. Now five feet four and one half inches tall and 111 pounds, the brown-eyed silver-blonde was considered one of the fastest rising young stars of Hollywood. And this promise was furthered in her next Goldwyn film.

The Magic and the Mystery

The Kid from Brooklyn when viewed today is still a pleasant comedy/musical. The premise involves a naive, bumbling young milkman named Burleigh Sullivan (Danny Kaye) who inadvertently knocks out Speed (Steve Cochran), the middleweight champion of the world, twice in public encounters outside the ring. In order to impress Polly, the girl of his dreams (Virginia Mayo), an unemployed singer behind on her rent, Burleigh becomes a boxing sensation and eventually knocks out the champ for real, thanks to a few twists of fate.

Kaye's character, the almost moronically innocent, sexually inexperienced young man with the mind of a child, is borrowed directly from Eddie Cantor's screen and stage persona known as "The Kid." Since Cantor was the Goldwyn film star of the '30s and

Virginia Mayo, Danny Kaye and Vera-Ellen in a publicity shot for *The Kid from Brooklyn*

was now too old to play the part, Cantoresque scripts were tailored to Kaye, who Goldwyn thought would succeed Cantor in the public mind. The Cantor/Kaye formula included the rapid-fire patter songs that had made both famous on the stage (Kaye occasionally even used Cantor's material). The idea of the young man who blushes when kissed, stammers and makes wisecracks, and then runs away is all pure Cantor but the story was a remake of Harold Lloyd's 1936 film *The Milky Way*, based on a successful play by Lynn Root and Harry Clork.

Vera-Ellen plays Susan (Susie) Sullivan, Burleigh's sister, and is given few acting chores. She is a nightclub entertainer who is worried about her brother's penchant for boxing and who falls in love with Speed. Her acting scenes are played as if she is on the Broadway stage. She uses exaggerated gestures, including an overly purposeful and particularly silly comedic walk, but she shows she can deliver a line and display effective emotional reactions to other actors. A better director would have worked with her and cut down her forced movements in the non-musical sequences, but Norman Z. McLeod was simply following the then current style of directing broad comedy. In fact, because of Vera-Ellen's slight resemblance to Shirley Temple at the time, McLeod allowed her to borrow from that moppet's 1930s gee-whiz enthusiastic screen persona. Years later Vera-Ellen would comment on how surprised she was to find that she looked so much like Shirley Temple when she was starting her career in film.

Vera-Ellen appears slightly pudgy in the film and she did not like the way her cheeks appeared to puff out on film. Goldwyn had a preference for women with mus-

Vera-Ellen displays her acrobatic dancing talents in *The Kid from Brooklyn*.

cular legs (a *leitmotiv* that fills his musicals) and by this phase of her career (1945-1948) Vera-Ellen's seemed almost muscle-bound. While her face suggested a waif or pixie about to improvise a dance, her legs revealed the enormous hard work and preparation that went into each number.

Her first specialty number in the film, choreographed by Bernard Pearce, is superb: "Hey, What's Your Name?" She appears to be singing along with a male chorus in a train station in the beginning of the Jule Styne/Sammy Cahn number (popular 1950s singing star Frankie Laine's voice can briefly be heard dubbed in among the males — it was one of Laine's first Hollywood assignments after arriving in 1945). Vera-Ellen's singing doesn't last long. It was actually dubbed by Dorothy Ellers, one of the busiest of the ghost-singers from 1944 through 1948, and not by Betty Russell as is usually stated in the general information on this film. Russell actually dubbed Virginia Mayo in the film. Ellers worked primarily for ultra low-budget companies such as Producers Releasing Corporation or in minor musicals for RKO, Columbia and Universal as the voice of Jinx Falkenberg, Evelyn Ankers, Leslie Brooks or Anne Shirley. This film was her only major color production of ghost-dubbing.

But although Vera-Ellen isn't singing she is soon revealing her talents at somersaulting and ballet, and her amazing ability to spin and turn, while throwing in several extraordinary splits and some fine prop-dancing. Prop-dancing is a special type of dancing in which the props can be small staircases such as Bojangles Robinson used in films of the '30s or objects like tables and chairs that become part of the dance. Even a flowing dress can be a prop if it is allowed to billow out in a highly controlled and decorative fashion, complementing body movements such as Cyd Charisse's flowing

The Magic and the Mystery   55

white costume in the *Singin' in the Rain* dream ballet sequence. Often props are intended to appear as if they are randomly encountered by the dancer but their use must actually be carefully planned into the performance. Fred Astaire was the ultimate master of prop dancing as carefully choreographed routines featuring top hats, canes, shoes, drums and even a hat rack in *Royal Wedding* prove.

Vera-Ellen was always able to integrate objects into her routines without breaking stride or letting them interrupt the rhythm of her number. In this number, suitcases are placed in a broad circle and she proceeds to knock each one down with a succession of kicks. The sequence is brief and appears effortless but really is quite remarkable. It shows her insistence that each step must be perfectly executed and the transition from step to step must also be flawless, fluid and seamless. There can be no hesitation or interruption of the fluidity of motion as each suitcase is kicked down; each must be struck in exactly the same way. She makes it seem easy as we watch her smile and float around in a circle, but in fact it is a difficult dancing assignment and requires precise rhythm, timing and extensive practice. It is a dancer's dance.

Each of her spins ends with her facing front, perfectly balanced and ready to make the transition to the next step without interruption. The dance concludes with her being lifted gracefully and flawlessly up into the air into a somersault, then ending up in a perfectly executed split. This is followed by a front somersault, again guided by the male dancers, down into another split. It is the sort of judge-pleasing performance that an Olympic skater might do with perfect fluid motion and a high degree of difficulty. Indeed she frequently compared herself to an Olympic athlete, training her body like a machine endlessly repeating a move to prepare for competition. Her work with the male dancers is equally remarkable. She appeared to float in their arms. In addition, no one could equal her ability of hitting precise marks on the floor so that the cameraman could center and effectively frame his composition.

Her image, now carefully guarded by the studio, was that of a precocious kid barely 21 years old. They hid the fact that she was 26 and that her singing was dubbed, although she had a perfectly good singing voice. She was the brilliant dancing pudgy-cheeked kid, suited to be the sister of Danny Kaye in the film but not glamorous enough to be the sexy heroine or love interest. That was left to the tall, lithe, classically beautiful Virginia Mayo (with whom Vera-Ellen became good friends). But her peers noticed the meticulous and flowing complexity of Vera-Ellen's routines that rivaled and, to some observers, surpassed the talent of Fred Astaire. He had the same ability to make every studied gesture seem improvised and spontaneous. In both artists, dancers knew they were witnessing something special.

Her second specialty in *The Kid from Brooklyn*, presented at the "Milk Fund Charity Dance," is a Goldwyn big-buildup number, designed to present his young dancing star in a spectacular way. She is introduced in a musical flashback as the old-time bombshell "Josie with the turned up nosy." Virginia Mayo "sings" her intro with "I Love an Old-Fashioned Song" as the Goldwyn Girls descend a staircase singing. They are surrounded by dancing males, building up the anticipation for the spectacular entry of Josie. Here Vera-Ellen displays toe dancing and tapping perfection, and again seems to burst down the staircase as light as a feather. The precision, crispness and fluidity of motion in her performance is remarkable and the number is climaxed by a swan dive from 13 feet in the air into the arms of the male dancers below. Vera-Ellen was an

Susan (Vera-Ellen) is romanced by Speed (Steve Cochran) in *The Kid from Brooklyn.*

excellent diver and swimmer and here we get a sense of her daring as she plummets headfirst toward the floor. This sort of plunge was reminiscent of her adagio dancing with the muscular Hightower troupe in New York a few years earlier. She had no fear of heights and, in fact, enjoyed them; this was one reason she wanted to become a solo pilot.

However, at this point in her career, Vera-Ellen's dancing lacked drama. She gave a light, airy performance, like the dancing in a Broadway revue or a talent show, showing her stuff, bouncing around the stage and smiling to the crowd. Vera-Ellen possessed the ability to be a total dancer but still lacked the ability to create a dramatic dance moment. That she would learn from Gene Kelly.

Her reviews for *The Kid from Brooklyn*, which opened April 17, 1946, were excellent. *The Christian Science Monitor* raved that she was "outstanding," "a sprite of a performer." Other critics deemed her "vivacious" and "spectacular," a "hummingbird or a butterfly or any other creature that defies gravity," and were "ecstatic" about this "dancing sprite." *Variety* noted that "Vera-Ellen gets in ably on the comedy and does some spectacular terpsichore in two equally spectacular production numbers." Eleanor Powell had just retired and Vera-Ellen seemed her heir-apparent. Arthur Murray, considered America's greatest ballroom dancing authority and proprietor of the Arthur Murray Dance Studios, was asked in 1947 who was the best all-around feminine dancer in the entire country. "Vera-Ellen," was the immediate reply. *The Police Gazette* reported even more incredible news. At a time when Hedy Lamarr and Lana Turner were the nation's proclaimed sex goddesses, their poll of the 10 women in Hollywood with

June Haver, Vera-Ellen and Vivian Blaine try to catch wealthy husbands in *Three Little Girls in Blue*.

the most sex appeal included neither one but did include Vera-Ellen, which was good news for all those girl-next-door types in the movie audience.

These two Kaye films are generally considered some of his best work and *The Kid from Brooklyn* was his biggest hit to date with the public (grossing $4,000,000). However, Vera-Ellen's contributions, readily apparent to American audiences, were never recognized by Goldwyn. Kaye was next booked for a non-musical, *The Secret Life of Walter Mitty* (RKO, 1947), in which he co-starred with Virginia Mayo—Vera-Ellen's talents were not required. She was loaned out to 20th Century Fox for *Three Little Girls in Blue*. She was billed fourth despite stealing the picture with a *tour de force* dance to one of the film's classic Mack Gordon/Joseph Myrow hit songs: "You Make Me Feel So Young." Lyric writer Gordon also produced the film. The premise was an old one, and was first a play by Stephen Powys before being filmed twice as *Three Blind Mice* (1938) and *Moon Over Miami* (1941), then later as *How to Marry a Millionaire* (1953). It was directed by H. Bruce "Lucky" Humberstone, who directed three of Vera-Ellen's 14 films, *Three Little Girls in Blue* (Fox), *Happy Go Lovely* (Criterion) and *Wonder Man* (Goldwyn)—all for different studios.

The plot involves three gold-digging sisters whose farm is going belly up in 1902. They pool their meager resources to head for Atlantic City and stay at a fine hotel where they hope to find rich husbands. The plan involves getting beautiful Pam Charters (June Haver) to pose as a wealthy young lady vacationer. Sister Liz (Vivian Blaine) will be her secretary and sister Myra (Vera-Ellen) her maid. Pam succeeds in landing

Vera-Ellen:

handsome George Montgomery (who replaced Victor Mature in the role before shooting started) and Frank Latimore, who, through a plot contrivance, is diverted conveniently to Liz. Vera-Ellen however is stuck with supernerd Charles Smith as Mike the comical wine steward. Unfortunately, Smith could not dance, sang with an extraordinarily high voice and was no great shakes as an actor. For this pairing, 20th Century Fox originally intended the Smith/Vera-Ellen characters to be portrayed by physically unattractive comedians. Smith might have been more appropriate for a Martha Raye or Judy Canova but Vera-Ellen is far too lovely for him and it doesn't work. In *Moon Over Miami* the role would be handled by character actress/comedian Charlotte Greenwood, who finally lands the unwilling Jack Haley.

While the other actresses receive more screen time, Vera-Ellen equals their dramatic abilities (despite being given lines such as "Zowie! That's a rip-roar!") and, since this is a musical, she easily blows them each off the screen with her dancing talent. The two other glamour girl leads seem vapid by comparison. *The New York Times* agreed, noting that the movie "...gives prominence to Vera-Ellen and Celeste Holm, two talented young ladies from Broadway, who have more charm than half a dozen Hollywood dolls." The *Times* also mentioned her singing, which was actually ghosted by Carol Stewart.

Vera-Ellen attended the premiere in Atlantic City, and at the box office the film did reasonably well. She worked on this film with Seymour Felix, Florenz Ziegfeld's famed dance director whom Ziegfeld had dubbed "The King of Dance." However, Felix, who had won an Academy Award for his staging of *The Great Ziegfeld* (1936), went bankrupt and had been working as a dance director for Fox since 1944. Since his work was usually considered a throwback to stage musicals of earlier times, lacking in cinematic qualities and creativity, it is surprising that he created for Vera-Ellen's specialty one of the greatest dance numbers in the history of film. And although it occurs in the midst of an otherwise unspectacular picture, that does not diminish its brilliance. It is certainly the most under-appreciated six minutes of musical film ever made and is seldom cited by musical film historians. The film has not even been released on video.

As a showcase for Vera-Ellen's gymnastic, tapping, prop dancing, toe dancing, baton twirling, comic acting and adagio abilities, the "You Make Me Feel So Young" production number is unsurpassed as she fairly bursts off the screen with charm and vivacity. When viewed in a movie theater as it was meant to be seen, the combination of Surrealistic set design (Thomas Little supervising Walter M. Scott borrowing from Salvador Dali), gorgeous Technicolor with its lustrous flesh tones, dark reds and ethereal blues (supervised by Nathalie Kalmus) and the magic of Vera-Ellen are overwhelming. Viewed repeatedly, the sequence reveals amazing technical virtuosity on her part and superior staging.

It begins with Myra and Mike strolling through a carnival. She is worried because their money is running out and the girls will soon be evicted and/or imprisoned without achieving their goal of finding rich husbands. Mike agrees to lend her the required $138 to get them out of the jam. She is ecstatic and her delirium segues to the production number where the two are shown initially with their heads placed above standing cardboard images of two kids.

Vera-Ellen wears her hair down and is dressed in a child's white ballerina outfit. Myra and Mike are dreaming about their love together, at a Surrealistic carnival where

Vera-Ellen is a super-energized Shirley Temple in this dance number from *Three Little Girls in Blue* with Charles Smith.

she dances through a "Guess Your Weight" stand, then jumps on top of a counter next to a giant Wheel of Fortune that spins about and moves its hand as she shakes her rear end at it. Next she grabs a musket from a shooting gallery, twirls it like a baton, and does some gymnastic twists before beating out a rhythm with her taps that sounds like staccato bullet fire as she aims the gun. This tap/shooting effect was "borrowed" from Fred Astaire's "Top Hat, White Tie and Tails" number in the 1935 movie *Top Hat*. Then she is handed two wrapped and boxed presents that, unknown to the film audience, are actually weights. She deftly places these on either side of her body to keep her balance as she is dragged by one leg (while she is in a split) up a ramp to a Ferris Wheel. From there she jumps onto the enormous keys of a giant organ and does a classical ballet dance to "I Love Mike," another recurring tune in the film, as balloons float by.

She grabs a male doll that Mike tries to stick with a big pin but as he does, it clones itself into six male dancers who seem to threaten her. With spins, leaps and staccato leg kicks she darts about them and leaps over them one at a time. Her single leg vaults over each male dance resemble alternate leg exercises on a vaulting horse, continuing until she has traversed all six dancers. This sequence takes place in a forest of giant cotton candy.

Then things get completely out of hand as the male dancers grab her and fling her about like a rag doll. It is difficult to describe the finale to this sequence since it is a blend of courage, extreme coordination and acrobatic dancing. She balances on one dancer who holds her ankles, does a complete spin while in the air and plunges forward one moment, and then the next moment she is flung upward into a complete somersault. Then, while held horizontally face up by her legs and arms, she is flung up into the air into a difficult forward somersault that is followed by giant reverse pendulum swings as the male dancers toss her back and forth.

Any miscue could have caused serious injury and she was completely dependent on the careful grip of her male dancers. This is Hollywoodized adagio dancing at its best and wildest.

Vera-Ellen, of course, executes all of this mayhem with a dazzling smile, which does not show the slightest trace of fear. Her attitude throughout this incredible dance number is that of a super-energized Shirley Temple with gee-whiz responses to everything that is

Vera-Ellen's ballet, done in bloomers to "I Like Mike," is sweetly silly in *Three Little Girls in Blue*.

done to her. Shirley was a teenager by this time, struggling to survive in more adult roles, but the Temple evoked here is that of the 1930s, a persona of optimism and fun. The facial resemblance to Shirley when Vera-Ellen's hair is fixed in a similar manner to that of the child star is striking. After this sequence the rest of the film seems flat. Although it is pleasant and charming, it never again reaches the pinnacle attained in this scene. One might ask if any other female dancer in Hollywood, or in the world for that matter, could possibly have executed this dance number in such an extraordinary manner? The answer is "no" — nobody but Vera-Ellen had the ability to carry it off.

Vera-Ellen also got a chance in the film to do some comic dancing, both solo and in an ensemble with the other female stars. Her brief ballet, done in bloomers to "I Like Mike," is sweetly silly (and sexy) and ends with her attempting to exit the front door but dancing beguilingly into the closet by mistake, a gentle spoof of slam-bang endings to dance numbers.

Forgotten today by all but diehard Vera-Ellen fans, *Three Little Girls in Blue* is an unappreciated high water mark in "The Hollywood Musical." Unfortunately it is only a slightly better than average film on the whole despite being pleasantly received and relatively successful at the time. It occasionally turns up on television's classic movie channels but hasn't been released on DVD as yet.

Vera-Ellen made several radio appearances in September 1946 for NBC, first from the Miss America Pageant in Atlantic City where she attended the premiere of the film and then in an interview with popular host Jinx Falkenberg about her skyrocketing dancing career.

Vera-Ellen with her proud parents on the set of *Three Little Girls in Blue*

For her next film she was again loaned to Fox for a role in *Carnival in Costa Rica,* a typical '40s "Good Neighbor Policy" musical. This film is also unavailable either in 16mm or on DVD but it is occasionally shown on television on the Fox Movie Network. It was designed to showcase the music of the 50-year-old Havana-born composer Ernesto Lecuona. Lecuona had become a legend in his native Cuba where he had been an accomplished pianist since the age of five. His fame spread through Latin America and Europe after a highly successful concert in Paris in 1927. His American following started with his performances for Samuel L. Rothafel at New York's Roxy Theater and he was largely responsible for popularizing Cuban music in America. America influenced him too for he settled permanently in New York City. He was most renowned for "Malaguena," considered a classic to this day, and another popular song of the time, "Andalucia." He was commissioned to write the score for *Carnival in Costa Rica* with the famous American lyricist Harry Ruby. It seemed like a great and novel idea, especially when the music was to be choreographed by one of the leading *avant garde* choreographers of the day, Leonide Massine.

The story involves two families arranging marriages between their children Vera-Ellen and Cesar Romero, but the children rebel because each is in love with another — Dick Haymes and Celeste Holm respectively. Location footage of Costa Rica's coffee festival was intended to spruce up the simple plot.

Before deciding to use her for the film, producer William A. Bacher made Vera-Ellen agree to three stipulations: no horseback riding, no ice skating at the Westwood

Vera-Ellen:

rink and no piloting of airplanes or even riding in them during the making of the movie. Vera-Ellen was a whirlwind of boundless energy and curiosity at this time; she often spent her mornings horseback riding, her afternoons studying for her solo flying permit at Rosemead Airport (she got it), and her evenings ice skating. According to aircraft historian Michael Day, no flight training other than military personnel or Civil Air Patrol had been permitted during World War II. But after the war ended, and apparently even slightly before, flight schools began to once again train a limited number of civilians and Vera-Ellen was at the front of the list. The studio ultimatum was issued to channel her energy onto the screen and to save the picture from costly delays due to injury.

Dick Haymes watches Vera-Ellen get ready for her movie wedding behind the scenes on *Carnival in Costa Rica*.

The production schedule required her to work 12 to 14 hours a day. As usual, she thrived on the work:

> I can still remember when I worked just as hard for $50 a week, and I wasn't merely on lay-off between pictures—I was just out of luck and out of a job. And when I did get one, there were four to six shows a day, rehearsing new routines between shows, making my own costumes, doing my own hair, applying my own makeup, writing my own lines and adapting and routining my own songs and dances. Now I'm getting co-star billing with Dick Haymes; I earn a Hollywood salary, my costumes are especially designed for me at studio expense, makeup experts and stylists and wardrobe girls keep me looking my best; instead of paying for dancing lessons my numbers in this picture are routined by the world's greatest and highest-priced ballet master—Leonide Massine; and on top of everything, I play to a film audience of millions instead of the hundreds, or occasional thousands who see a stage show. With a set-up like that, I'd be plain stupid or ungrateful or both, to gripe about anything, wouldn't I?

But it was a grueling schedule. She was up at 6:00 a.m. and in makeup by 7:00, then dressed, coifed and ready for work at 9:00. There was an hour for lunch and another for dinner with all the time between consumed by such things as interviews,

Vera-Ellen helps with chores on her aunt's farm in Minnesota over the holidays in 1946.

still pictures, costume fittings and hair changes. Evenings were usually spent with Massine going over her numbers for two or three hours, after which she went home and studied her script before turning in at 10:00 p.m. Song recording was also done at night, which in her case meant synchronizing her mouth to another star's voice, although the studio continued to go to great pains to deny this, even claiming she was actually singing (a few years later an exposé of this practice was done in the movie *Singin' in the Rain*). Her singing voice in the film was Pat Friday, who was a regular on the Roy Rogers radio show and was used extensively in Fox movies, especially for actress Lynn Bari.

Before beginning the film, Vera-Ellen, who was very close to her family, flew to Wadena, Minnesota to visit her 87-year-old paternal grandmother Mary Rohe and her uncle and aunt Fred T. Maurer and Julia Rohe Maurer for the 1946-1947 holiday season. She hoped to get some home cooking and to "enjoy" the bracing -35° F climate for 12 days. The tiny town (population 4,000) declared a "V-E Day," not for the holiday commemorating Allied victory in Europe during World War II, but for Vera-Ellen's visit. While there she helped out shoveling snow and milking cows. She went skiing and sledding but the bitter cold kept her from flying out of Wadena airfield as she liked to do on other visits. The town had no dance instructors and a young girl complained to her that children there couldn't ever hope to become tomorrow's Vera-Ellens without instruction. During the 12-day stay, Vera-Ellen gave a dancing class every day to 12 students. Although this sounds like studio cooked-up hokum, friends and family con-

Vera-Ellen takes a sleigh ride during her family visit.

firm that this is exactly what she was like throughout her life with people. She was known for secretly giving money to needy people or charitable organizations, insisting that her gifts remain anonymous. She especially loved children and hoped to make instructional 16mm films of herself giving dancing lessons for viewing by youngsters without access to dancing schools, but so far as is known, these were never made.

Dale Stedman, later a professional photographer from Wadena who worked most of his professional career in Fort Wayne, Indiana was there, on Christmas break from Carleton College, when Vera-Ellen came to Wadena and, like everyone else in the town, he was smitten by her charms:

> I was flattered that she accepted a New Year's Eve date with shy me, turning down, I have since heard, two much more extroverted school mates. It was quite an honor. My dad drove us to the dance, but couldn't get the car started in the 22 degrees below zero weather to pick us up, so the two local policeman on duty drove us to our homes. I later received a letter or two and a stuffy-formal autographed portrait, which were greatly appreciated.... I had a fascinating time over several days making some delightful publicity-type photos of her during the holiday season when she was visiting the Maurers. She was delightful to photograph, and knowing her in her prime was a privilege, although she wasn't the ultra-slim girl that the Hollywood studios demanded. We made pictures of her playing in the snow, riding in her uncle's horse-drawn cutter, with her grandmother, giving a dancing lesson to little local girls.

The Magic and the Mystery

Vera-Ellen dances with J. Carroll Naish in *Carnival in Costa Rica*.

The legendary ballet master Massine who choreographed the dance sequences in *Carnival in Costa Rica* was enamored of the amazing dancing talent of Vera-Ellen. The Moscow-born Russian Ballet star had been discovered by the great Diaghilev in 1913 when he was just 17. A dominant figure in international ballet of the '30s and '40s, he became ballet master of the *Ballet Russe de Monte Carlo* from 1933 to 1941 and, like the film's composer, also triumphed at the Roxy Theater in New York. He directed the prestigious *Ballet National Theater* during the war years and hoped to create a special ballet for Vera-Ellen in a proposed Technicolor feature film to be entitled *The Blue Danube* in which he would also dance with her. The project was much discussed but eventually considered financially unfeasible and was never made. It was one of the first of a stream of proposed but unrealized projects for Vera-Ellen that would have been of the highest artistic value.

Vera-Ellen was excited about working with the master:

> I've studied dancing since I was nine—ballet, acrobatic, eccentric, adagio, tap, ballroom—practically every type but the type I've been doing in this picture: Spanish. I was lucky enough to have the world-famed ballet master Leonide Massine to teach me that, and if you've seen him dance the Miller in *The Three Cornered Hat*, you know there's no one who knows his ballet or his Spanish dancing as thoroughly. No wonder he's been called the greatest dancer since Nijinsky!

Vera-Ellen:

But working with Massine, who lived in Spain for two years studying every type of native dance, gave me the idea for my second ambition (touring the world studying dance of each country). Everyone wants a trip around the world but I think a trip with some working basis is apt to be more fun than a pleasure trip. When you have a definite aim, you contact definite people, go to definite places and with native guidance learn and see more than you would do on a large unmotivated tour. Anyway, although I'm definitely a low-brow, I like learning something new....

Massine actually dances with Vera-Ellen in the film's "Bridal Night" sequence.

Vera-Ellen had another reason for being excited about this film. Back in 1932 when Massine took over the trendy and prestigious *Ballet Russe de Monte Carlo,* which succeeded the famous but now defunct *Ballet Russe* of the Russian master Diaghilev, he assembled the greatest names in the world of ballet to work with him. In 1934 he helped to mold the career of the great Zorina, Vera-Ellen's role model, and for two torrid years he was also Zorina's lover even though he was married at the time. The destiny Alma Rohe had envisioned was becoming reality. Vera-Ellen seemed to be following

Vera-Ellen and Cesar Romero on tour for *Carnival in Costa Rica*

directly in Zorina's footsteps. Furthermore, Gregory Ratoff, who had directed Zorina in *On Your Toes* and who was Zorina's good friend, was now *her* director.

In 1947 Vera-Ellen was hopeful that better roles, and, particularly, more varied acting assignments might come her way:

> By the time I'm 25 (she was actually 26 at the time she said this), I should be ready to do justice to a straight acting role without a song or dance. After all, this is just my fourth picture, and while my acting scenes in each of them increased in length and number, I still have plenty to learn about acting. By the time I'm older, I'll be more experienced and more tired. Doing a musical is about the most strenuous schedule you can have in pictures, you know.

Being goal oriented, she vowed one day to fulfill her wish to star in a non-musical film and she candidly assessed her capabilities and her future plans in 1947:

I'm no glamour girl, but I'm going to keep on working hard enough at being a good actress so maybe someday I'll rate at least an Academy Award nomination. My first goal is to lead a normal life, including having children. The second, which should take only a few years out of my life and consequently, not affect the first, is to tour the world with a view to studying the dancing of every country in the world.

She never fully accomplished any of these dreams. Her desire for a normal life with husband and children remained a constant ambition, especially since her own marriage to Robert Hightower had fizzled. George Sidney, the famed film director, remembered why the marriage ended:

Their marriage was happy at first but Vera-Ellen could not give up her solo dancing and I suspect that that engendered some jealousy on his part.

She thought a lot about having a child and frequently would baby-sit for her married friends and even read books and took courses to prepare herself for raising a family: "I think nothing is as glamorous as a normal life."

But for now it was career first and full speed ahead.

Unfortunately, *Carnival in Costa Rica*, which should have been a major launching pad for her career, bombed with audiences and critics alike, partly because of a stale plot and dull direction by the erratic Russian eccentric Gregory Ratoff. There was also a problem with the leading man. Dick Haymes had been Frank Sinatra's successor with the Tommy Dorsey band and a major crooner (40 top-10 hits 1943-1951) but 20th Century Fox could not make Haymes into a big-screen sensation à la Sinatra, despite his having the ability to deliver dialogue like a breezy leading man. He had slightly odd looks and a stiff presence on the screen and his shoulders were not broad and seemed to point upward. Careful tailoring and photography by director Gregory Ratoff could have compensated for the problem but Ratoff didn't do this. In one sequence Haymes, wearing an oversized sombrero as he serenades Vera-Ellen, looks like a hideous parody of a scarecrow, certainly not a sex symbol for bobby soxers. In addition, the fact that Haymes had dodged the draft in World War II by relying on his British citizenship rather than applying for American citizenship and serving the country that had become his home was an even greater problem and caused many Americans to boycott the film. There were also rumors of his arrogance and nastiness to women.

The picture begins horribly, weighted down by location footage of the happy Costa Ricans gathering coffee and smiling amid their carts and fields so that it resembles a tedious documentary. Massine's boring choreography coupled with Ratoff's clueless direction are disastrous. The film features tireless dancers bouncing up and down in large groups, singing and smiling endlessly and pointlessly. Too many of the characters have thick, hard to understand accents and the basic plot of families arranging marriages seems tiresome and dated. The dialogue is stilted and most of the characters behave like insensitive imbeciles. Particularly astounding is the use of an annoying character, a priest who dispatches advice based on his deep knowledge of the commu-

Unfortunately, *Carnival in Costa Rica*, which should have been a major launching pad for Vera-Ellen's career, bombed with audiences.

nity and its customs. But the advice turns out to be totally worthless. Ratoff has no idea how to pace the film, which resembles a failed dry run for *Black Orpheus* with all of the endless jumping and none of the power of the later film. And the scenes choreographed by Massine are all identical in style.

This debacle is all the sadder because it wastes a beautiful score by Ernesto Lecuona. One song, "Another Night Like This," should have become a standard and is beautifully sung by Haymes, but with all the visual clutter, it is hard to appreciate the subtle beauty of the music of this legendary composer. *Carnival in Costa Rica* is boringly ethnic, with cardboard characters that aren't truly ethnic at all. And each ethnic sequence seems to run on much too long.

But at least Ratoff does show respect for Vera-Ellen as an actress. The film is worth seeing for her charming performance as a romantic lead and light comedienne, even though the dance numbers hide her under so many garments it is difficult to see exactly what she is doing. Her eyes twinkle and she injects the film with a special vivacity and sweetness that reveal her natural talent for acting. Her words are expressed with gentle compassion and sincerity, conveying the impression of a real person and not an actress in a role. The ladies—Vera-Ellen and Celeste Holm—anchor this film as they did *Three Little Girls in Blue*, but Ratoff fails to protect Haymes and makes the talented Cesar Romero just seem foolish.

In Ratoff's obsession with carnival crowd scenes, it is evident that he was strongly influenced by director/cinematographer Josef Von Sternberg in films such as *Devil is a Woman*. Von Sternberg specialized in crowded carnival scenes and masquerades with

Vera-Ellen won over the *Carnival in Costa Rica* film crew with her homemade fudge, note the heart shaped fudge box.

streamers, horns and interacting characters whose tensions and delicate emotional states were revealed by the action of inanimate objects and arranged accidents. In his films, indifferent characters bump into one another, streamers seem to strangle and catch characters in their snares, costumes gleam and sparkle menacingly, horns blare warnings that go unheeded. In a Von Sternberg film the entire visual environment is quivering with passion, governed by the loves and hatreds of the characters. Ratoff tries to emulate this but has no idea how to patch the thing together and the result is boring.

Howard Barnes of *The New York Herald Tribune* on March 29, 1947 called the film "a florid and witless extravagance." Nevertheless, he praised Vera-Ellen's performance in the flop: "Of the principals, Vera-Ellen alone succeeds in capturing fleeting attention by the sheer bounce of her hoofing and make-believe." Bosley Crowther agreed: "...The discomforts outweigh the fun....Vera-Ellen is a pleasant chick who dances with stimulating vigor and has a nice way with a song."

Despite the film's failure, Vera-Ellen appreciated the interest shown in her by 20th Century Fox in first trying to buy her contract and then seeking a share-in-the-contract deal because she had been doing loanouts to Fox. They had also done a lot more for her in terms of press releases and general public promotion. Still, she found herself with a lot of "layoff" time after the film and was devastated by its failure and her inability to get work. The greatest dancer of her generation found herself participating in local Lutheran church activities, taking part in a bowling league that met one night a week and taking 12-mile walks, but she never let herself get out of training:

> I'm a dancer and I can never really get away from my career. On the days when I don't dance at the studio, I have to practice for at least an hour in the evening to keep in shape. Dancing is like breathing— missing a day doing either is very bad.

Meanwhile, at her home studio, Goldwyn did nothing for her career. He saw her only as a "second banana" with no possibilities as a leading lady. He continually claimed to be casting her in second-tier projects that then were never made. Had she done something to offend him?

One possible source of problems in her career came from her personal life. The stable, happy marriage with Bob Hightower had lasted from their wedding day on February 4,1941 (some sources say February 1942 or March 17, 1943) to their official separation in February 1946, not long after his return from military service. The pert 25 year old, who was only 20 according to studio publicity, was not living up to her goody two shoes image by being a divorcee. This cannot have sat well with Goldwyn, since his name was directly connected to her in her epithet "the Samuel Goldwyn dancing star." Gossip columnists like Hedda Hopper had a field day with this sort of thing. On February 14, 1946 Hopper wrote about the separating Hightowers while Vera-Ellen was filming *Three Little Girls in Blue*. The Goldwyn studio had released her official statement to the press the day before:

> We are definitely separated and have been since before I came to Hollywood. There is no possibility of a reconciliation. Neither of us has retained legal counsel in the matter but the parting is final. The rift between us really began when I came to Hollywood.... But Robert couldn't take Hollywood, I guess.

By July 10, 1946 Vera-Ellen had filed for divorce while her husband was in Blackpool, England fulfilling a dancing engagement. He was served with papers (via a registered letter) for mental cruelty, a standard, often routine complaint used to avoid further paperwork, but the added details confirmed persistent rumors that Hightower was unstable, domineering and given to violent rages. She accused him in a Superior Court complaint of compelling her to make verbal and written statements against her wishes. He was called "stubborn, obstinate and unreasonably jealous" of the men with whom her profession required her to associate. He was also highly critical of her "ability and art." The suit, filed under the name Vera-Ellen Rohe, asked for no alimony. Seven years later she would refer to herself as "immature" during this period and shouldered some of the blame for the failure of the marriage.

During this period Vera-Ellen's mother was staying with her and her closeness to her mother may have been another wedge in the marriage. In any case, Hightower's response to the suit was sent to her mother from England on June 20, 1946. It was then, oddly, released in part by Alma Rohe to the press. It stated:

> I don't tell people here that Vera and I are married, as I don't think it
> would do her any good to have her name linked with mine. I'm sure
> you know I love her and always will.

Photos of a pouting and distraught Vera-Ellen hit the newspapers on November 28, 1946 when a default divorce was granted in Los Angeles. In a candid interview she revealed perhaps more than she should have about her unhappy life with Hightower:

> He had an overestimated opinion of himself. I had to remind him that
> I earned more money than he did. He was jealous of my career, had a
> violent temper and twice knocked men down in public, and always
> tried to use physical force to make me sign written statements. I was
> frightened to death of his reckless driving. My friends were afraid to
> have me ride with him.

Vera-Ellen was careful not to date anyone until after the divorce papers were served. After her divorce the Goldwyn studio attempted to pair Vera-Ellen with various male stars in their pantheon but because of her strict religious convictions she did not consider dating assigned men appropriate. At this time she and her mother were members of Hollywood's Lutheran Bethany Church and she was spending her Sunday mornings in a black and white robe singing in the choir and her Wednesday nights attending choir practice. Her disobedience coupled with her very public divorce may have irked Goldwyn and may have encouraged him to abandon her. Later in life she recalled: "After Mr. Goldwyn set me up in pictures, he really ruined my career."

20th Century Fox, on the other hand, was interested in making her a true star. In *Three Little Girls in Blue* they touted her "piquant sense of comedy, that no one ever suspected she possessed." Press releases stated that she "bubbles with enthusiasm and charm, and 20th Century Fox, who borrowed her for this picture, have already realized her possibilities and borrowed her for *Carnival in Costa Rica.*" But the stubborn Goldwyn would not release her to Fox. It was a critical moment in her career and a terribly disappointing one as she was perched on the verge of superstardom with Fox. Between Goldwyn's obstinate shortsightedness and neglect and the failure of her second Fox film, another golden opportunity slipped away.

One major project announced as a starring vehicle for Vera-Ellen was *Billion Dollar Baby*, which was supposed to be produced in 1947, but it quickly vanished into thin air. Originally produced on Broadway, this musical by Betty Comden and Adolph Green was to be tailored especially for Vera-Ellen immediately following her success in *The Kid from Brooklyn*. Goldwyn actually distributed publicity kits about it. Finally, after the failure of *Carnival in Costa Rica*, she was released from her contract. Finding herself without a studio, she broadened her talents, taking a lesson from the failure of her heroine Zorina (who was also flopping in films such as *Follow the Boys* and *Lover Come Back*). She used the time during this freelance period to prepare for straight dramatic roles by formally studying acting. Despite her feeling that "a musical is about the most strenuous schedule you can have in pictures," she realized that Holly-

Vera-Ellen in a 1946 swimsuit pinup pose

wood dancing stars such as Ginger Rogers and Rita Hayworth had gone dramatic with considerable results. In fact, Ginger had won an Academy Award for *Kitty Foyle* in 1940.

One project repeatedly dangled in front of her as a possibility by Goldwyn was the lead in a musical version of the life of Marilyn Miller, a role she desperately wanted. Miller had been the darling of Broadway musicals of the 1920s and had died tragically in 1936 at the age of 37 after being medicated for a severe sinus infection. She had been a singer, dancer and actress on Broadway and, less successfully, on film. And she was another role model for Vera-Ellen who, with her slim build, cute persona and flashing eyes, physically resembled her. The project was discussed for years in Hollywood and a film of Miller's biography was finally made in 1949 as *Look for the Silver Lining* starring June Haver (from *Three Little Girls in Blue*), who at the time was being groomed as Betty Grable's successor. Haver resembled Grable, was perhaps even lovelier (and 10 years younger), and had a passable singing voice and a fair ability to play the piano. But she lacked Grable's vivacity, onscreen charm and acting ability and never attained Grable's popularity. With the decline of the musical in the early '50s, Haver retired in 1953 to enter a convent for some months until she fell in love with and married actor

The Magic and the Mystery

Vera-Ellen, an accomplished pilot, poses circa 1946 with a PT-19 or PT-26. The pose, according to Michael Day, is a little joke: "A PT-19, like most other low-powered aircraft of the period, did not have a starter motor. The engine was started by someone grabbing a propeller blade and pulling it. This is a 'prop start.' At the time Vera-Ellen was flying it was common practice (but not recommended) with larger engine planes to raise a leg and then kick back for additional force as you pulled the propeller. So Vera-Ellen is doing a parody of the engine start-up using one of her famous high kicks!"

Fred MacMurray. In the hands of Vera-Ellen, who would have poured her soul into the role, the story of Marilyn Miller could have been a legendary musical and dramatic performance with magnificent dancing. Unfortunately, Vera-Ellen lost out again and Haver's lackluster portrayal and a weak script garnered few notices. The film is all but forgotten today.

After wrapping up *Carnival in Costa Rica*, Vera-Ellen spent three quiet weeks vacationing mainly in Northern California, riding in a San Francisco cable car for the first time, almost falling off Morro Rock and enjoying Lake Tahoe and Yosemite. Due to the postwar boom, she was unable to find hotel reservations, so she slept in the trailer she had used at Fox for her last film during the trip. While passing through San Jose, California she telephoned to her number one fan, Dorothy Hashimoto, President of the Vera-Ellen Fan Club, that she was going to drop in on her. This was the way Vera-Ellen was with her fans and she always loved to sign autographs, stop on the street when recognized, chat and answer fan mail.

But on her return to Los Angeles she still found herself with no offers. She immediately enrolled at UCLA's summer school for six weeks of typing classes, Gregg shorthand and Spanish. And her 87-year-old grandmother, Mary Rohe, came to visit her in Hollywood for the first time. Her interest in Spanish had come from Costa Rican technical advisor Miguel Ruiz, who started teaching her the language between takes on the set of *Carnival in Costa Rica*. Since the film was to premiere in San Jose, capital of Costa Rica, she hoped to go there and speak to the local people in their own tongue. She wanted to use her typing skills to answer fan mail faster and the shorthand was important for taking notes more quickly on dance steps she saw in the movies or at the ballet or for taking better notes in her classes. She also sought to learn French (she had taken some classes at Hollywood

Vera-Ellen:

High) and German (Gregory Ratoff had tutored her briefly) well enough so that if her career dry spell proved permanent she could establish herself as a multi-lingual typist. But the real reason behind all this academic activity was that the ever-motivated ball of energy that was Vera-Ellen just "liked learning something new" all the time.

During this period Vera-Ellen was continually encouraged by her mother, who lived with her in California. "Mother" was her principal adviser and personal secretary, helping her to deal with fan mail that continued to pour in. Vera-Ellen's father Martin, who continued to work at piano tuning in Norwood, was only visiting the family twice a year, but moved out to join them late in 1946 or early in 1947 at the Argyle Avenue home. When his piano tuning business was nearly wiped out in the Great Depression, Vera-Ellen had became the family's principal source of income. He had stayed in the business until her future appeared bright enough for him to join his family in California. By 1947, he had developed a heart condition and was unable to do much physical labor. A.C. Lyles remembers being with them all back then:

> Her mother was a wonderful lady. I can picture her like a little sparrow and they had this nice home out in the Valley. I knew her father…he was alive when I first met her and he passed away and she and her mother lived there. I just got along great with her mom and we'd go sometimes down to Palm Springs.

Vera-Ellen was realistic enough to understand that in the post-war period movies were not drawing the way they had before or during the war. By the later 1940s, television was becoming increasingly popular and a family could entertain itself at home far more cheaply than it could by going out to a theater. At first television featured second-line performers such as Olsen and Johnson, Doodles Weaver, Arthur Godfrey (who quickly became a star of his own show, *Arthur Godfrey and His Friends* in 1949) and Faye Emerson. But by 1948 with the popularity of Milton Berle's *Texaco Star Theater* cinemas all across America became abandoned on Tuesday nights for "Mr. Television, Uncle Milty." *Ed Sullivan's Toast of the Town* that same year and the popularity of Godfrey and other shows soon to come crippled the movie theaters further. Actors who had formerly been seen only in the movies or onstage were obliged to do television or risk not working and being forgotten.

Vera-Ellen had become the victim of a studio head who had lost all faith in her during a period when that Hollywood staple, the musical, was going into eclipse. In a year particularly disastrous for musicals, Vera-Ellen told *The Herald Tribune*:

> When Hollywood hit a depression, I was known only for my dancing, so I went to work on everything I could think of that might help… Singing, dramatic courses, dancing in every form, speaking voice.… I realized I had to get out of the class of being a specialty artist. The studios do not sign people under long-term contracts who can supply just a single ingredient for a picture.

This desire to make herself a complete entertainer helped her personally and professionally:

Vera-Ellen successfully changed her image to help her win better parts.

I shall never be sufficiently thankful for the blessing in disguise this sudden lull in activity meant for me. I took stock of everything. Above all I tried to learn what Hollywood was really like....I had been known as a dancer when I was engaged by Mr. Goldwyn. The roles that I played in Danny Kaye films were secondary. I had other opportunities in the two 20th Century Fox films but these did not seem to help for one reason or another, and in one film of these two [*Three Little Girls in Blue*] I was in a secondary spot again.

So I decided that I would school myself for young leading roles, if possible, and would try to become associated with a studio where musicals were regularly made and where my dancing talents could be used and then hope for the opportunity to act as well. I knew above all that I must qualify as somebody who could be built up from their standpoint, that there was no hope of a regular contract otherwise.

And with that she was back on the road to stardom.

Chapter Four
MGM Heyday

It is amazing that Vera-Ellen was as successful as she was in the late '40s and early '50s because the old Hollywood was rapidly crumbling around her. Almost all the musical stars of the '40s had made their final appearances in Hollywood musical films by the middle of the '50s: Gloria De Haven (1955), June Haver (1953), Donald O'Connor (1957), Tony Martin (1957), Betty Hutton (1952), Betty Grable (1955). Between 1943 and 1953 the number of musicals dropped from 65 to 38 and for those 38 the budgets had fallen considerably. In 1963 only four were made.

With her movie future so uncertain, she thought of returning to the Broadway stage. Constantly being compared to Marilyn Miller as the cutest, most vivacious and premiere popular dancer of her day, Vera-Ellen was offered the starring role in a musical revival of Miller's enormous hit music *Sally* to be produced by Hunt Stromberg Jr., husband of actress Hedy Lamarr, and William Berney. Richard Barstow was to do the choreography and former silent film comic star Billy Gilbert would direct, while legendary comic Willie Howard was set to star in the role made famous by Leon Errol on the stage in 1920.

Through the early part of 1948 she agonized about whether to stick it out in Hollywood or do the risky show and risk being forgotten in Los Angeles:

> It was a great part and a fine chance to dance and sing and do some acting, but I couldn't make up my mind. I carried the script around with me for three weeks. I was afraid to leave Hollywood, though, because I thought if I were away from pictures too long I'd lose out entirely. I hadn't established myself well enough to take such a chance....Just after I turned down *Sally* I was offered the MGM contract and *Words and Music*.

The role of *Sally* was eventually given to dancer Bambi Lynn, primarily a ballerina, who was less than a sensation, even though Willie Howard got some of the best notices of his career. The show opened in May 1948; it closed in five weeks.

In the meantime Vera-Ellen was indeed approached by the greatest of musical studios, MGM, to do *Words and Music* with Gene Kelly in 1948. Robert Alton, who had loved working with Vera-Ellen at Casa Manana and in *Panama Hattie*, was the choreographer and was also responsible for staging the musical numbers for the film. He reminded Kelly of her outstanding capabilities and availability and lobbied for her selection. Kelly had seen her dance on Broadway and was already impressed. Not everyone, however, was impressed with her during this period. Director George Sidney had little admiration for her dancing form at this time and told us so in an interview shortly before his death on May 6, 2002:

> As a dancer she was not that proficient but was rather a trickster. She seemed to be good but wasn't the best. Her movements were too

jerky and lacked fluidity. She liked to do her points and high kicks. She did however have no peer in acrobatic dancing.

Fortunately, Alton and Kelly did not share Sidney's assessment of her work. The seven and a half minute jazz ballet "Slaughter on Tenth Avenue" from this film became her all-time favorite dancing role, completely regenerated her Hollywood career, achieved landmark status in the history of the musical film, and became the single work of art for which she is most remembered today. Rehearsing with Gene Kelly, her first worthy film dance partner, and studying with studio voice and acting coach Marie Bryant proved to be a great learning experience for the starlet. Bryant coached her on "screen personality," convincing her to lose her girlish dress and innocent, easy-going Shirley Temple facial expressions and go for something deeper:

> Until I got the part of the Bowery girl in the number with Gene Kelly, I had just danced in a thoughtless, easy-going way. But Marie made me "think" about my dancing and Gene made me take it seriously. Altogether, I spent six weeks rehearsing the number and three more weeks with Gene shooting it—all for seven minutes on the screen.
>
> It was worth it though. I got a seven-year contract from my studio, an offer from England and a number of proposals, including one from a man who enclosed an engagement ring as an introduction. The Museum of Modern Art in New York asked for a copy of the dance number and, best of all, my fans made it plain that they liked my new personality better.

Robert Alton's task in the "Slaughter on Tenth Avenue" sequence was to choreograph Vera-Ellen and coordinate his moves with those of Kelly, who found it surprisingly easy at first to collaborate with him. Kelly said:

> Bob Alton was a very underrated choreographer. Years ago he was the first fellow who really knew that what I was doing dancewise was different; he recognized it and said, "Go ahead and do it." He was a great help to me and always encouraged me very much.

Vera-Ellen's work ethic was legendary and Kelly was a notoriously severe taskmaster, but she could take everything he could dish out. During the filming of "Slaughter on Tenth Avenue," she had to have her delicate, tiny feet packed in ice at the end of each work day and she regularly worked with bleeding and severely blistered feet. She lost so much weight on this production that her costume had to be altered. She was determined to make the most of the opportunity with Kelly even though she was billed 14th on the film credits due to the alphabetical listing of stars. MGM meanwhile kept the pressure on for her to slim down her thighs. Her long-time friend A.C. Lyles remembers Vera-Ellen's attitude on the set:

> I've been with Paramount since I was 10 years old and in those 70 years I've known and worked with everyone in this business: writ-

ers, directors, producers. I think everybody who has been successful has been obsessed and extremely talented, and I've never know anybody who worked harder or was more dedicated to her task than Vera-Ellen. I'd talk with her at 7:30 a.m. and she'd either be in the gym or class—she just worked constantly. For her it was like having a 9 to 5 job everyday but it was extended earlier and later and on weekends.

When she first arrived on the set she wore her usual rehearsal costume of fluffy ballet skirts and her necklace of hearts for luck. But this image of the girl next door wouldn't do. Gene Kelly sought to revamp her look and image and contributed to her education by teaching her to exemplify what she called "a sort of earthy, sexy quality—toward modern." She reportedly became so obsessed with her character that she was observed in church walking in a

sultry fashion, prompting her mother to say to her in a shocked whisper: "Vera-Ellen, you're slinking!" She began to show up on the set in what became known on the MGM lot as the Vera-Ellen rehearsal costume: tight turtle-neck sweater, tight satin blue jeans.

For her performance, which was to have been a one-picture deal, Vera-Ellen earned her long-term MGM contract and went on to work with Kelly again in the classic *On the Town*, and Fred Astaire in *Three Little Words* and *The Belle of New York*. Vera-Ellen had reached the big time and was entering her "Golden Age." Critics praised her dancing versatility, noting that "she could do acrobatics, characterize, step gracefully and eccentrically." The secret of her success was not just talent but also a lot of plain hard work that left her black and blue and bleeding.

Vera-Ellen's growing legion of fans was stunned by the Vera they saw in "Slaughter on Tenth Avenue." The number had been originally staged more comedically by George Balanchine for Ray Bolger in the 1936 Rodgers and Hart stage musical *On Your Toes* and it had also been used in the 1939 film of the same name, which had starred Vera-Ellen's inspiration Zorina and Eddie Albert. Now the number, as staged by Gene Kelly, was serious, different from Bolger's slaphappy dance routine. It has been termed the first *dance noir*, echoing the popular *film noir* genre of the '40s. Kelly stated:

> I changed the libretto from the comedy which Balanchine had done to a tragic ballet....We rehearsed the number for four weeks and shot it in three days.

Vera-Ellen and Gene Kelly in "Slaughter on Tenth Avenue," which stole the show in *Words and Music*.

It was also a landmark in that it was the first attempt to show a lengthy stretch of ballet, indeed a complete dramatic story, in a major Hollywood film, something that no one believed general audiences would sit through, let alone enjoy, the whole thing having been given the feel of a Parisian Apache dance bathed in glaring red and yellow lighting.

Kelly had gotten the idea to change the original concept of the dance, as exemplified in the 1937 Broadway performance, from the original plot which featured a young dancer holding a dead girl's body to avoid a gangster's bullet. His new idea was a self-contained ballet within the overall film featuring a gangster and his pickup girl who are followed by a jealous rival and shot dead in a Manhattan Hell's Kitchen saloon.

Gene Kelly has stated to several writers that he considered Vera-Ellen among the very best dancers in films.

Vera-Ellen portrays a super-tough, saucy Bowery girl with a wild blonde wig, a too-tight yellow top and a bright orange skirt slit almost too far up the side, all cinched with a thick black belt with overlarge ring buckle. As she struts in under the Tenth Avenue overhead El, swinging herself alluringly from side to side, she attracts the attention of a local thug (played by famed choreographer/dancer Jack Baker) who makes a crude pass at her. She rebuffs him with flamboyant gestures, virtually hissing in his face, then pauses to adjust her clothing in a provocative manner, and she straightens her stocking.

Quickly we learn her interest is focused on Gene Kelly's tenement flat and with one intense stare she suggests she will do all she can to attract his attention. Kelly, at his most muscular and athletic, rises from bed and climbs down to the street where Vera-Ellen is strutting, preening and slithering around him, even rubbing herself up against a phallic pole. It is a mating call and Kelly takes the bait. They interact as she falls to the ground and rises up toward him, then falls back as he moves down toward her. Once again she moves away from him, but they finally end their teasing courtship and come together in a sensuous dance as he dips and drags her body along the street.

Passing to another set by rotating the stage rather than by using editing (a curious technique which was deliberately apparent to the audience and made the proceedings actually look like a staged Broadway production), they enter the swinging doors of a saloon where couples are dancing. Descending a long staircase, they begin to dance too, but the same thug who had accosted her before is still waiting. Her daring wrig-

The charming North Hollywood home of Vera-Ellen and mother Alma Rohe on Camellia Avenue as it looks today.

gling dance and the sight of Kelly gyrating suggestively with her incite the thug to grab her and a fight ensues. Then the police arrive. Kelly has knocked down and dazed his opponent but now kicks him gently, a humanitarian act to warn him that the police are coming. After they leave, however, the troubles continue and the thug shoots at Kelly at the top of the stairs.

Vera-Ellen gets in the way, takes the bullet, and falls. She crawls, then flips upside down, landing in the foreground where a diagonally placed camera captures her unconscious head as Kelly rushes to her. This was filmed with a 28mm lens lowered into a pit at the bottom of the staircase and caused deliberate distortion of her face, which Kelly later stated he was not only trying to achieve but had insisted upon. Louis B. Mayer tried to prevent the use of the lens by arguing that it would make an MGM female star appear in an unflattering way. But Kelly got his way. The fight then continues and Kelly hurls a chair that lands very close to the camera, almost in the viewer's face. The thug shoots him and he staggers about, finally grasping and carrying Vera-Ellen to the top of the stairs, kissing her and falling dead.

Despite the downbeat theme, the pair do some difficult synchronized dancing with angled, jagged steps, a far cry from anything Vera-Ellen had done before. The dance number stole the picture from the rest of the MGM cast and was a springboard for her career. Gene Kelly has stated to several writers that he considered Vera-Ellen among the very best dancers in films and the excellent reviews helped to launch the $2,799,970 film to a gross of $4,552,000. This new sexy Vera-Ellen, the girl next door with an attitude, revealed a range and dramatic intensity that was unexpected. Suddenly, after the film's opening on April 4, 1948, she was a hot property. Louis B. Mayer called her into his office at MGM and told her she would star with Kelly in *An American in Paris*. However, when Arthur Freed found out about this, he persuaded Mayer to change his mind. Freed and Kelly insisted on casting an actual French girl and Leslie Caron got the part. Nonetheless, between 1949 and 1950 she had three musicals in release simultaneously and was considered a major young star. And the best was yet to come.

During this period, Vera-Ellen was feeling more secure about her future and purchased her home at 4557 Camellia Avenue in North Hollywood where she lived with her increasingly ill father and her ever present and dominant mother. At this time also, reports of her having a "nose job" began to surface, but it is hard to see that anything significant was done to her. She always had a relatively ample nose which could be downplayed with makeup, hair styling and lighting, but if a tiny nip or tuck was taken when she

got her MGM contract, it can hardly have merited the behind the scenes gossip it got in Hollywood at the time, for so many stars were having much more done to themselves. More likely, Vera-Ellen was simply growing into a beautiful young lady just when her dancing talents were peaking. Her next film proved she was no one-hit wonder.

Vera-Ellen made a decision that ultimately did her no good in 1949. She decided that if she was going to have a new image in Hollywood and a new contract with MGM, she might get dramatic roles and therefore she would have to know how to handle a cigarette. She practiced smoking in order to learn how to seem more sophisticated for possible upcoming roles. She also believed that smoking might help to keep her weight down and there was at the time no public evidence that it was harmful. In no time at all she was hooked and became a chain smoker. Friends say that she liked to start her day with a cup of coffee and a cigarette.

All historians of Hollywood musicals consider *On the Town* to be one of the definitive, ground-breaking examples of the genre and most rank it as one of Gene Kelly's three cinema masterpieces. It also grossed three times its $1,500,000 budget, breaking the house record at its debut at Radio City Music Hall. Released in 1949 in time for Christmas, it once again featured Kelly and Vera-Ellen "deliciously coupled in the singing and dancing of 'Main Street' and a new Leonard Bernstein ballet, 'A Day in New York,'" according to *The New York Times*. *The Herald Tribune* added that Vera-Ellen's solo work was "the show's dancing sensation."

Typically, MGM gave Vera-Ellen poor billing, even dumping her below the film's title along with Broadway newcomer Jules Munshin, despite the fact that her work was critically important to the film and she was one of the six ensemble players. It was another slap in the face and a vote of little confidence in her, this time by MGM. And it was even noticed by her fans, many of whom wrote the studio asking why she was given such poor recognition by her studio. She never seemed to worry about billing. Nor did she ever try to jockey for position in the credits of her films. She simply believed in doing her work and letting the chips fall where they may. She told her friend A.C. Lyles that she felt fortunate to have been in the film at all.

The salaries for *On the Town* reflect how MGM valued its talent. Gene Kelly got $2,000 a week and took home $42,000 while Betty Garrett, who was considered a hot ticket at the time from her Broadway work, got $1,750 a week but only totaled $6,250. Jules Munshin, who spent a good portion of the film terrified of the heights of New York he had to perform in, received $1,500 a week and a handsome total of $20,250. Ann Miller received $1,000 per week and totaled $16,833. The director Stanley Donen got only $400 a week and a total of $8,400. Vera-Ellen received the lowest pay of any of the stars, receiving the same weekly salary as bit part comedienne Alice Pearce, $750 per week. Vera totaled just $8,875 for the film while Pearce, who was seldom on screen and had little to do, took home $6,250.

On The Town was originally conceived for the Broadway stage by an almost unknown young choreographer named Jerome Robbins, with music by a rising star named Leonard Bernstein working with Betty Comden and Adolph Green. The idea had originated as a ballet with music by Bernstein called *Fancy Free*. The story involved the use of song and dance (and little spoken dialogue) to describe the adventures of sailors on a one-day leave in New York City. For the film Kelly and his friend co-director Stanley Donen kept two Bernstein songs but scrubbed the rest for a new score with lyrics by Comden and Green and music by Roger Edens. And they decided to film it largely on location in New York. The myriad setups all around the town were highly effective and the frantic pacing made the film different from all other musicals that came before.

The making of *On the Town* was part of MGM's Silver Anniversary celebration in 1949. As part of this occasion 59 of the 80 great stars and promising performers from their stable were assembled for a photo session. Vera-Ellen sat directly behind Fred Astaire and in front of Van Johnson, and next to Errol Flynn and Jimmy Durante with Gable just a seat away and Hepburn nearby behind her. It was quite fancy company for the young lady from Norwood, Ohio.

Ads for *On the Town* proclaimed it was "Twice as Gay as *Anchors Aweigh*," which, many forget, was the less artistically successful forerunner of *On the Town*. It featured two sailors (again Sinatra and Kelly) on leave in Los Angeles. That film had been successful at the box office and won two Academy Award nominations. But the new film was much more fun.

In the film, Kelly sees the vision that is Vera-Ellen on subway posters that celebrate her as the winner of the "Miss Turnstiles" contest. She is the principal focus of the film. He fantasizes about her in two dream sequences: the "Miss Turnstiles Ballet" and "A Day in New York." In a "real life" sequence, Kelly sings "Main Street" and dances with Vera-Ellen. She also joins the cast for the famous "On the Town" finale.

The male stars set up the highly effective opening solo by Vera-Ellen. As sailors on leave, Kelly, Sinatra and Jules Munshin ride the subway and stare at the poster of lovely Ivy Smith (Miss Turnstiles), and Kelly fantasizes about what she must be like

Gene Kelly and Vera-Ellen as young lovers in *On the Town*

from the written description. In his fantasy, she is singled out from among all the lovely girls who ride the subway. Next she pantomimes the many-faceted description of herself that Kelly is reading on her poster. She is home-loving and so dances happily behind her ironing board, then leaps and brings the newspaper to her man. She loves the social scene so she whirls about in a fashionable evening gown and gloves. She is seen dating the Army and the Navy, but her heart belongs to the Navy (Gene Kelly served in the Navy during World War II and slips in a plug for his branch of the service). She is studying painting at the museum and dancing at the Symphony Hall so she

The Magic and the Mystery

Vera-Ellen as the ideal sports-loving woman in *On the Town*

appears doing both at once: toe dancing and painting in a ballerina costume. She is described as a frail and flower-like creature who is also cited as being athletic, triggering frantic sequences of hurdling, running and winning a victory cup, huddling with a football team and catching and running the ball, boxing, wrestling and flipping male opponents and pulling their hair.

This sequence gives the picture a big lift right at its beginning and establishes Vera-Ellen as a charming comedienne at what used to be termed "eccentric dancing." Her girl-next-door good looks and stunning flashing smile, coupled with her impressive dancing in the sequence, not only sell the number but make it an American film musical classic. It is also important for the history of dance on film for it is the first time that a female lead in a film was introduced and had her complete character presented through dance.

Later there is another charming dance number as Kelly finds her standing on her head while she is taking dancing lessons and he warbles "When You Walk Down Main Street With Me," a salute to Meadowville, Indiana, their common home town in the film. In this routine she mimics Kelly's typical swagger, shoulder shrugs and jaunty manner as they tap together, and the dance is tossed off effortlessly and without a false step. Here we see Vera-Ellen's uncanny ability to complement her partner perfectly. Ginger Rogers, within a limited range of tap, ballroom dancing and light ballet, could also do this but Vera-Ellen could effectively partner any male dancer in Hollywood or on Broadway in *any* type of dance, something Rogers could not do. That was one of her unique talents. The dancing continues as Kelly and Vera-Ellen go out on the town, but their nightclubbing ends abruptly when she leaves him at precisely 11:30 p.m. with no explanation.

Kelly finds Miss Turnstiles standing on her head while she is taking dance lessons in *On the Town*.

Near the end of the film, Kelly daydreams about what has transpired between himself and Vera-Ellen on this day in New York. The segment is called "A Day in New York Ballet." In his fantasy, he meets Vera-Ellen, who is exercising at a ballet practice bar dressed in a leotard with black fishnet stockings. They are attracted to each other and dance slowly and sensuously together, kissing and then parting. Next, he relives seeing her again, taking her out on the town in New York with his two buddies (being played here by dancers/choreographers Lee Scott and Alex Romero, replacing Munshin and Sinatra) and their dates (dancers/choreographers Carol Haney and Jeanne Coyne).

The Magic and the Mystery

"A Day in New York Ballet" in *On the Town*

They do a frenzied happy dance now with the skyline of New York silhouetted in the background but suddenly it is 11:30 p.m., Vera-Ellen disappears and Kelly returns to reality to ponder why his fantasy and real-life girl has vanished.

In the finale, Kelly finds out that Vera-Ellen is really nobody important at all, just a kid, like himself, from Meadowville, Indiana. But she is gravely upset when he finds out she is making her living at night as an exotic "kootch" dancer at Coney Island; this was her dark secret and the reason why she had to leave him at 11:30. In this sequence Vera-Ellen is seen bending completely over backwards about to pick up a handkerchief with her teeth. The term "kootch" dancer had become common vernacular during the 1893 Chicago World's Fair when such feminine midway attractions packed them in. Originally known as carnival "hootchy-kootchy" dancers, the term became shortened over time to "kootch."

Shortly after the release of the wildly successful *On the Town*, Vera-Ellen mused about her career, which finally seemed to be in high gear, and mentioned the roll of destiny in her life, a concept that her mother had always cited as important:

> It's always the slow way with me. That, I've learned, seems to be my
> life pattern. I've never been able to get where I wanted without

preliminaries. There's a certain fate about the way things develop for me, and I've learned that patience is the best solution.

She was dating producer A.C. Lyles at the time and today he still remembers *On the Town* vividly:

> When she did *On the Town* with Frank and Gene and Ann and Betty she'd say to me, "my God how fortunate to be working with all these people and learning"—and yet she was herself as good as they come! *On the Town* was so great for her because she had that wonderful part of being almost like the girl next door. When every fellow saw this, I would imagine, he would say "that's the kind of a gal I'd like to take home to mother" and every mother who saw her would say "that's the kind of a gal I wish my son would bring home."
>
> It was because that part she had there was as much the way that Vera-Ellen was in her personal life as anything that she did—she was so vivacious. That was a good part for her—she looked great, she danced well, she was happy in it, and she was so delighted to be working with all of them.

Frank Sinatra, a close friend of A.C. Lyles, was particularly impressed with Vera-Ellen's work in the film, as Lyles remembers:

> Frank often said to me: "God, she was so lovely and so sweet." She had a wonderful wholesomeness about her. If you looked at her and you didn't know about her background, you'd probably think she was born on a farm in Utah and went to town and won a contest.

Donald O'Connor watched Vera-Ellen's work in the MGM musicals with great admiration:

> I know for a fact that Astaire and Kelly truly respected her as a dancer. You can tell from the way they danced with her that they felt she was someone truly special.

Ann Miller told us:

> She was a lovely girl, a darling girl, very hard working and a beautiful dancer.

There was talk of her dancing again with Kelly in a musical version of *Topper* which was to be called *Ghost of a Chance* but it never materialized. Instead, her next film was a comedown, a limited role in a lesser Marx Brothers comedy, entitled *Love Happy* (1950) that is mainly remembered today as the film that introduced Marilyn Monroe to the screen via a two line saucy walk-on. Monroe's small part led to the film's re-release in the mid-1950s when it was advertised as "The film that introduced

Vera-Ellen gets to do a sexy "Sadie Thompson" dance number in *Love Happy*.

Marilyn Monroe." But it is usually considered by critics to be a featherweight comedy because the brothers are seldom allowed to perform together and bounce comedy off one another as was their trademark. It has its high moments, but it is not up to the golden age of the Marx Brothers.

The plot concerns a million dollar necklace stolen from the Russian Romanoffs and smuggled into New York by villainous Ilona Massey (in a scenery chewing over-the-top performance) and her henchmen, including a young Raymond Burr. Harpo, whose function is to steal food for a starving cast of a Broadway show in production called *Love Happy*, accidentally pilfers the necklace that is hidden in a sardine tin

Harpo Marx and Vera-Ellen in *Love Happy*

marked with a Maltese cross. Hopelessly smitten with Maggie Phillips (Vera-Ellen), principal dancer of the show, he gives her the necklace when he finds it in the can. The thieves end up backing the show to try to get the sardine can with the jewels and the whole mess ends in a rooftop chase among New York advertising signs with swinging pendula and belching smoke.

Vera-Ellen gets to do a sexy "Sadie Thompson" dance number, based on W. Somerset Maugham's story and the famous John Colton and Clemence Randolph play. With this number she joins the ranks of Gloria Swanson, Joan Crawford and Rita Hayworth, who starred respectively in the three film versions of this story, playing the prostitute in Pago Pago who ruins the life of a missionary during an epidemic. Vera-Ellen looks beautiful in one of the few black and white films in which she appeared— but unfortunately she hasn't much to do. Her dance work is limited to strutting and spinning like a whirling dervish at the finale, and she is not well photographed. Her male dancing partners are not paired well with her and seem at times to be dancing in another number altogether. All this may be laid at the feet of the normally reliable dance director Billy Daniel but to be fair, he had 10 major film choreography assignments within a two-year period and perhaps was either burned out or did not have enough time to devote to this project.

Nonetheless Vera-Ellen has a pleasant if small featured role and was billed third (if you count the Marx Brothers as one). The film is a loosely constructed mess of gags, thin plot and weak musical numbers but once again she anchors the film by giving a solid and sweet interpretation of a sad ingenue whose boyfriend has gone off with sultry Ilona Massey to discuss funding for the show. By playing her role straight, she allows the mayhem around her to ensue but lets the viewer identify with a realistically portrayed character. Love-happy Harpo befriends her and the two have several charming scenes together. She is more than up to the challenge of her Cinderella-like role. Her sweetness, long flowing hair, lovely smile, effective crying scenes and pleasant toe-dancing give her the demeanor of a storybook princess. Although thin, she looks much more robust than she does in her next film, *Happy Go Lovely*, filmed a year later in which she had become frighteningly emaciated, to the point of losing muscle tone. She also has a lovely, silly and well-delivered monologue about uniting with Harpo to scale the heights of Broadway.

Although she was largely ignored on the set by Chico and Groucho, who spent a lot of time cutting up and refusing to follow the planned script, she was treated most graciously by Harpo, whom she adored: "He treated me just as if I were his daughter."

Among the promotional tie-ins for the film, United Artists had Vera-Ellen endorse Royal Crown Cola in a *Life Magazine* ad, featuring a photo spread of her taking the taste test with brands X, Y and Z and supposedly declaring: "I'm convinced RC tastes best—for I compared the leading colas and RC rated best with me…"

Even before *Love Happy*, MGM vowed to give her more non-dancing screen time as a comedienne and dramatic actress, casting her in *Three Little Words* in 1949. This was a busy and exciting time for Vera-Ellen, but it was marred by the death of her father at her Camellia Avenue home on June 21, 1949 from hypertrophy of the heart. He was four months shy of his 67th birthday. Martin Rohe was buried at Glen Haven Memorial Park in San Fernando, California.

Her career, on the other hand, was booming. Prior to starting work on her new movie and just at the time of her father's death she was starring in the Laguna Playhouse production of *A Highland Fling*, a comedy by Margaret Curtis, in which she portrayed Jeannie McKenzie. With her acting skills thus sharpened, Vera-Ellen was ready for a meaty screen role. She was at last to work with Fred Astaire and his friend and choreographer Hermes Pan. Astaire had retired in 1946 but was coaxed out of it to star in *Easter Parade* with Judy Garland after Gene Kelly had broken his ankle. At first she was overwhelmed but they all got on famously and Astaire taught her "exhibition, ballroom stuff." Vera-Ellen was actually a more complete dancer than Fred but she was not permitted in their paired dancing to show him up in any way. So there were seldom any super high kicks, splits or flamboyant acrobatics when the two of them danced together. Those moves had served her well in her pairings with Danny Kaye when there was need to make him look as if he could dance. With Astaire, she had to dance his style, which was easy for her. She was amazingly adaptable and by far the most versatile partner he ever had. The actress Vivian Blaine once noted that Astaire had told her that Vera-Ellen was the best dancing partner he ever had and Hermes Pan, Astaire's doppelganger and choreographer, considered her one of the most talented dancers he ever worked with.

She was amazed at how much Astaire was like her. He worried over a routine obsessively and felt that it never seemed to look exactly right and always had to be rehearsed and rehearsed again. Apparently she worked hard enough because *Variety* gave her the best notices of her career on July 12, 1950:

"Vera-Ellen...becomes the undisputed premiere *danseuse* of the screen..."

Vera-Ellen with this picture becomes the undisputed premiere *danseuse* of the screen. She matches Astaire tap for tap in their terping duets, which is no mean achievement, and looks to be possibly the best partner he's ever had.

The London Evening Standard described her as "infectiously happy as a new partner for Fred" and *The Herald-Tribune* said that both dancers were "at the top of their form." Philip Hamburger of *The New Yorker* wrote that "Astaire never had a more charming associate" and Astaire himself called Vera-Ellen "a brilliant dancing star."

Many critics realized that the chemistry between the two was extraordinary and matched the Astaire-Rogers pairing in grace and unity of movement while excelling it in technical virtuosity. Vera-Ellen later offered her theory on partnered dancing:

The Magic and the Mystery   *93*

I like to vary partners, but with any partner, it's two people moving like one, if you know what I mean. She should practically breathe only when he does, and the audience should feel the romantic bond between them and not be conscious of the steps. It's different when you're given your own number. Then you can get out there and stop the show.

Three Little Words is a Vera-Ellen high-water mark. She got third billing after Fred Astaire and Red Skelton and she was part of an acting ensemble foursome that included both of them and Arlene Dahl. The rapport among all four was remarkable and gives the film a more believable and warm family quality than any of the other MGM biopics. Chronicling rather fancifully the ups and downs, Broadway hits and romantic breakups of girl crazy, baseball-loving composer Harry Ruby (Skelton) and the magic-obsessed Bert Kalmar (Astaire), the film is full of fine acting and lovely music. Behind the scenes Skelton kept everyone entertained with non-stop gags.

Vera-Ellen's acting is particularly wonderful in this film. Her gentle and subtly nuanced performance is the glue that holds the film together (she would be given the same type of role four years later in *White Christmas*). She proves herself not only adept at making an ensemble scene work but at reacting to the dialogue of others with understated but effective emotion. It seems unbelievable that MGM still found her acting talents marginal after this effort, but they did. She projects a sexier image here too, than in previous films with her deep, throaty voice, elegant designer gowns and dancing costumes, and a dance number that allows her to be a racy French can-can dancer. Yet she still projects the image of the girl next door as she sits home knitting (she was such a perfectionist she actually studied knitting so her stitches in the film would be real). Her lovely smile and golden skin tone were never shown more effectively or beautifully in Technicolor than here and after the release of the film her popularity soared as the major stardom she sought seemed hers for the taking. She was light years away from the bouncy young girl of *Wonder Man* and *The Kid from Brooklyn*. And gone were the puffy cheeks of her early years, thanks to maturity, makeup and the extreme diet forced upon her by MGM.

She always had difficulty with a lisp for "s" sounds but her general softness of tone and breathy delivery, particularly in her opening closeup in the dressing room with Astaire, turn this slight speech impediment into a positive attribute. *The New York Times* noticed not only her marvelous dancing but also her fine acting performance:

> In talking of the fine dancing contributed by Mr. Astaire and Vera-Ellen, we forgot to mention how engagingly they carry off the romantic interest and burst into song when the script demands it.

It was fashionable at the time for actresses like Martha Raye, Betty Hutton, Bette Davis and Joan Crawford to overplay their scenes. Vera-Ellen's performance holds up today and is more appreciated now because natural acting has become increasingly fashionable in recent years. Every word she speaks, just like every step she dances, is the result of careful study and thinking and comes from the heart. Her quiet sincerity is

Vera-Ellen as Jessie Brown in *Three Little Words*

the gentle core around which *Three Little Words* spins and it allows the film's characters to achieve true warmth and charm.

The film opens with a charming old-time vaudeville tap routine with Astaire and Vera-Ellen in top hat, white tie and tails. She looks sweet and adorable as she shakes her head and mimics Astaire's style. They perform a synchronized cane dance, tapping as they throw their canes back and forth and slam them down on the ground, only to catch them again—in unison. Of course Vera-Ellen had no difficulties with cane twirling, having been a high school majorette.

Balletic flourishes are thrown into this routine that is supposed to echo vaudeville circa 1919 with Kalmar-Ruby songs such as "Where did You Get That Girl."

The two dancers toss off this number with an effortlessness that astonishes. But once again Vera-Ellen's singing is dubbed, this time by Anita Ellis.

As Jessie Brown, later Mrs. Kalmar, in the film, Vera-Ellen next appears in an unusual and renowned duet of two married dancers with Astaire: "Mr. and Mrs. Hoofer at Home," which has remained one of her most famous and best-loved routines. Vera-Ellen shows a flair for comic dancing while domestic life is parodied, including frantic breakfasting and an extremely odd sequence of abusing and throwing around a baby like a football as the child is popped out of her crib into the air. Astaire uses several

"Mr. and Mrs. Hoofer at Home" in *Three Little Words*

beautiful hurdling lifts (swinging of the partner over an extended leg that is resting on a chair or table) as he had done for Ginger Rogers in *Carefree*, and the sequence ends with the pair crashing wildly through the wall of their home. Thomas M. Pryor of *The New York Times* raved about this dancing pantomime:

> Mr. and Mrs. Hoofer at home for purity of motion would be hard to equal. With Vera-Ellen as his adept spouse, the incomparable Mr. Astaire nimbly demonstrates the domestic life of a pair of married dancers. The hyphenated young lady beautifully complements her partner in this imaginative, exquisitely conceived and executed number.

Then she is given a brief solo as "Sweet Marie from Gay Paree," just long enough to do a bit of can-can, lip-synch "Come On, Papa," fall into a split that is transformed by dancing males into a somersault, and execute a series of remarkable turns, acrobatic twists and leaps. But it is over far too quickly. This segues quickly into another number with Astaire and Vera-Ellen, briefly ballroom dancing to "Nevertheless."

The masterpiece of the film is the Astaire/Vera-Ellen dance to "Thinking of You," certainly one of the most elegant and beautiful dances in the history of the motion picture (it was selected for inclusion in the 1985 compendium film *That's Dancing*). Although it is filmed at normal speed, it seems to be in slow motion as every movement is perfectly matched between the two and they seem to be floating above the ground.

There is a hot, still quality about it that reveals that the sum of these two together is much more than the parts. It is nothing more than ballroom dancing, yet a still picture taken at any moment during the dance would reveal the two in total synchronized motion, elegant flowing visual curves echoed by the movement of Vera-Ellen's gown. Reflecting on this number later, she would observe that Astaire had taught her how to dance "like the floor was hot—suspended off the ground." He was "a more ethereal partner, willowy, smooth—in ballroom, ballet and tap." At the end of the sequence they glide to rest on the piano where the routine had begun. The fluidity of this final move-ment and their total synchronization are breathtaking. It is two gifted souls in love with the art of dancing and dancing as if they were one. Astaire noted:

> She can do anything—lush dances, tap, comedy. She's quite good at eccentric dancing, and a good comedienne.

A United States film poll in 1950 listed Vera-Ellen fifth among the top-10 new screen personalities likely to achieve major stardom. Even more amazing was a *Life Magazine* poll in the same year which listed Vera-Ellen high among the top-12 most admired people in the history of the world, along with such dignitaries as General Douglas MacArthur, Louisa May Alcott, Joe DiMaggio, Roy Rogers, Babe Ruth, Franklin D. Roosevelt and her former Ohio dance class companion Doris Day. She even got her image on Dixie Cup lids and if you sent 10 of these ice cream lids to Easton, Pennsylvania, you could get an 8x10 color photograph of her. Yet MGM, like Goldwyn, never realized what they had in Vera-Ellen. They never fully considered her a leading lady and believed that she could not act well enough to get out of the second lead or specialty dance category. Only later, in *The Belle of New York,* did she get the full co-star buildup by MGM and most unfortunately that film bombed—through no fault of hers. This lack of attention to the promotion of her career is hard to understand today. Screening her films reveals a most capable actress who listened well onscreen and was a fine dramatic or comedic anchor when given half a chance, as seen in movies such as *Three Little Words*, *The Belle of New York*, or *Happy Go Lovely*.

During this period, Debbie Reynolds remembers that MGM held dancing classes early in the morning for their female stars that included calisthenics, bar work, stretch-ing and ballet with instructor Janet Bennett. The class usually included Vera-Ellen, Cyd Charisse, Ann Miller, Leslie Caron, Zsa Zsa Gabor (!), Debbie Reynolds and some-times Zizi Jeanmaire. Cyd Charisse and Vera-Ellen amazed the young Miss Reynolds with their fabulous extensions, and the way they placed one leg and then the other over their head pointing to the sky. They did everything perfectly. But Vera-Ellen had lots of time for dance classes because MGM wasn't creating starring roles for her. They were a lot more interested in sultry, long-legged Cyd Charisse, whose big break would come when she was assigned to do "The Broadway Melody Ballet" in *Singin' in the Rain* in 1951.

Vera-Ellen was hoping for dramatic roles during this time or at least more musical work but she faced a rival being brought along by MGM named Sally Forrest. The latter was also a dancer, although not in her league, but she was considered to have more sex appeal by the authorities at MGM and they began to put Sally in a string of dramatic roles that Vera-Ellen would have loved to have played: *Mystery Street,*

Rock Hudson and Vera-Ellen in 1950

Valentino, Hard Fast and Beautiful, Vengeance Valley. All of these were shot in rapid succession so that Sally was working constantly (six films in 1951 alone) while Vera-Ellen was not, and Ms. Forrest was regularly mentioned around MGM as Vera-Ellen's principal rival for parts. Finally, Vera-Ellen was offered a role in *Excuse My Dust*, a small Red Skelton gay nineties vehicle about a small-town inventor. When she hesitated about doing it, the studio immediately cast Sally Forrest and Vera-Ellen wondered if she would ever do anything significant again for MGM.

It was about this time that Vera-Ellen began to date Rock Hudson regularly and they appear to have become serious about one another after first being simply close friends. She was aware of his homosexuality but there was nonetheless considerable affection between them. Together they attended the Hollywood Press Photographers Ball in 1950 and caused a sensation, appearing as Mr. and Mrs. Oscar. In an effort to gain notoriety and publicity for themselves, both of them wore skin-tight gold outfits (she wore a bathing suit) complemented by gold body paint and prop swords. A few years later she reflected on the event:

> We went into a paint store for the gold paint and when the salesman wanted to know *what* we were going to paint, Rock said "ourselves." I'll never forget the expression on the man's face. We went as Oscars, you know, and it was easier to put the stuff on than it was to get it off. For a week afterward we'd stop traffic when we drove with the top down on his car, our tarnished faces peering into the world.

They couldn't keep the paint on for very long as they risked poisoning themselves. Her comment to reporters was: "I wanted to dress like Oscar." *American Movie Classics* host Nick Clooney reflected on the event: "I couldn't believe it. This shy sweet young thing showing up dressed like that. It was really something."

With so little for Vera-Ellen to do, even in later June 1950 when she was so popular throughout America, she sold her car to Rock Hudson and made her first trip abroad in July for a starring role in the British-made *Happy Go Lovely,* written by the much underrated writer, director, producer Val Guest and co-starring Cesar Romero and David Niven. She was concerned about leaving her mother alone, but Rock Hudson promised to look after her and even helped with yard work such as fence painting while she was away. MGM was against the move and tried to dissuade her from doing the film.

The lofty aim of the executive producer and director of *Happy Go Lovely* was to create the first decent British musical by importing American talent. This genre became known as the "Anglo-American musical" and had its roots back at the turn of the century when American plays such as *The Belle of New York* were brought to London. The imported talent included the veteran Bruce Humberstone, known for directing musical hits with Betty Grable, Alice Faye and Sonja Henie and Vera-Ellen (in the hit *Wonder Man*). It was a risk for the Americans because in the early '50s, if an American took a starring role a British movie, it was seen as a sign that his/her Hollywood career was on the skids or even that he/she was washed up.

The movie had an extremely low budget by Hollywood standards, only $840,000. A Romanian named Marcel Hellman (a Vera-Ellen fan) had been signed to produce it, and it was made in a country not noted for making musicals that were well received on the other side of the Atlantic.

Hellman was from Bucharest, but was headquartered in London where he had organized Criterion Film Productions in 1935 with the help of Douglas Fairbanks, Jr. A number of small-scale productions followed among which was *Happy Go Lovely*. The film is claustrophobic—the sets are small, the stages are small, the costumes look cheap, as if creditors will repossess them at any moment (of course that was supposed to be the case in the show). But RKO agreed to release the film and Hellman was ecstatic about landing Vera-Ellen to star: "I couldn't have done it without her."

Set during the Edinburgh, Scotland Arts Festival, the plot concerned an out-of-funds American stage musical director (Cesar Romero), desperate to find money before the creditors close his production of *Frolics to You*. Through a mix-up, he mistakenly believes that Vera-Ellen is the girlfriend of the richest man in Scotland (greeting card magnate David Niven) and he gives her the lead in his show when the star quits. Niven is irate, and Vera-Ellen discovers that Romero is only using her, but she decides to do the show anyway so she can become famous. By the end of the proceedings both Niven and Romero have fallen in love with her, but due to yet another misunderstanding, she thinks Niven is actually a newspaper reporter. The typical Hollywood mistaken identity plot could have come straight from an Astaire-Rogers film of the 1930s but actually was lifted from the 1937 British picture *Paradise for Two*.

The film gets off to a shaky start with a Scottish musical number featuring British players. Vera-Ellen is barely visible in the background as chorus girl Janet Jones. The number is entitled "Macintosh's Wedding," and it is ragged enough to send audiences heading for the exits demanding their money back. But once this is endured and the

David Niven courts Vera-Ellen in the musical comedy of mistaken identity in *Happy Go Lovely.*

story begins, it is so charmingly played by all three principals that it becomes delightful viewing. Unlike the MGM and Goldwyn films, this is a starring vehicle tailored completely for Vera-Ellen, even though David Niven is top-billed. For once, the producer has been willing to respect her talent and give her a chance to display her burgeoning dramatic skills. And Val Guest's witty script makes the most of the ridiculous mistaken identity plot and generates real laughs. Her low-key acting and fine dancing carry the film and infuse it with the same sort of warmth that typified *Three Little Words.*

By refusing to overplay her lines, she becomes again the pivotal center around which the wild over-the top-acting of Cesar Romero and the wonderfully exaggerated, mannered performance of David Niven revolve. She makes the viewer care about her character and she makes her role believably sweet rather than frantic or simply comedic. Vera-Ellen has the chance to show herself as a talented romantic comedienne and she generates real chemistry with Niven. In one scene, she lies about her relationship with a millionaire, not realizing she is speaking to the millionaire himself. He asks where she met the millionaire and she replies: "We met near the pyramids, just a little to the left!" Vera-Ellen is in virtually every scene of the film either dancing, acting or reacting, generating sweetness and sincerity (even when she is lying), and chiefly for these reasons *Happy Go Lovely* remains a charming low-budget surprise.

The time spent in London was hard on the Cincinnati-turned-California girl. Although she wanted it known that she wasn't belittling the English or their filmmaking, she complained about British life and culture. Missing the sunshine of her San Fernando Valley home, she claimed that London fog was suited to a mystery film but not at all conducive to "animated performance." She also found the post-war lack of available meat in London a problem since her special dancers' diet called for unusually large amounts of it to keep up her energy. Instead, she existed largely on grapefruit and scrambled eggs during the production and, amazingly, stated at the time: "I like to feel fragile and undernourished when I work."

Though pencil slim, she kept up her search for the virtually nonexistent meat and didn't enjoy the British afternoon habit of filling up on tea and little cakes. Her weight began to drop substantially and in the film she appears frighteningly thin. Her 20-inch waistline had become a Vera-Ellen trademark and she was determined to keep it at all costs, and her measurements at the time were widely advertised as 33-20-32. At 5 feet 4 inches tall she weighed 108 pounds until constant rehearsal made her weight drop closer to 105 as she wore out over 30 pairs of dancing shoes during the filming. But following the shooting she put weight back on while vacationing in Italy when she ceased her maniacal work schedule for a time. When she got back to California, she became obsessive about mowing lawns — not only her own but her neighbors' — in order to exercise and keep off weight. She gradually adopted the practice of wearing Saran Wrap when she mowed to maximize weight loss.

Her greatest dissatisfaction with London was the scarcity of proper rehearsal equipment and Hollywood comforts:

> They have no idea over there how much equipment a dancer needs for film work. Since shoes and full-length hose wear out at an astonishing rate and since these articles are just not to be had in England, I had to put in a rush order to Hollywood for 50 pairs of each. Costume materials are hard to get, too. I wear a cotton costume in *Happy Go Lovely* that the average American star wouldn't be caught dead in — and do you know — it looks pretty good on the screen. Marcel, the producer, always had us report at 6 a.m. for work which meant I would arise about 4:30, breakfast (one egg a week) and then dogtrot around Hyde Park to limber up.... Sometimes I would exercise my leg muscles atop the hotel....

It must be noted that Vera-Ellen felt appropriate costumes were essential for she had learned from Kelly, Astaire, Hermes Pan and especially Robert Alton that costumes were not just clothes but props. The displaying of the costume, its flaring and billowing, and its decorative emphasis of the movement of the dancer is integral to the routine. Such costume movements were Vera-Ellen trademarks. There has never been any female dancer who could use costumes in a routine with the grace of Vera-Ellen, so much so that they seem to behave as a dance partner with her, rather than as a raw material.

As if all the problems of food, weather and working conditions weren't enough, Vera-Ellen was attacked by the British press for declining to perform in a command performance for the Royal Family. But doctors had forbidden her to perform because of exhaustion and injuries received while driving herself too hard on *Happy Go Lovely*'s routines. Val Guest reports that she seemed as if she would kill herself with her preparations. She agreed to attend the command performance and walked down the aisle of

Meeting Princess Elizabeth in 1951

the theater on crutches with bandaged feet. Princess Elizabeth recognized her and she smiled and exclaimed: "Look! There's Vera-Ellen!" This royal gesture helped soothe her ill feelings toward Britain and was the highlight of her visit.

Everything about *Happy Go Lovely* is so much smaller and shoddier than a standard MGM production that Vera-Ellen's complaints seem justified today. The critics spotted this too. Bosley Crowther of *The New York Times* wrote on July 26, 1951 that it was a "featherweight" musical. The film would be unendurable but for the work of the three principals and especially Vera-Ellen's dancing and acting. There is particular emphasis placed by director and cinematographer on her ultra-thin waist and every opportunity is seized to show off her long legs.

Her charming performance infuses the modest production with what Crowther called "a certain limpid charm" which he noted was "due in the main, we would reckon, to Vera-Ellen's youthfulness and grace." *Variety* was similarly enthusiastic about the overall pleasantness of the film and especially Vera-Ellen who "sings and dances her way through the picture with poise, artistry and grace. But at all times she remains a warm and colorful character, handling the romantic scenes with much delicacy."

Why did she do the film?

> Well, there wasn't anything doing right at the moment for me at MGM. I had never been abroad and thought it would be quite fascinating. Executives at Metro tried to discourage me but I went anyway. It was fun, in a way. I enjoyed Scotland very much, Edinburgh in particular, where I picked up a cute little dog (her Pomeranian Happy) with a burr in his bark.

She also wanted to show everyone that she could really act and that *Three Little Words* was no fluke. Nonetheless, MGM, just like Goldwyn, paid no attention to her dramatic skills. And even in her British film she was not permitted to sing; her voice was dubbed this time by Eve Boswell. Screenwriter of *Happy Go Lovely,* Val Guest, reflected in July 1998 on the experience of working with Vera-Ellen:

> It was pleasant fun but we didn't get to know her well. She was really a loner. But I remember several things about her. She was very very professional, 100% into her work. She rehearsed like a lunatic. London had no good locations for dancers, no proper training bars so it was very hard for her to find good spaces to work. I remember her dancing, practicing on the roof of the Dorchester Hotel. She really was a very good actress of what I call the natural school, a type of acting like Spencer Tracy did. It was a sort of throwing out your dialogue without seeming studied at all.

She wrote the president of her fan club on July 30, 1950 from the Dorchester Hotel in London:

> Well Yvonne I'll have to get busy and hustle to bed as I have a very, very early call in the morning 5:15, oh boy! I'm so tired now I don't know how I'll ever be able to get up so early, but I'll have to.

Happy Go Lovely featured four major numbers, coordinated and supervised if not entirely staged by Jack Billings, the British actor and choreographer, with ballet sequences by Pauline Grant who went on to great fame as ballet mistress of the Sadler's Wells Opera and director of the English National Opera. That notwithstanding, the ballet sequences of the film are dull, particularly the initial dance to the waltz entitled "1-2-3," staged in period costumes that seem pointless and probably were pilfered from some other film. In the sequence an attempt is made to recreate poses used in the French Rococo painter Fragonard's *The Swing*. Although there is little new here, Vera-Ellen executes the standard toe-dance with her typical flair, making beautiful transitions from step to step and never interrupting the graceful fluidity of her dance with a false move. In one part two male dancers wrap a long scarf around her minuscule waist and twirl her charmingly back and forth, the sequence likely cribbed from *Three Little Words* where Fred Astaire had done virtually the same thing in the hoofers at home sequence. But the overall concept of the piece is fuzzy—why is everyone in period costume and what does the song have to do with it? The final short ballet to "Would You, Could You," yet another of the uninteresting songs in the film, also presents little that is new and contributes a cheap, setting sun backdrop as Vera-Ellen does another pleasant but very brief classical toe-dance.

The fascinating set piece of the film, however, falls in the middle. It lasts over six minutes and is clearly an attempt to create a British "Slaughter on Tenth Avenue" by telling a complete dramatic story through dance. Despite being an *homage* or blatant rip-off if you prefer, it is very good. Vera-Ellen learned from Gene Kelly how to dance with deep-felt emotion. One of the joys of this sequence (or any post-1947 dancing

Vera-Ellen and David Lober in the "Slaughter on Tenth Avenue"–inspired number in *Happy Go Lovely.*

sequence with Vera-Ellen) is to watch the emotional expressions on her face change and her body language attempt to portray the deep feeling she is experiencing at each moment. She has become a complete dancer.

The sequence opens, "Slaughter" style, with a crowd milling about a London street corner (Picadilly Circus?). There are tough street girls, a newspaper boy, a thug or two, people out with their family for a stroll, a bicycle rider, etc. Vera-Ellen appears taking in the sights and photographing local color. She tries to photograph a paperboy but a woman with packages keeps getting in her way. Next she photographs a prostitute adjusting her stockings and the woman attacks her and smashes her camera. Undaunted, Vera-Ellen flirts and tap dances with two men in bowler hats carrying canes. They dart around a streetlight pole and dance up and down some stairs. But soon she attracts the attention of a young street punk (further shades of "Slaughter") danced by Jonathan Lucas. Making repeated gestures of alarm and trying to escape these unwanted attentions, she flees as he rips off her skirt. As the young bounder grabs her, the prostitute laughs derisively and Vera-Ellen slaps the man. Before he can strike her, a nice-looking young man (David Lober) comes to her aid. The police arrive and drag the thug off, leaving a happy Vera-Ellen to dance with her handsome rescuer. Unlike "Slaughter," this liaison ends happily (but also on a long, wide staircase) with the couple staring lovingly into each other's eyes. Although the male dancers in this sequence do not have the stage charisma or emotionalism of Gene Kelly, it is a memorable sequence with lovely steps in the Kelly/Alton style, and it repays a second (and third) look despite its derivative nature.

David Lober, dancer and choreographer who worked with Vera-Ellen in this film, recently corresponded with us most candidly about his experience with her, which was not altogether positive. He notes some good things about her but on the other hand found her not entirely cooperative, not entirely capable and not at times particularly pleasant to be around:

> It's been a while since I worked with Vera, but there may be some snippets that might be of interest to you. The male dance members of *Touch and Go*, a Broadway musical playing at the Prince of Wales Theater in the West End of London, were involved in the "Picadilly Circus" number in the film. They were doing two shows a night, 11 performances a week.

> To prepare her for the modern dance number, I would be driven to the studio at 8 a.m. and give Vera an hour's class every day. It was a way of moving that she was not familiar with. She worked at it diligently, if not totally successfully. As you know she was a private type of individual, with several idiosyncrasies. It was her habit to eat one soda cracker and drink coffee during the day. Then she would eat at night. She was concerned about her legs appearing heavy. Her costumes were constructed, that is padded, to give her body more of a V shape at the top of her torso. Another thing I recall was her cultivation of a low voice in speaking.

> Between her willingness to work and self-destructive diet she ran herself into the ground. Because of fatigue, one section of the dance took 26 takes; five or six are normally more than enough.

> She spoke of Rock Hudson, and I believe she said that she had hoped to marry him, so there was obviously some involvement.

> In the section with Jonathan Lucas that preceded mine, her skirt was torn off, leaving her in a peblum. Since I considered our section to be a lyric romantic dance, I insisted it be done with her original and longer skirt. This is why it magically reappears. She had wanted to do the dance in the peblum showing her elegant legs. It became an issue which revealed her part in it. I was willing to walk, and she made the concession.

> Each section of the number was choreographed by the people involved, and coordinated by the dance director. Jonathan choreographed his section. I did mine and I believe Doug (Douglas Scott with his group, the Debonair Boys) and Jack (Jack Billings), the dancers in the next sections, did theirs.

> The choreographic direction for my section was that it should be like *Slaughter on Tenth Avenue* that she did with Gene Kelly.

> I had heard that while filming her toe number that she had worked so long and hard that her feet were bloodied and blistered during the shoot.

> Dance credits were given in the European release of the movie, but not in the American. The filming must have been in July and August of 1950, because my wife worked in the film and didn't arrive in England until the end of June.

The Magic and the Mystery

After being criticized for her style, Vera-Ellen remade herself once again.

There was the sense that Vera was working hard at being a movie star. She seemed to have mastered the façade, and was driven beneath it. Hard working, private, attractive and ambitious were the impressions I got.

Not long after the release of *Happy Go Lovely*, a reporter once again insulted Vera-Ellen for no good reason and hurt the insecure and eager to please young star very deeply. In 1952, Mike Connolly of the *Hollywood Reporter* wrote:

> Somebody should award Vera-Ellen a special Oscar for being the worst dressed off-screen actress in Hollywood.

This reporter claimed Vera-Ellen hid herself behind beads, jangling earrings, jeweled gloves, bows and flowing draperies. When she went to an Academy Awards event in a full-skirted pink evening gown with ballet slippers and a pink velvet "tam," Connolly let her have it. She was heart-broken by these harsh words, and her long time friend, protector and frequent date, the legendary Paramount producer A.C. Lyles, went after Connolly at a party: "That was a nasty thing you wrote. The poor kid's been heartbroken ever since."

At the same party Vera-Ellen, now in a simple green cocktail dress, mink stole, plain gold necklace, ring, wristwatch and high-heeled shoes, told Connolly:

> It took your item to straighten me out. First I bawled. Then I went to Sam Kress, head of wardrobe at the studio, and to Helen Rose, who helped me by designing some less frou-frou dresses. They were the kind, Helen explained, that would let people see me. No ribbons, no bows! Then I talked with Ann Strauss of MGM publicity. She said that when I dressed to go out I should give myself one last once-over and take something off. Now if I deck myself in earrings, bracelets, rings and necklace, I take off the earrings — and sometimes *both* necklace and earrings! In addition, I learned plenty from Claudette Colbert, Gloria Swanson, Marlene Dietrich and Irene Dunne, with whom I attended the Command Performance in London. I studied not only the way they walked and talked in public and the clothes they wore, but the way they wore them.

She blamed her lack of style on her rustic roots:

> I think my own gaudy taste in clothes was a throwback to my childhood. We were a rather poor family. Mother and Grandmother made over my clothes and I guess I always thought I knew what was right. I wanted to glitter like the movie stars did in those days. Besides I was a skinny little kid and the ruffles covered up a lot of ugly angles. Then when I became a dancer high heels were uncomfortable. So I always wore ballet slippers. I've discovered it's important to spend time on your looks rather than concentrating strictly on your talents.

After this episode, Vera-Ellen became one of the most elegantly dressed women in show business both onscreen and at functions around town. But her problems went far beyond clothing.

Chapter Five
The Belle of New York

In 1952, before the much-anticipated opening of her recently completed film, *The Belle of New York,* which featured her exciting re-teaming with Fred Astaire, Vera-Ellen did something she had not done since the 10th grade. She went home to Ohio for two days. It was February and she was both promoting the film's March premiere at Cincinnati's Palace Theater and celebrating her 31st birthday. Her former dancing teachers, the Hesslers, met her at the airport along with a police escort. Mrs. Hessler exclaimed, "My little girl!" and threw her arms around the star. Vera-Ellen replied: "I could just squeeze you to death. I'm so happy." Her homecoming was marked by a student assembly at Norwood High School, an extraordinary honor for the woman who never finished her classes there. Deeply touched at being remembered, honored and cheered so warmly, she was reduced to tears. She told the thrilled audience as the tears streamed down:

> Just look at me now. I'd really planned to be glamorous. But I'm so excited—I've never been so happy in my life.

As more cheering followed this and more gifts were brought, the tears kept flowing. The president of the Student Council honored her royally with flowers, the head of the chorus in which she once sang brought her a bracelet, and the president of the Girls' Council produced a birthday cake.

She came down from the stage to greet friends as the Norwood High School Band she had once led as a majorette thundered the school's anthem, "Love and Honor to Old Norwood." On the following day a wonderful reception was held at the Children's Convalescent Home in Mount Auburn for her birthday. She spent much of that day serving cake and ice cream to the young patients. Vera-Ellen also found time to lend support to the Heart Fund campaign in Norwood before leaving for more promotions for her film in Miami, Florida, New York, Los Angeles and Baltimore:

> Funny, but when I suddenly found myself in the places I had spent my childhood, it seemed like I'd never been away. I felt like it was only a short time ago that I'd played hopscotch and tag with the kids at Norwood View Grammar School.
>
> And when I stood on the stage at Norwood High School and saw the school's drum majorettes twirling their silver batons, I was reminded of the days when I used to do the same thing to the tune of the school song. And all the kids were singing a song they had written especially for me. I don't mind admitting that the enthusiastic demonstration really touched my heart.

It was also strange to revisit her old home, and the neighborhood where she grew up and dreamed of becoming a Hollywood star:

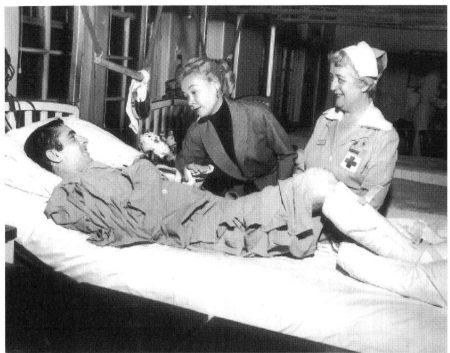

Vera-Ellen visits injured Korean war soldiers in 1952.

I can't explain the exact feeling, but I'm sure that anyone who's been away from home for a long time can understand the experience. However, I'm certain of one thing. If I ever have to return home and live with mom and dad, I would have no trouble getting into the swing of things again. I'll always have that feeling no matter what. I'd fit in with the neighbors—and they'd get along with me.

At the ceremony she was given her transcript, showcasing her perfect grades in Latin and her 98% in everything except for Physical Education. She had become the Belle of Norwood!

At this time in America fans were recognizing Vera-Ellen everywhere she went. Her friend A.C. Lyles remembers being with Vera-Ellen when she would be stopped frequently by admirers:

It was interesting when I'd go out with her to see how much attention she got from fans and the complete sincerity in her response to them. She was so kind and nice to everybody wherever you went: waiters, parking lot attendants, just everyone. They'd say that they had just seen her in some picture and she was so great and she would reply something like: "Have you seen this picture where Cyd Charisse was dancing with Gene Kelly; they had this wonderful dance and if you love dancing so much you'll love this picture." Or she would say, "I

Vera-Ellen and A.C. Lyles take in a scary movie in 1952.

was on the set yesterday and I saw Ann Miller do this wonderful routine." She would say how she was enthralled about it. It was interesting how she was always extolling the abilities of other performers.

In February 1952, Vera-Ellen was at the pinnacle of her career and took time to write an article about how she had gotten to this point on the strength of her religious faith. She noted:

> Actors live in the spotlight. We must think of ourselves all day and all evening. How do I look? How does my voice sound? What are people thinking about me? What should my next role be?

Vera-Ellen:

Vera-Ellen accepts a plaque and citation of merit presented at San Diego's Hotel Coronado to MGM and the cast of *Above and Beyond* (1952) at the April 19th Airpower Banquet for the California Wing of the Air Force Association. Standing is James H. McDivitt, outgoing Wing Commander. Seated left is Lt. Gen. James H. Doolittle, USAFR, who attended with many of his Tokyo Raider airmen. Vera-Ellen was "Miss Golden Flight," official hostess to the raiders.

> It's natural for people to think of themselves but actors do more of it. We're always in danger of becoming self-centered. Then too actors are emotional people, with emphatic ups and downs. We feel everything deeply, or we couldn't act. When something depresses us, we're very low indeed. That's when prayer helps.

During this period she had sent out Christmas cards to servicemen in Korea who had written her, with the 23rd Psalm and a photograph of herself:

> There was a time in Hollywood when I made no movies for almost a year. Nothing is more discouraging to an actress than to be idle. I

The Magic and the Mystery

prayed hard and often, and prayer brought me the faith that the Lord was really shepherding me, and I could trust in Him no matter how gloomy my predicament seemed to be....Sure enough, my luck turned—only I think it was Providence, not luck!

I've always had this faith in prayer, because my parents were deeply religious and as a little girl I often saw their prayers answered almost miraculously.

On March 20, 1952 a radiant Vera-Ellen presented the Academy Award for Cinematography for black and white film (*A Place in the Sun*) and color (*An American in Paris*) at the Pantages Theater in Hollywood. By now she was touted as Fred Astaire's new partner and a worthy successor to Ginger Rogers and she had never looked lovelier. Her life was a whirlwind of activity. In the early '50s her hobbies included gardening, going to stage shows (especially to see comic Phil Silvers who became a smash in the 1952 show *Top Banana*) and movies (especially drive-ins), golf, swimming, making fudge and taking unplanned automobile trips. Her San Fernando Valley home was more like a farmhouse and she was relaxed there, never dressing up but wearing mainly gingham slacks. A great animal lover, like her fellow Norwoodite Doris Day, she had kept over the years a pet chicken, rabbit, three goldfish, a white canary (that died at the close of *The Connecticut Yankee*), a beloved toy Pomeranian named "Nip" and another named "Happy" she found in England shooting *Happy Go Lovely*. She liked to curl up by a fire and toast marshmallows and eat home-cooked meals (except those with eggs) and save dimes in a piggy bank.

Vera-Ellen:

The Astaire–Vera-Ellen re-teaming in *The Belle of New York* promised to take her career to dazzling heights, especially so since dance numbers, either her solos or partnered dances with Astaire, filled nearly half of the film's running time. The film was based on a successful (at least in its European tour) operetta that had been produced in New York in 1897. It was much beloved by the film's producer, Arthur Freed, who had seen the original as a boy and dreamed of one day making the definitive film version. It had been originally filmed by Vitagraph as *Salvation Joan* in 1915, then redone as *The Belle of New York* in 1919 by Select Pictures Corporation, starring Marion Davies as Salvation Army Lassie. The original New York stage musical had featured 19-year-old ex-chorus girl Edna May as the Salvation Army girl Violet Gray but the show was not particularly successful in America. Only when it was transported to London's Shaftesbury Theater did it become one of the legendary musicals of all time, with an initial run of 697 performances and successful London revivals in 1901, 1914 and 1942. May, who was the cute, sweet-voiced daughter of a Syracuse, New York mailman, became the toast of two continents and started the fashion vogue for Violet Gray Salvation Army bonnets, candy and cosmetics. She also starred in the 1915 film version.

Astaire had planned to make the film with Judy Garland in 1946, when turn-of-the-century musicals were more popular and the World War II British stage revival of the musical was still remembered. But the plan was put on hold when Astaire announced his retirement. Then in 1947 the planned film was advertised as the first MGM starring role for Ann Miller but this effort was also dropped. An extraordinarily creative group toiled on the project. Hit songwriter extraordinaire Harry Warren wrote the music and multi-Oscar winning Johnny Mercer the words, and several of the tunes are charming and fun. The impressive set design came from the workshop of Cedric Gibbons, one of the premier designers in the history of film. One of the more fascinating ideas in the film was that it was supposed to take place in the four different seasons, each one inspired by a Currier and Ives print from the turn of the century. Each change of scene would be introduced by a still picture which would unfreeze into the actual scene. The forced perspective of the prints made this conversion difficult.

For her part in *The Belle of New York,* Vera-Ellen had managed to gain the weight and leg tone back she had lost in England. She was eating again, lots of meat, plus seeking out health food stores in Beverly Hills to buy gluten bread, yogurt and "healthful" candies and cookies. At age 31 she had developed into a stunningly beautiful woman and a fine comedic and dramatic actress, but her singing was again ghosted by Anita Ellis. William Tuttle's makeup made her look breathtaking and the transformation from the apple-cheeked Shirley Templesque doll of *Wonder Man* to the "Naughty but Nice" Hollywood glamour girl of this film is nothing short of astonishing. Her old classmates and the Hesslers who well remembered the pint-sized baton-twirling entertainer of Norwood View Elementary must have been amazed.

The plot involves a spoiled, turn-of-the-century New York playboy, Charles Hill (Fred Astaire), who proposes to many young ladies but cannot follow through to marry any of them. He does not wish to give up his delightful bachelorhood, much to the consternation of his guardian Aunt Lettie (a role cartoonishly overplayed by Marjorie Main) and his lawyer (the almost equally overstated Keenan Wynn). He falls in love with Angela Bonfils (Vera-Ellen) who excites him so much that he quite literally walks

Fred Astaire is a playboy who falls in love with proper Vera-Ellen in *The Belle of New York*.

on air. She is, however, a prim Salvation Army (or in this case Daughters of Right) worker who has inherited her organization's building from her late mother.

She insists that he get work on a regular basis in order to prove he is sincere in his affection for her and he attempts to hold down job after job without success. Finally, she falls in love with him, is swept off her feet into the air, and they plan to marry. However, even though he is truly in love, Charles still cannot bring himself to marry her, and he deserts her at the altar. This is all the more surprising for the sight of Vera-

Vera-Ellen:

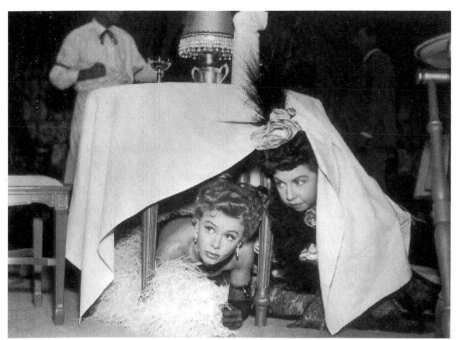

Vera-Ellen and Alice Pearce try to avoid notice in *The Belle of New York*.

Ellen in a bridal outfit should have immediately convinced any mortal man to marry her instantly. In an especially forced and inexplicable plot contrivance, Angela decides to pretend to be a fallen woman who visits cafés unescorted. Her hope is that Astaire will sweep in to save her from her newly found evil ways and commit himself to marriage. For no clear reason, this all works out and they float off into the sky together.

Vera-Ellen vigorously promoted the film across the country, gaining a reputation from theater managers as one of the nicest and most cooperative stars, being punctual and signing large numbers of autographs. She also did a great deal of charity work on these tours, promoting blood donations for the Red Cross. There were radio promotions too, including her starring role on *The M.G.M. Musical Comedy Theater* on the Mutual Broadcasting System, with her guests the song belter Georgia Gibbs and actor/singer Johnny Johnston. This show was aired on January 30 and repeated November 12. But it was all to no avail. *The Belle of New York* was a box office disaster, taking four months to make at a cost of $2,606,644 but grossing only $1,993,000. It was the first Astaire film to lose money. This came as a shock to Fred Astaire:

> The less said about it the better....It bothered me to think I could try so hard with enthusiasm only to realize afterward that everything amounted to nothing....There were some awfully good dance numbers in that thing.

Reportedly, he detested the gay nineties setting in which he felt audiences did not appreciate him but he still felt that this was one of his best efforts:

The Magic and the Mystery

Arthur (Freed) had this idea—and we all had this feeling—let's do the impossible: an old New York show with fantasy. As my partner I had a girl who was a good dancer, Vera-Ellen. And some of the best dance numbers you could ever get. It was just a musical show that did not make it, and it makes me so mad, because *The Belle of New York* was one of my favorite films....When the English critics lambasted a play by Noel Coward several years ago for being "thin," Coward retorted with: "Very well—from now on I will write nothing but very fat plays for very fat critics."

The director, Charles Walters, reportedly hated making the film, and was disturbed by what he perceived to be the lack of chemistry between the two stars. He later claimed that anyone who liked the picture must be "sick." This alleged lack of chemistry could perhaps be explained by the fact that Astaire was 52 and starting to look it, and Vera-Ellen was a youthful and radiant 31 (and pretending to be 26). But in fact the chemistry seems fine when the film is viewed today.

Variety found that the film was stuck with "an even lighter plot than usual, and the numbers are just ordinary." But Bosley Crowther, ever the Vera-Ellen and Astaire fan, wrote more favorably in *The New York Times*:

> The two nimble performers have just about all they can do to keep this slight musical moving. Mr. Astaire gets first go with a dizzying...tap, in top hat and tails, while perched precariously atop the arch in Washington Square. This is put in the shade by Vera-Ellen when she does a delicious pantomime, in opera-length hose and ruffled scanties... And just when you're starting to pity the old master for being outclassed, Astaire pops back in a honey of a soft-shoe sand dance that takes the prize.

Crowther was ecstatic about Vera-Ellen:

> Add to the list of young ladies who have danced on the screen with Fred Astaire the name of Vera-Ellen, and mark it with a star. For this agile and twinkling charmer, who accompanied the ageless Mr. A in his latest if not his greatest Metro musical... is as graceful and pleasing a dancer as any that has gone before.

Newsweek added:

> Possibly none of the opposites has ever matched Astaire's personal style so brilliantly.

From Gilbert Seldes of *Saturday Review* came:

> Vera-Ellen dances always as well and sometimes better than any other partner of Astaire's.

Vera-Ellen:

A glamourous Vera-Ellen promotes *The Belle of New York*.

And yet despite the critical praise for their pairing, Astaire and Vera-Ellen never teamed again.

When viewed today *The Belle of New York* is one of Vera-Ellen's most impressive screen achievements. Second-billed and put on true equal footing with Astaire even if the letters of her name aren't quite as large as his, she never looked lovelier than as the *Belle* who has men falling for her in droves. Thanks to superb choreography by her guru Robert Alton, she turns in a remarkable dancing performance in solo and partnered work. In fact each of her numbers repays multiple viewing by catching nuances in her onscreen dancing and her dramatic acting as she dances. Throughout the film her acting shows skill and range plus a flair for comedy as she falls in love with Astaire, transforming herself from a straight-laced prude to a sweet lovestruck girl and then, incredibly, to the sexy siren of the final scenes. Astaire and Vera-Ellen partner first for the song "Baby Doll," a charming example of her new understanding of adding dramatic attitude to her dancing. Here she must act prim and proper as she dances with Astaire, maintain extra-erect posture while trying to keep him at arm's length as he makes advances.

As a determined social worker, she cannot allow this flirtatious man into her life. She maintains her stiffness throughout the early part of the number, but as it continues she has periodic lapses when she begins to smile, obviously enjoying the dancing courtship. She unveils an easel sign that reads "Evil has many disguises" but he flips over a sign reading "Spread a little kindness." She replies by easel that "Satan is at your elbow" but he counters with "Love thy Neighbor." The number ends with her fending off his advances by raising a protective hand between herself and her pursuer.

The Magic and the Mystery

The next number "Oops" is not only a charming song but a true Astaire/Vera-Ellen classic. In the routine they are slowly falling in love as he attempts to reform and drive a horse-drawn streetcar for a living. The number features Vera-Ellen in partnered comic dancing, a spoof of the normally rigid synchronization of their usual dances. Here, they seem clumsy and they cannot get in synch on any move they make. But that lack of synchronization must in reality have been carefully planned and rehearsed. The comic dancing here is vaudevillian in style, with broad movements, exaggerated foot placements and frequent collisions, a type of dancing perfected by Ray Bolger on the Broadway stage. In fact, Vera-Ellen would have been intimately familiar with his style since she had worked with Bolger in the comic Broadway smash *By Jupiter*.

Here the streetcar is used deftly as a prop and they climb on and off of it darting around the seats. But as they dance, the streetcar moves along at a slow and steady speed so that their dancing must be coordinated smoothly with the rolling streetcar. Timing is crucial. Poles must be grabbed and movements must be gauged and timed to mesh exactly. Yet on the screen it looks effortless, with no hitch or hesitation in either partner's movements. During the sequence, Astaire offers her a flower that she takes as a symbol of their growing love. They dance about celebrating the joy of their relationship and finally she finds herself in love with Astaire and literally floating on air. During the rehearsals, Astaire was supposed to end up on a horse near the end of the routine but in jumping off the animal he twisted his ankle, forcing a substantial shooting delay on this number.

Next up was "A Bride's Wedding Day," a charming salute to the art of Currier and Ives whose famous prints of the four seasons come to life, one by one. In this captivating and refined sequence we see the characters of Currier and Ives taking pictures of the couple—a slightly wary Fred Astaire ice skating in Central Park with Vera-Ellen, who seems much more at home on the skates than her partner (which she was). In another sequence she plays badminton and demonstrates that she must have been a killer on the court in real life, even returning a serve after spinning around. Sequences include swinging on swings and a Coney Island boardwalk clog dance to the tune of "When I'm Out With the Belle of New York." Gilbert Seldes in *Saturday Review* wrote:

> There is a series of scenes after Currier and Ives, all of entrancing
> beauty; one of them, a skating scene, has a breathless quality not
> achieved by the best of the ballet scenes in *An American in Paris*.

Finally, her "Naughty But Nice" number is a stunner. Elegantly costumed as a fallen woman and sexy flirt (or stripteaser, with black undergarments and sequined evening gown), she prepares to head unescorted to a café. She does a high-kicking dance (one kick is done extra-slowly to demonstrate phenomenal leg control) in which her flowing dress is used as a partner. She flares it, twists it and makes it do everything but jump through a hoop, splaying decorative patterns across the screen. Her facial attitudes are that of a repressed beauty who has unleashed her pent-up wild side and is making the most of it. It is the sort of dance that Marilyn Monroe attempted in *Gentlemen Prefer Blondes*, but where Marilyn projected raw, blatant and vulgar sex appeal (which to be sure had a pronounced effect on most males in the audience), Vera-Ellen

Fred Astaire and Vera-Ellen use the streetcar as a prop in *The Belle of New York*.

raises her flirtatious dance routine to the level of high art. Every movement, facial gesture and prop contributes to the mood of this seemingly simple dance. With this film, and especially this number, Vera-Ellen is transformed into a glamorous movie star. This scene concludes her dancing in the film except for the fadeout sequence with Astaire but her acting throughout is notable. A sequence in the café where she is slightly tipsy, complete with exaggerated comic hiccup, is a delight.

Reassessing Vera-Ellen and this film in his book *Astaire Dancing* in 1985, John Mueller noted:

> If the quality, vivacity and virtuosity of the three duets in this film are any indication, Vera-Ellen is the partner in the post-Rogers years who most stimulated Astaire's choreographic genius. Like most of his film partners after 1951, Vera-Ellen was an extensively trained dancer first, an actress second, and a singer not at all. Light, lithe, strong, and quick, she seems capable of doing anything Astaire chooses to dream up, and there is an unfettered quality to the choreography in the duets in this film that suggests the dancers were trying to push themselves to the limit.
>
> Vera-Ellen's ballet background may also have suggested certain ideas that recur in several dances in the film—the frequent use of a version of the crooked-leg ballet pose known as attitude being the most notable. And there are a few places in which Astaire seems to be gently parodying ballet.

The Magic and the Mystery 119

What, then, killed *The Belle of New York*? Unfortunately, in 1952 people preferred to stay home and watch free musical entertainment on television. Louis B. Mayer had been fired as studio head at MGM and replaced by Dore Schary, who had little interest in musicals. Box office receipts were plummeting, theaters were going out of business all across the country. Period musicals were well past their heyday of the late '30s through the later '40s when this film was first conceived. Nonetheless, there are catchy songs, fine acting and top-rate dance numbers of both a solo and partnered type.

But the film is hampered by the dreaded Alice Pearce who portrays Elsie Wilkins, a member of the Daughters of Right. Pearce had almost destroyed *On the Town* with her one-joke routine as the ugly, whiny and unwanted young lady who constitutes every male's nightmare of a blind date. A little of her went an awfully long way.

Her comedy consists of dreadfully overplaying each line with an irritating nasal twang that makes *The Nanny*'s Fran Drescher seem like Maya Angelou. In *On the Town*, she provided comic relief for Vera-Ellen as Gene Kelly's blind date substitute while Vera-Ellen ran off to her "kootch" dance engagement. In that film, in a mercifully brief interlude, her manic, garish comedy stylings proved popular. However, in *The Belle of New York*, she appears throughout the film every few minutes, with that same endless ugly duckling joke. Any scene with her is already too much, but here, each time the movie generates energy and artistry either through the dramatic acting and/or dancing of Astaire and especially Vera-Ellen, Pearce has a pointless comedy scene that derails the flow of the film and cheapens it.

Viewed today, the picture has considerable visual beauty and achieves a true artistic elegance but it is repeatedly marred by this low level of comedy. Along with Marjorie Main's overstated performance as Lettie Hill and the cardboard performance of Keenan Wynn, Pearce torpedoes the film. The blame must be placed at the feet of director Charles Walters for lacking the confidence that his audience could appreciate a higher level of entertainment. By his own admission, he never believed in his own assignment. He should have.

The failure of *The Belle of New York* was a setback to Vera-Ellen's career from which she never fully recovered professionally or personally. Astaire abandoned her as a partner, not wishing to repeat disaster. The experience must have traumatized her, for it is after this debacle that her weight plummets and she begins to age rapidly. She was supposed to be in a number of films in 1952 but the opportunities all vanished. She was slated for a major supporting role in *Skirts Ahoy* and, not long after *The Belle of New York* was released, she had begun rehearsing a dance number with Ricardo Montalban. But reportedly, the star Esther Williams vetoed her and replaced her with Vivian Blaine or Joan Evans. Howard Strickling of the publicity department of MGM issued Vera-Ellen's name in a pre-production publicity release for the film. She had also been mentioned for a possible starring role in *Everything I Have Is Yours* (1952) but it went to Marge (and Gower) Champion.

After *The Belle of New York* she was announced to be teaming again with Gene Kelly and Marge and Gower Champion in a musical called *Give the Girl a Chance*, to be followed by an unnamed straight drama. The musical sounded very exciting and was to be choreographed by Bob Fosse and Gower Champion while Ira Gershwin was to write the score with Burton Lane. Stanley Donen was to direct. The story involved three girls competing for a role in a Broadway musical. The film was actually made in 1954 under the title *Give a Girl a Break* but the part of the pert and vivacious ingenue went to Debbie Reynolds, another MGM rising starlet who could sing and dance enthusiastically. Gene Kelly didn't participate in the film either. It was yet another setback and a bitter one since Reynolds, despite a certain peppy onscreen charisma, was by her own admission nowhere near the dancing talent that Vera-Ellen was.

Although musicals at MGM were generally drying up at this point and many stars would get axed in the future, only Vera-Ellen seemed to be the scapegoat after this production. Perhaps MGM felt she was not a significant draw and the studio publicity on her began to tail off once the receipts for the film came in. There is much more energy spent in promoting Cyd Charisse as the studio's lead female dancer. The one problem for Cyd was her height, for she was taller than Gene Kelly (who was barely 5 feet 9 inches) and Fred Astaire,

Vera-Ellen in a studio holiday publicity shot in 1952

but it was clear that Vera-Ellen's star was falling fast at the studio.

Vera-Ellen had been slated for a guest spot in *I Love Melvin*, a comedy featuring Donald O'Connor being filmed in 1953, and her specialty number was actually filmed. The idea was that the leads Debbie Reynolds and O'Connor go to the movies and daydream as they watch a musical number sung by Howard Keel to Elaine Stewart. Then the number is danced by Vera-Ellen and the graceful non-dancer Ricardo Montalban. In the film only a few seconds of a Spanish number are glimpsed. Montalban was just as happy to have it cut—he was terrified that his dancing would look dreadful on film, especially when he was matched with MGM's greatest dancing talents, but for Vera-Ellen, another golden opportunity had gone out the window. She would never again be the star of a major film for a major studio. She would shine as the second lead in two more excellent films, but her chance for legendary superstardom passed with the failure of *Belle*.

The Magic and the Mystery

Chapter Six
Ups and Downs

Vera-Ellen's film career rebounded with her next film, *Call Me Madam* (1953), a strong dancing and supporting role with her former stage colleague Ethel Merman. Unfortunately, the film cannot be seen commercially today, except primarily in grainy pirated editions sold on E-Bay from television tapings made circa 1980, because of a dispute within the Irving Berlin estate. This is a great tragedy because Vera-Ellen does some of her finest dancing and acting in this film. She had been loaned to 20th Century Fox for the movie, where she had worked so happily six years before. MGM paid out $30,000 to Fox for the arrangement. The movie was based on the highly successful stage comedy by Howard Lindsay and Russell Crouse which had been the hit of the Christmas season in 1950 on Broadway. It had run for a year and a half and was still playing in road companies when Vera-Ellen got word of the exciting new project on May 6, 1952. She was already promoting it on radio, appearing on NBC's Dean Martin and Jerry Lewis radio show on June 23 as their only guest star. And by the end of the year the Vera-Ellen Fan Club was still in high gear and she issued a 45 rpm recording to all the members, personally signed by her and stickered with a Santa Claus.

Irene Sharaff of New York designed the beautifully regal costumes for *Call Me Madam* for which she won an Academy Award, and Vera-Ellen always loved to dress royally. The dresses were primarily Dior New Look fashions designed for ultra slim waists, accompanied by skirts with frilly petticoats and crinolines, the latter giving a stiff tiered petticoat look to lend volume and flare. One outfit, which was composed of 17 yards of material and required more than 400 hours of labor to sew, cost the studio $1,250.

And Vera-Ellen was thrilled to be working with choreographer Robert Alton again, one of the greatest dance directors of American stage, movies and later television. Alton had helped to define the careers of Ray Bolger, Gene Kelly and Betty Grable, among others, and liked to work improvisationally. Vera-Ellen was keen for whatever he could dish out. Her ability to get it fast, change it or just try it and reject it allowed him enormous staging flexibility within a short period of time. He was like a Svengali for her but she had ideas too, and together they hit some amazing highs in American dance. Alton was always amazed at her dedication and found her to be a choreographer's dream. Despite being habitually late for everything in her personal life, she would

Vera-Ellen, pictured with co-star Donald O'Connor, got to wear a royal wardrobe designed by Irene Sharaff in *Call Me Madam*.

arrive at the studio ahead of all the other players and would stay far into the evening. Before she felt she had her routines down, she had worked off 10 pounds from her already dangerously thin frame. Alton commented on her work ethic and character:

> Vera learns a number faster than anyone else I know but she is her
> own severest critic, never satisfied until each move is a masterpiece
> of classical perfection.

Now Alton was to cook up specialty numbers not only for her but for another MGM star, Donald O'Connor, who had been dancing in films since he was a child. O'Connor was a graceful, talented, charismatic, skilled and often comedic performer and it seemed a new team might be created. He had made his mark as a comic dancer in the "Make 'em Laugh" number in the 1952 classic *Singin' in the Rain*, but few besides Alton realized he was capable of brilliant partnered dancing and an Astaire-like grace. He shared with Vera-Ellen a wholesome kid-next-door quality that won over family audiences.

Call Me Madam is an unusual cinematic experience, for it is like watching two completely different films within one: an annoying account of a rich, vulgar oil heiress getting an unmerited political appointment and a fairy-tale romance between a princess and a commoner. The fundamental story concerns Sally Adams (Ethel Merman), whose

George Sanders (Cosmo Constantine); Billy De Wolfe (Pemberton Maxwell); Ethel Merman (Mrs. Sally Adams); Donald O'Connor (Kenneth); Vera-Ellen (Princess Maria) in a posed publicity shot for *Call Me Madam*

father found oil in Oklahoma which made the whole family rich, but not educated. Like her prototype Pearl Mesta, she become Washington's premier partygiver, offering large-scale shindigs where leaders of society and government could meet. A Democrat, Sally is supposed to be a widow with a huge fortune and time to kill. She is also a large contributor to the Harry S. Truman campaign and there are frequent jokes about Harry's daughter's efforts to succeed in the entertainment field. This "Hostess with the Mostest on the Ball" is suddenly named ambassador to the small grand duchy of Lichtenburg, as a reward for her contributions. Because she is so ill-suited for the position due to her crude and brazenly obnoxious ways, she desperately needs a press attaché. Sensing this, an unemployed reporter named Kenneth Gibson (Donald O'Connor) saves her during an embarrassing press interview and gets the job. The plot was intended to recall Truman's making Mesta the ambassador to Luxembourg, an act which raised eyebrows at the time due to its blatant rewarding of political contributions instead of merit, a process which is still almost as widely followed in Washington today as it was then.

Merman's performance is over the top and suited more to the stage. Her characterization is so intentionally low class and vulgar that Sally seems repellent when viewed through contemporary eyes. Ethel Merman's singing is, of course, always a matter of personal taste. No doubt on a stage she would have been larger than life and, with her leather-lunged power, certainly audible. But onscreen she seems to be over emphasizing every gesture. When Sally comes to Lichtenburg she quickly falls for the Foreign

Minister General Cosmo Constantin (George Sanders, replacing Paul Lukas of the stage version) and their talky courting scenes together lack chemistry, to put it mildly.

Along side of the Merman-Sanders romance is a wonderful sub-plot (the much better movie within the movie) which involves Kenneth falling in love with the Princess Maria Hammenschlafen of Lichtenburg (Vera-Ellen). The accents used by the court of the fictional country posed a problem for director Walter Lang until Vera-Ellen came to him, imitating the way people talked in her Norwood, Ohio hometown:

> I'm from the old German section of Cincinnati where everyone spoke with a thick Teutonic accent — so much so that I didn't realize until leaving the neighborhood a number of years later that everybody didn't speak that way.

In the story, the love affair is doomed because the princess must endure an arranged marriage to the lecherous Prince Yugo (Helmut Dantine, whom Vera-Ellen was dating in real life) of the neighboring Duchy of Mitteldorf.

In order to cement relations and link family and political lines, a huge dowry must be obtained, hopefully from a "loan" from the United States ambassador. To this end several ministers of Lichtenburg try unsuccessfully to flatter and court Sally (among them Walter Slezak) and through a misunderstanding Sally thinks Cosmo is in on the flattering, when in fact he does not want the loan to be given and for some reason he genuinely loves Sally. Meanwhile, Kenneth and the Princess Maria cannot stop their love affair, even though it can never lead to marriage. By the end of the film, Sally is fired for messing up American and Lichtenburg relations by helping her secretary to see the princess, and she returns to party-giving in Washington where she is visited by Cosmo and they presumably decide to marry, although it is unclear who will live where. In a particularly unrealistic last-minute plot switch, the Princess' family decides their country's future alliances don't matter after all and she is allowed to give up her throne for the commoner Kenneth and live in America.

The generally uninteresting plot is spiced up by some marvelous dancing: two partnered dances between O'Connor and Vera-Ellen, one solo by O'Connor and one by Vera-Ellen. The first partnered dance occurs at the royal palace reception where Kenneth and Maria dance off from the main room into the gardens. The song they introduce is Irving Berlin's bouncy "It's a Lovely Day Today" with Vera-Ellen's voice dubbed by Carole Richards. The accompanying dance is unforgettable and one could argue that there are actually three participants in the Astaire-Rogers type dance: O'Connor, Vera-Ellen and her lovely petticoated skirt, which flutters and floats under her careful control as they dart about, light as air.

Throughout this dance, Vera-Ellen projects dramatic expressions of attraction and resistance as she struggles between her sense of duty to her country and her passion for O'Connor. Her ability to listen and react while dancing is highly developed here and the dancing is so well coordinated between the two that it is difficult to find any movement that they do which is not perfectly matched. As the drama of the dance unfolds, Vera-Ellen progresses in her persona from someone sheltered and shy to someone rejoicing in the joy of the moment and the beauty of the music, and yet she periodically stops and tries to resist. It is not only a dance, but a true dramatic performance within the dance. O'Connor proves himself the equal of Astaire as they perform matched twists, turns and hand movements, and dance around each other, moving from step to step with an elegance and smoothness that can only be the result of enormously long practice sessions. Like Astaire, they have labored intensely to make the performance seem effortless.

It is this particular duet that O'Connor, normally a modest, considerate man not prone to exaggeration, told us he considered "one of the greatest dance numbers ever put on the screen." Repeated viewing of the sequence confirms he was correct. He enjoyed telling about one rehearsal for the number:

> All the dancers adored her. She was so nice and concerned about everyone's health and happiness. And in that number I twirl her around and she goes under my arms a couple of times. Once I hit her solidly in the back. I thought I killed her and she was a person you would never ever want to hurt. But she never said a thing and went back to rehearsing. But she paid me back later. Her dress had little plastic sea shells and every once in a while she'd give me an elbow and a shell would go up my nose! She got even!

They worked so well as a team because each was pencil thin, similar in size, versatile in all forms of dance from tap to ballet to props to acrobatics to comedy, fluid of movement, and capable of total sensitivity to the other's performance. She tries to match him but he can consistently repeat his movements in the same manner. When partners can do this, synchronicity is achieved. Under Bob Alton's watchful eye, it occurs here and he must have considered it one of his greatest choreographic efforts.

Vera-Ellen is given a lovely solo dance to "The Ocarina," a pseudo-Bavarian ethnic clapping and slapping song and dance about the sweet potato-shaped wind instrument. Here Berlin has tried to write a traditional-style folksong in which Germanic peasants cavort and smack their elbows, hips, feet and knees vigorously with their hands and engage in ring dancing. During this light and bouncy sequence, Vera-Ellen employs some rather stiff-legged dancing, punctuated with leaps and high kicks.

In the most memorable sequence of the dance, the male dancers lie down on the ground with their legs extended and Vera-Ellen must whirl continually and at the same time pick her way through the outstretched legs, which she does with total precision, remaining perfectly centered with the camera and exhibiting total fluidity of movement, her constant trademark.

For the finale of the specialty number, Robert Alton hit upon the idea of staging her peasant specialty number by having her dance as if she were a human cannon ball, being hurled through the air at the end of it, as in the spirited routines from her Hightower days. Therefore, she is hurled forward through the air as if shot from a cannon into a swan dive, ending up in the arms of several of the men. Before she is caught by them, and while still in midair, she already begins her graceful transition to the next step and seems almost to be floating like a feather through the air, not allowing the viewer to realize the danger of the stunt. While not a dramatic dance, it is an expression of joy and celebration which is fully expressed in the radiant, flashing-eyed performance by Vera-Ellen.

Donald O'Connor considered this number from *Call Me Madam* "one of the greatest dance numbers ever put on the screen."

Following one of Donald O'Connor's vaudevillesque dances in which he imitates a drunk and does several dangerous pratfalls and some marvelous prop dancing, breaking balloons on cue with his feet, the twosome reunites for another song and dance to "Something to Dance About," a lovely tune that takes place at the lovers' secret rendezvous in an underground tunnel and dark wine cellar of the palace. Here they perform tap, ballet and prop dancing up and down steps, while bouncing off of wine casks and at the same time expressing dramatically their joy and love at being together. Their movements in this sequence are so perfectly blended as to seem almost supernatural, like something perhaps added in as a special effect. Vera-Ellen considered this number to be one of her all time favorites, ranking it after "Slaughter on Tenth Avenue."

The Magic and the Mystery 127

The two paired dances in *Call Me Madam* are all the more surprising due to their being little known or appreciated, but they are worthy of the best paired dances in the history of film and certainly up to anything produced by Astaire or Kelly with any of their partners. In fact, O'Connor's reputation as basically an eccentric dancer and fine acrobatic tapper really must be reappraised once he is seen in the two partnered dances in *Call Me Madam*. They are of a level of artistry seldom seem in the movie musical. Once again fate has dealt Vera-Ellen an unfortunate hand—some of her finest dancing is in this movie and almost nobody gets to see it.

An added bonus in this film which no Vera-Ellen fan should miss is the farewell sequence in the wine cellar between the two lovers. During this sequence Vera-Ellen exhibits her fine ability to listen to another actor and react with her face and eyes as they speak. Like Virginia Bruce, another unheralded dramatic actress of the 1930s, she was a great screen listener. As if to express the hopelessness of their love and her need to fulfill her duties as princess, she searches his face with her eyes. Then Vera-Ellen begins to cry and at one point, exactly on cue at maximum closeup, lets fly a tear practically the size of a golfball. Two more ample tears follow. In such a lightweight film, it would be a moment tossed away by any other ingenue, but Vera-Ellen makes it riveting and true. Anyone who believes that she was not a real actress should observe this sequence, for she has poured herself so much into this role (as she did with any role she was allowed to do) that her face is full of emotion and she seems to have become this young girl. Of course she manages all this while still maintaining her German accent.

However, throughout the production Alton and director Walter Lang worried about her weight loss, so much so that Lang kept tempting her with weight-building snacks between takes. But nothing seemed to work and her weight kept dropping as she maintained her seemingly round the clock activity. Despite all efforts to fatten her up for the part, she looks dangerously thin and frail and yet her energy in the dance sequences is amazing. When first glimpsed she is lovely, yet seems all lips, with a skeletally thin body and a head too large for it. Furthermore, she seems dwarfed by her clothing in the dance sequences. At this time Vera-Ellen's waist size was 18 inches and through unnecessary dieting she was down to about 100 pounds. She prided herself on her ability to maintain a high energy level while eliminating all fat from her body:

> I work to keep my energy. I can keep this (energy) up until sunrise. I often go dancing at night when there's a good orchestra around. You don't need fat for endurance. It's so nice to be thin. My feet scarcely seem to touch the ground when I dance.

Years later however she would admit:

> I was really getting carried away with the exercise during this period.

Nonetheless, for viewers who can get beyond these limitations, *Call Me Madam* has extraordinary moments of great dancing artistry. But the magnificent grace of O'Connor and Vera-Ellen only make Merman's movements in the film seem all the

The love story of the Princess and the commoner holds *Call Me Madam* together.

more ungraceful and crude. While Merman's character was supposed to be this way, it nonetheless increases the feeling that one is watching two different movies simultaneously, and the better one is the one without Merman.

By this time Vera-Ellen had danced in films with the greatest male partners in Hollywood: Kelly, Astaire, Ray Bolger and Donald O'Connor. Most remarkable was her ability to adapt to the style of each, whether in a graceful ballet, a jaunty tap number, a routine with tough stunts or dramatic expressive dancing. In her typically kind, diplomatic fashion she assessed each one:

> I learned something from each partner. It wouldn't be fair to say one was more important than another. I tried to adapt myself to each man's style. In that way I learned their rhythms and dancing tricks.
>
> From Gene Kelly I got the modern — knee drops, slides, and the earthy, almost brutal, approach to rhythm. It was a big change for me. At the moment I think dancing with him did the most to advance my career.

The Magic and the Mystery

Fred Astaire and I rehearsed for two and one half months before *The Belle of New York* started. I was so overcome when I learned I was going to be with him I couldn't think of a thing to say when I met him. But we got on famously and from him I got the high hat and exhibition ballroom stuff. And he taught me to dance like the floor was hot! From Ray Bolger I learned lightness and comedy routines. And Donald O'Connor taught me the sheer joy of dancing [with him].

The Donald O'Connor/Vera-Ellen pairing in *Call Me Madam* was understandably popular with critics and fans and MGM planned to reunite them in two more movies. O'Connor had been concerned about doing the partnered dancing and credited Vera-Ellen with helping him a great deal, calling her "a marvelous gal who made me look good." They worked together beautifully during the production and he spoke with us not long before his death:

I want readers of your biography of Vera-Ellen to know what a truly wonderful gal she was. She was extremely sweet—so very sweet—and she always had that smile on her face. She was like a den mother and kept everybody's spirits up. She was outgoing and right up front always. She was wonderful. She was special.

Vera was a physical dancer like me. She could adapt her style, and *Call Me Madam* had every kind of number you could think of. When we danced together the great thing about her was that she didn't try to upstage you. Women dancers sometimes try to lead. We worked together and every movement we did meant something.

I first noticed her when she did that "Slaughter on Tenth Avenue" ballet. It was the first time I had seen her dance. She worked so hard. It takes a toll on your ankles and knees. She had so much energy and was so dedicated but I did not know her at all offstage and we were never good friends away from work. But that's normal, when you work all day with someone.

O'Connor/Vera-Ellen were soon announced to star in a biopic based on the lives of dancers Gaby Deslys and Harry Pilcer. Deslys had been a glamorous Parisian fashion plate, and stage and movie star in America in the 1910s until her untimely death at 35 in 1920, perhaps from tuberculosis. For another project, the pair was to be loaned to Paramount for *White Christmas* after Fred Astaire withdrew from it because he didn't like the script (although he gave illness as his official reason for refusing). But O'Connor couldn't do the film and Danny Kaye got the part. Gossip columnist Hedda Hopper, a Vera-Ellen fan, called the O'Connor/Vera-Ellen pairing in *Call Me Madam* "one of the most exquisite dancing teams of many years." Sadly, Donald O'Connor passed away in September 2003, another loss for the classical Hollywood musical.

Following *Call Me Madam*, Vera-Ellen hoped to gain more varied film roles. She remained completely devoted to her dancing at this time but still actively sought to fulfill her personal goal to star in a non-dancing drama:

My career at the moment is my life. I have naturally sacrificed many things for it: pretty clothes, when I needed the money for dancing lessons; quiet evenings at home, when I practiced; and romance, when I had to concentrate on studying new parts, dance routines or songs. But I have never lived a hermit's life. As far as happiness is concerned, well, what is happiness, anyway? To some, a little white bungalow with roses creeping all over the place. To others, a family. As for me, I have my career, my friends, my neighbors, my opportunities to travel and see the world.

She also enjoyed, upon occasion, visiting her Aunt Julia and Uncle Fred Maurer in Minnesota where she helped out around the farm. And when the weather permitted she would go flying solo at the Wadena airfield.

For some time Vera-Ellen had been supportive of the California Wing of the Air Force Association. As one of few women pilots who were also movie stars (we can only think of one other, the acclaimed actress, writer and director Ruth Chatterton in the 1930s) she served as "Miss Golden Flight" for the organization. Her duties included being official hostess at the Annual Convention Airpower Banquet and giving speeches honoring deceased heroes or aviation pioneers. She sometimes worked with the legendary Jimmy

"Miss Golden Flight," wearing her favorite lariat necklace, waits behind Jimmy Doolittle in 1953 at a ceremony honoring Californian John J. Montgomery who made the first controlled wing glider flights near San Diego in 1883. Left to right are seated Earl V. Prudden of the California Aeronautics Commission, Air Force Association national president Arthur F. Kelly, and Sherman Platt, president of the San Diego Junior Chamber of Commerce.

Doolittle and his Tokyo Raider airmen, famous for their spectacular daylight raid on Tokyo with 16 B-25 bombers in 1942. Her goal was to promote support and enthusiasm for the Air Force, which had officially formed in 1947.

Her punishing schedule included swimming 100 laps in a neighbor's pool each day and tap lessons and singing lessons taken as soon as she finished an engagement or

Vera-Ellen turns on the heat for this studio glamour portrait.

had a little time off, though she was never considered good enough to sing in one of her films. In her offscreen time she was not interested in shop-talk or gossip, and most of her friends were either outside the entertainment business or entertainment people not involved in making movie musicals. She also enjoyed spending time at church and church-related functions:

> I'm not a social outcast because I don't live like the popular conception of a movie star. Nobody cares if I don't have a swimming pool, and never go near the night spots. When I asked to be excused from working and rehearsing on Sundays, no one tried to argue me out of

it, and my practice of eating health foods has only brought on a flock of funny little stories.

Nonetheless, she was quite concerned about younger competition edging her out if she didn't stay on the top of her form:

> I always study between pictures. Anyone who stays up there works continually. Remember, the world is full of girls who take a lesson every day; they're coming up all around you and they're amazingly good.

But she did not seem envious of the competition, for she loved to watch all kinds of dancing. A.C. Lyles recalls:

> One thing that was unusual about her was that she loved to watch other persons dance. I never ever heard her say anything unkind about another dancer, like the fact that something was a little wrong or a little off, because she felt that anyone who could dance was great. She'd see people dance and she'd say to me "weren't they great" and I'd say they were fine. If you had the ability to dance you were great in her book.
>
> I know sometimes we would go to the ballet and she'd say all these wonderful things and she'd say "that's so difficult" because you had to do this or that, and I learned more about ballet than I'd ever learned before just from listening to her comments. She was the most non-envious person I've ever known.
>
> When she was on a contract at Metro and a picture would come up and Cyd Charisse or Ann Miller or Eleanor Powell or someone would apply, she'd say "this is such a great part for them."

Vera-Ellen believed that she had to keep in tip-top shape and compared herself to someone preparing for the Olympics, needing to always be in peak form for upcoming competitions. She was still an obsessive perfectionist about everything and stated in 1953:

> I'll start out playing a few games of tennis, just for the sake of finding an outdoor sport, and it won't be long before I'll decide that I've got to improve my backhand or strengthen my serve. Bingo, I've got a whole new series of lessons on my hands.

Critics and columnists in fan magazines began to note how thin Vera-Ellen had become and it began to affect her career and cause talk about her being a bit strange. A.C. Lyles advised her to "gain 15 pounds" and *Screen Life* magazine said:

> A stickler for artistic perfection, Vera-Ellen drives herself mercilessly, has lost too much weight.

The Magic and the Mystery

But there seemed to be no way to slow her down. She somehow found time to continue her dancing lessons even when she was still doing *Call Me Madam*, and she seriously studied knitting two nights a week. By 1953 she had studied piano, French, Spanish, cooking, baby-raising, singing, horseback riding, tennis, golf, knitting, swimming, calisthenics, butterfly collecting, gem polishing and book-binding in an effort to fill every spare hour in her life with something. Out on a date she was known as an easy laugher who would crack up constantly and make people with her feel truly at home.

She had a gracious manner and winning, warm smile. A.C. Lyles reports:

> She laughed all the time. She was as jovial and sweet as anyone I've ever known. She was just a sweetheart.

Despite her thinness and increasingly frail appearance, lacking the voluptuousness she had in *The Belle of New York*, Vera-Ellen had matured and been glamorized into a true screen beauty. The critics said she had "the blonde prettiness you see on candy boxes" and that she was a "sprightly bundle of energy" who "dances like a sprite borne on the wind." Much was made of her incredible lightness when she danced and the way she seemed to float across the stage. Although she could be reclusive and private, she had a number of good friends, among them Marie Windsor, the great '50s character actress and specialist in tough-girl roles. They were about the same age and had both worked their way up the ladder from small-town America, one step at a time (Marie had been Miss Utah and was from Marysvale), and each shared a great passion for animals (Marie was a noted horsewoman). They talked a lot about finding Mr. Right, getting married, having babies and raising a family.

Gossip columnists in Hollywood between 1950 and 1953 speculated that Vera-Ellen's future husband would be Rock Hudson. They made a curious couple since he was 12 inches taller. At this time Hudson's homosexuality was not well known in the Hollywood community. Movie magazines such as *Modern Screen* made a big deal out of their supposedly torrid love affair that was actually a publicity stunt designed to perk up both their careers. It had been engineered by Hudson's publicist, Henry Willson, who was also a good friend and the long-time agent of Vera-Ellen. Hudson had a reputation for being a gentleman on a date and she was a good girl with a strict religious upbringing. They enjoyed each other's company and were happy to let the screen magazines do features on them as lovers, and Alma Rohe adored Rock too. The "big affair" was particularly helpful as a career boost to Hudson who was just starting out. However, he later admitted that they had become so close, such warm friends, that he seriously entertained thoughts of marrying her. After they went their separate ways, Hudson's "people" could point to his carrying the torch for Vera-Ellen as the reason why he had never been married until then (he was married for a short time from 1955-1958).

Nonetheless a persistent rumor has circulated over the years that Vera-Ellen and Rock Hudson actually were in love and that Rock, although principally homosexual, was actually bisexual, a fact attested to by a number of females in his life. Her relationship with Hudson remains a mystery, for she told some close friends that it was a platonic affair, that there was nothing between them but friendship and the desire for a pleasant evening out and that he "didn't prefer women." But she told others that they were serious about each other. She told her cousin's wife Toddy Maurer that they were

Cousin Fred Maurer and wife Toddy dine at Ciro's with a very handsome Rock Hudson and his frequent date and dear friend Vera-Ellen in November 1950.

not lovers because, she whispered very very softly, "he's queeeeerrrrr." She couldn't say the words above a whisper even though no one else was around. Rock and Vera-Ellen were extremely close, either as friends or possibly lovers, and the truth about their relationship may never be known. However, she confided late in her life to close friend Bill Dennington: "The best thing about Rock was that his mother was a wonderful cook!"

Two different sources have mentioned that a male child was born to Rock and Vera-Ellen either after her role in *The Belle of New York* or, more likely, after *Call Me Madam* but before her appearance in *Big Leaguer*. Supposedly, the baby was born in 1953 but the birth was covered up because of the scandal that would have destroyed both of their careers. Vera-Ellen reportedly had an extremely difficult childbirth with resulting serious medical complications which caused the haggard look she had in *Big Leaguer* and the sharp change from her physical peak in *The Belle of New York*. The birth also explains the fact that she did little work during the period between *Call Me Madam* and the baseball film. However, other close friends say that there was not enough time for the pregnancy between her public and film appearances and no one remembers seeing her pregnant, but the possibility, however unlikely, cannot be ruled out.

Her friends remember that during this period, pregnant or not, Vera-Ellen continued to be big news in the film magazines; she had been reported engaged half a dozen times:

> I've never been engaged since I lived in Hollywood. Not to Rock Hudson or anyone. I was married when I lived in New York—his name was Robert Hightower. I was less a career girl then than I am

The Magic and the Mystery   **135**

now. I'm really less of a career girl than many people I know, but I think it's better to have a successful career than an unhappy marriage. If I married now I couldn't dash around as I do. But I wouldn't pass up happiness — the real thing — if I found it. When I marry again I want it to take. And I *want* to marry.

With Rory Calhoun

With Dean Miller

She was seen around Hollywood with many eligible young men during this period. Most were just good friends, not romantic involvements. The list included actor Richard Anderson and hotel heir Ernie Byfield, Jr. as well as her long-time friend and confidante A.C. Lyles. There were also dates with Farley Granger, Rory Calhoun (before his marriage to Lita Baron), and Henry Willson. The latter, however, was not only her own agent but also a homosexual friend and may have been responsible for cooking up not only the Rock Hudson/Vera-Ellen "love affair" but also the Oscar dress-up episode described earlier. The brief fling with Rory Calhoun was struck down by Alma Rohe, who considered him too unrefined and rough for her daughter, and she referred to him as "that convict" because he had a minor prison record in his youth.

Another of her beaux, perhaps the greatest love of her life and her constant companion in the evening and even during the shooting of *Call Me Madam* later in 1952 was MGM contract player and fellow Ohian Dean Miller, who had grown up not far from her native Norwood. He was a handsome, dark-haired personable fellow who had started in radio and television in the midwest but was signed in 1951 to a long-term contract by MGM. Little came of this, however, and eventually he made more of a mark in television than in the movies, first as the emcee of a New York children's show called *Choose Up Sides* in 1953 and then more memorably as young architect Matt Henshaw on the highly successful series *December Bride* beginning in 1954.

By December 1952 it seemed that Dean and Vera-Ellen would marry early in January and build an early American house with lots of grass and trees:

I've never felt this way about anyone else... I wouldn't let people know me too well. I really walled myself in, although even I hadn't realized how much until I began going with Dean... It was April 18 when he first told me he loved me. We had spent the evening at home and he said it just as he was leaving. Almost as an afterthought. On April 22, I told him the same. We were both in the business office at the studio when I told him. Which shows you we don't know where we are or who's around... We have some weighty problems, but we're working them out... I wouldn't leave Hollywood for anyone else but Dean.

But even though the two lovers were in a dynamic, worldly business, religion was the stumbling block to their relationship:

I think we could have worked it out very well but there was one problem which was of paramount importance and which seemed incapable of solution—the fact that we are of different religions. When I get married, I definitely want to raise a family, a large one. If only Dean and I were concerned, with no youngsters to consider, I feel we could have reached an adjustment about our beliefs.

Later she would elaborate a little further:

Actually, we only went steady—saw each other exclusively—for about two months. We were never formally engaged. We hadn't set a date... I don't think I would have gone on them (i.e., trips for personal appearance tours) if I'd actually thought that things would have worked out with Dean. But when you don't feel sure, your sort of try to get away from what's troubling you... We felt very deeply about each other. But we didn't think there were all the ingredients for a lifetime marriage. We didn't feel it would last. We're both cautious types—which is a good thing.

Like so many of the sadly ironic statements Vera-Ellen made, this one stands out dramatically since she ultimately would never see a child of hers live past infancy. She and Dean Miller could have worked things out together after all, if only they had known the future. But, of course, lacking foresight, the couple discussed what could be done and tried a voluntary separation from romance for three months. After just a few weeks they were talking on the phone and after four weeks they were back in each other's arms. But they just could not resolve the situation. She had had a strict Lutheran upbringing, was a regular churchgoer and even choir singer both in her hometown of Norwood and in Hollywood. She was at heart an old-fashioned girl who believed that the virtues and truths learned in her childhood were just as necessary in adulthood. Her mother in particular did not believe in interfaith marriage; it was a common feeling in those days, so the romance hit the rocks:

We couldn't reconcile our differences after all — and we finally parted. It hurt, a lot! I didn't want, in the final analysis, to give up my religion and Dean felt the same way about his.

But once Vera-Ellen believed something was right or must be done, she stuck to it to the end, even if it cost her love and happiness. In this case it did.

In 1953 she elaborated on what she wanted in a man and how her thoughts had matured along this line over the years, giving some insight into what had attracted her to Bob Hightower when she was so young:

> When you're 16 you want the world's best rumba dancer. At 20 you want something else. Above all things I want to be certain. Sometimes the prevalence of divorce frightens me. This work takes a great deal of time, and marriage is a job that requires time and thought too. I want a home and children though, so one of these days...

After parting from Dean Miller she began dating more men, among them a second-rung nightclub singer named Russ Severin whom she had met in St. Louis during a personal appearance tour. A more serious companion was Helmut Dantine, a ruggedly handsome Viennese refugee who had become a member of the Pasadena Community Players and made a career of playing villains, especially Nazis, in Warner Bros.

Vera-Ellen warms up for *Big Leaguer*.

films of the war years. They met during the filming of *Call Me Madam* when she played glamorous Princess Maria of the Grand Duchy of Lichtenburg and he played the prince to whom she is betrothed by official arrangement of her court. The relationship between Vera-Ellen and Helmut Dantine, like so many of her courtships, lasted only briefly. Unfortunately, her vision of happiness, although it would finally come, would last but a decade.

After *Call Me Madam*, the dramatic role Vera-Ellen had been promised by MGM turned out to be not much of a role at all. She played Christie, niece to John Lobert, in a semi-documentary baseball drama called *Big Leaguer*, featuring Edward G. Robinson at the lowest point of his film career as John B. (Hans)

Vera-Ellen:

Lobert, running a baseball camp and grooming young hopefuls while being forced into lines like "What I am expecting you to do is give it everything you've got" and "One game is worth 10,000 words." For several years Robinson had faced major problems as an alleged Communist sympathizer and was dragged before the House Un-American Activities Committee during the notorious McCarthy Era in 1950 and again in 1952. His reputation was smeared, although he was never convicted of anything. He had been known in the 1930s as a soft touch and lent support to a wide variety of causes. In 1947 *The New York Post* reported that among the organizations he supported were what were termed Communist front groups. Later in 1952 he was finally cleared by HUAC, but was still considered a risk and he was forced to accept very poor material in order to keep working. A role extolling the virtues and dedication needed in playing American baseball seemed to be just what he needed to clean up his image. MGM knew that Vera-Ellen sought straight roles but they still lacked faith in her abilities. They dumped her off into their sports feature film unit. Producer Charles Schnee gave her little to do in this programmer. It remains her sole dramatic film and she tried to make the most of it, for Vera-Ellen would never give a second-rate performance, even in a third-rate film.

The MGM sports unit specialized in bottom of the barrel, low-budget sports pictures such as the horse-racing film *Fast Company*. This is where musical leading man and singer Howard Keel got trapped between musicals. Schnee had charge of a seven-man unit making all sorts of B (or even C) films. Matthew Rapf, who wrote the trite story of *Big Leaguer*, was one of the members of the team. *Big Leaguer* was the first film directed by Robert Aldrich, who later developed a reputation for high drama focusing on the dark and violent side of life. He was one of the first big-name directors to come out of television. Indeed the film looks like a TV docudrama, something like *Dragnet* meets baseball. Production was simplified through the use of long stretches of narration by Robinson.

Much of the film has all the excitement of an airport waiting room but the drama, such as it is, comes as the baseball hopefuls wait to learn who will be cut from the squad. Some are cocky (such as Richard Jaeckel in a fine performance as a pitcher with guts, class and latent talent), others are fearful, while still others are just trying to learn enough English to figure out what is going on around them. The successful ones get $150 a month and it was possible to become a "bonus baby," getting up to $50,000 for signing.

Vera-Ellen plays Robinson's niece Christy, who works in the front office for the New York Giants. She falls for a talented rookie recruit and potential big leaguer, the rugged, handsome and broad-shouldered third baseman Adam Polachuk (Jeff Richards). She helps her "Uncle Hans" keep his tenuous job as a talent recruiter at the New York Giants' training camp in Melbourne, Florida by helping Polachuk deal with his personal problems. Polachuk is upset about going against his immigrant father's desire that he go to college and not play baseball.

Vera-Ellen receives equal billing with Robinson, the first time in her career that this was done for her by MGM. Unfortunately that only confirmed that Vera-Ellen and Robinson were equally consigned to a C picture. Carl Hubbell, the famous pitcher, makes his acting debut in this film, conclusively proving why he never pursued an acting career. In a finale that can be predicted light years before it finally arrives, Richards

Vera-Ellen and Jeff Richards in *Big Leaguer*

saves the big game versus the Dodgers with a clutch hit. His father, who has come to pluck him away from all this, gets excited and supports him and Richards and Vera-Ellen unite.

With no set design (only drab training camp facilities were needed — and used) and outdoor shooting on a simple baseball diamond in mid-day glare, there was little expense. However, Vera-Ellen is not well photographed in black and white and in the harsh natural light. When she makes her sultry entry into the training camp, she looks

Vera-Ellen:

years older than she did in *The Belle of New York* which was filmed just the year before. Which suggests the great toll the dismal reception of that film took on her or that something had happened in the meantime to affect her health. Her body is extremely slim and lacks the great tone of the year before, evidenced in the swimsuit sequence. Her face seems puffy and her cheeks falling, and placing her next to Edward G. Robinson, who is himself awash in jowls, did nothing for her looks. It also did little for her career since MGM thought so little of *Big Leaguer* that it never even gave it a proper opening in New York.

Vera-Ellen's part was actually written for a disposable 18- to 25-year-old ingenue, rather than for a 32-year-old woman. Jeff Richards, a former University of Southern California and Portland Beaver baseball player who gave up the game when he tore a ligament in his leg, was 31 at the time the film was made but looks younger. The harsh lighting, poor choice of clothing, and overstated lipstick draw attention to Vera-Ellen's slight speech impediment and she seems to have difficulties saying her "s" sounds, something a more skilled director would have gotten around as directors used to do for actresses such as Kay Francis and Lizabeth Scott. Generally, Aldrich fails to protect his star and show her in the best possible light. Still, Vera-Ellen manages somehow to project her warmth and sincerity into even this limited portrayal. We believe that she really loves Richards and cares about helping the young man's career and saving her uncle's job. She throws herself into this sweet little performance earnestly—despite the lack of quality around her and her own miscasting. Her role centers the picture and makes us care about its principal characters, even just by simply walking along and talking to Edward G. Robinson. Her cousin Fred Maurer noted:

> Vera always wanted to do drama and that is why she agreed to do *Big Leaguer*. Even though it wasn't her best film it helped her attain a personal goal of doing a film without any dancing.

A.C. Lyles watched the film recently and observed:

> Most any kind of part that you could give her she could do... She did this baseball picture with Eddie Robinson and there is a wonderful scene where she did a trucking shot with Eddie and it was so wonderful, so great.

The one truly poignant scene in the film has Vera-Ellen lecturing Jeff Richards about how baseball is a fine way to make a living, how he must follow his heart even if he goes against his family, and how he shouldn't quit:

> Don't talk about baseball like it's something you read in the want ads...Maybe you're running out on your father, but that's not as bad as running out on yourself.

The shy Richards nonetheless gives up and gets on a bus. As it pulls away, leaving Vera-Ellen (and us) watching it head down the road, we hope it will stop and he will get off and come running back. Finally, it does, he does, and the lovers kiss!

Chapter Seven
Christmas Joy

To fill in the time after *Big Leaguer* while she was waiting for her announced starring role in MGM's *Seven Brides for Seven Brothers*, Vera-Ellen promoted the baseball film by doing a magazine ad for Cameo stockings. However, the photos used in the ad seemed none too recent. She also toured with actor Tom Drake in *I Am a Camera*, the John Van Druten play about life in Berlin in the '30s. Vera-Ellen played the wild English girl and Drake the English writer who has a platonic relationship with her. It was a strong role but didn't advance Vera-Ellen's career and in the film version of the play the part went to Julie Harris. Later it was transformed into the Broadway show and movie *Cabaret*. *Seven Brides for Seven Brothers* was in the meantime recast as a vehicle for Jane Powell. Bob Hope's radio show helped Vera-Ellen begin 1954 on a positive note as she guested on his 15-minute, five-day per week program for a full five days from January 4 to 8.

Vera-Ellen was to have appeared dancing and singing with Gene Kelly in the biography of composer Sigmund Romberg known as *Deep in My Heart* (1954) and this sequence was actually filmed. The songs dueted were *Falling in Love With Love* and *You Took Advantage of Me* and Vera-Ellen used her own singing voice. The recording survives and has been issued in the MGM Composers Collection Laserdic Set with her voice coming through perfectly well and offering no reason why MGM felt the need to dub her singing. Unfortunately, the sequence was cut from the final film, another major disappointment for her. Regrettably, as 1954 wore on, MGM still had nothing for her to do, so she was sent over to Paramount where she would have her last big hit, in fact the biggest Hollywood movie of the entire year.

How did she get the role in such an important picture at this stage of her career? All indications point to the team of Irving Berlin and Robert Alton, who had rescued her once from MGM oblivion in *Call Me Madam*, and brought her back a second time in *White Christmas*. They obviously admired her talent and were happy to work with her again. That Berlin okayed her twice for his most important film work could never be an accident.

In *White Christmas* (1954) she was once again paired with old friend and partner Danny Kaye and a wonderful ensemble group that featured Bing Crosby and Rosemary Clooney. Broadway's John Brascia did the serious dance numbers with Vera-Ellen, filling in for Kaye. The aim was to film another *Holiday Inn*, a big Paramount success of 1942, which featured Astaire and Crosby. Astaire was set to do the film but was not optimistic about the project and Donald O'Connor, who had been a hit with Vera-Ellen in *Call Me Madam*, was brought in to fill his part. O'Connor was eager to do it and Robert Alton's choreography was prepared especially for him but he told us recently that his illness caused the part to be given to Kaye:

> Bob Alton had already put a lot of the choreography together for me but I got this strange disease and the doctors couldn't diagnose it and it turned out to be Q fever. They waited two months for me. I was

Danny Kaye and Vera-Ellen rehearse one of the most charming numbers in *White Christmas,* **"The Best Things Happen When You're Dancing."**

terribly disappointed. And Danny Kaye made twice the money I would have gotten and he got a piece of the picture. You can see that the movements used look like something I would have done.

Q fever brought O'Connor headaches, fatigue and severe muscular pains. The disease, transmitted by contact with an infected person or spread directly through microorganisms transmitted by tick bites, rendered him unable to do this important film.

As it turned out, Kaye works surprisingly well with Crosby and seems to be a cross between Astaire and Bob Hope. This was the first and, so far as we know, only movie in which Vera-Ellen dropped the hyphen from her name for the credits even though it

The Magic and the Mystery   **143**

John Brascia and Vera-Ellen rehearse the "Abraham" number from *White Christmas.*

was retained in the advertising for the picture! Some columnists such as Louella Parsons began to dehyphenate her as well but soon after the release of the film the hyphen was mysteriously back.

When shooting began Paramount only had three star dressing rooms and Vera-Ellen was assigned to a small, drab cubicle. When Bing Crosby learned of this, he immediately paid to have it redecorated and new wallpaper put in so that it was ready before she reported to work.

White Christmas was the first film shot in Vista Vision and was also in Technicolor. Supervising production was none other than Irving Berlin himself, who wrote a number of new songs for the work in addition to recycling several old standards. The director of this family film was the bombastic Mr. *Casablanca* himself, Michael Curtiz, who was infamous for wrapping up morning shooting in time to have sex with wannabe starlets over the long lunch hour. Robert Alton was again on hand to choreograph but, as the movie musical was becoming a risky venture, rehearsal time for numbers was cut short. Economy was used in the set design, which is appalling throughout the film. The set for the initial sequence set during a bombing in World War II looks like the sound stage it is and the New England inn stage backdrops are extremely spare for the dance numbers.

Still, *White Christmas* is well worth seeing today, even though its values seem alien in today's cynical world. It is an old-fashioned family film, extolling the importance of loyalty to one's friends, and promoting reverence for the United States Army, in this case the 151st Division and Major General Tom Waverly played by Dean Jagger. Everything that evokes a traditional American Christmas is thrown in, as if someone

Vera-Ellen and Rosemary Clooney in the "Sisters" number from *White Christmas*

was going down a checklist to make sure it was all included. One finds pseudo-precocious child ballerinas, snow that miraculously appears when wished for, and family gatherings around the Xmas tree. Although at times it becomes a bit too gooey for many of today's unsentimental audiences, it still charms if you allow it to. It was the highest grossing movie of 1954.

Its plot concerns two war buddies/entertainers who hook up when Kaye saves Crosby's life. They later become superstars and producers vaguely resembling Rodgers and Hammerstein. Vera-Ellen as Judy, the younger of the two singing and dancing Haynes sisters (although she was actually seven years older than "sister" Rosemary Clooney), uses the fact that their brother was in the same army unit as Crosby and Kaye to persuade them to catch their act. Appropriately, they sing "Sisters" with Rosemary Clooney actually dueting with Trudy Stabile (wife of popular bandleader Dick Stabile), who sang under the stage name Trudy Stevens and who had been personally recommended for the dubbing part by Clooney. Originally, Gloria Wood was going to do Vera-Ellen's singing until Clooney intervened on behalf of her friend. "Sisters" became quite a popular hit song for Columbia Records, thus making Vera-Ellen one of very few singers to lip-synch two songs which became hits (the other was "You Make

Danny Kaye and Vera-Ellen as the meddling matchmakers in *White Christmas*

Me Feel So Young" in *Three Little Girls in Blue*). The soundtrack album from the film gives credit to Stevens as singer. She was a frequent voice double at Paramount and Columbia from the later '40s through the late '50s, dubbing Lizabeth Scott in three films.

Vera-Ellen and Danny Kaye eventually get together in *White Christmas*, but much of the film is occupied with the on-again off-again and extremely boring personal relationship of the bickering and posturing Clooney and Crosby. They are both so pig-headed and dense throughout that one wonders how they think they would get along *after* marriage. Thirteen complete songs and bits of others fill up the time until everyone (along with a fresh batch of snow) unites to save the inn for its owner, the former Army Major General, who is about to go under financially.

One of the most charming numbers involves, of all people, Danny Kaye dancing with Vera-Ellen. "The Best Things Happen When You're Dancing" was written for Astaire and would have been a natural, graceful Astaire/Vera-Ellen or O'Connor/Vera-Ellen classic. But Robert Alton let Kaye attempt a real dancer's part and, though his steps are simplified, he proves that just about anyone who dances with Vera-Ellen can be made to look good. The result is a beautiful and surprisingly long dance that is remarkable not only for her floating, graceful movement but her expressive facial gestures, the sort of dramatic dancing that became her specialty. Here she flirts with Kaye and projects the passion and romance of new love. It is also an excellent example of Vera-Ellen using her dress as a dancing prop—making swirling patterns into the camera and complementing her body movements magnificently—proving again that she is

Vera-Ellen:

Vera-Ellen, Danny Kaye, Rosemary Clooney and Bing Crosby in the "Gee, I Wish I Was Back in the Army" number in *White Christmas*

the queen of "dress dancing." And by hiding Kaye behind Vera-Ellen for much of the dance, Alton tricks Kaye fans so that they will say: "Look how well he can dance!" But to be fair, Kaye actually worked hard and did a fine job.

White Christmas is a true ensemble acting film. Vera-Ellen is onscreen with the others through most of the film and gives another of her sincere and natural performances. She works especially well with Clooney, who gets her first chance to do serious acting in this film and makes the most of it. Vera-Ellen's role as a relentless gold-digger pursuing Kaye is a charming light comedic performance. The chemistry among all the principals makes this schmaltzy film work and keeps the viewer interested. And for once the comic relief in the film is brief and provided in a more natural, tolerable vein by veteran Mary Wickes as the inn's receptionist.

Once at the inn the ensemble performs a minstrel number featuring a solo by Vera-Ellen. Throughout the film her super-thin waist and lovely long legs are featured and her neck, which was beginning to show signs of age, is carefully covered up. This is never more true than in her "Mandy" feature with dancer John Brascia. Here, although appearing frighteningly thin and frail, she dances energetically and with amazing flexibility, executing extraordinarily high front and back kicks, along with somersaults and splits, and ends by being hurled through the air like a torpedo.

A humorous but not fully realized highlight in *White Christmas* is the routine to "Choreography" that makes fun of the tendency in the '50s to develop odd theories about dance that led to peculiar postures and angular, disjointed moves. Kaye portrays

The Magic and the Mystery

John Brascia, Vera-Ellen and Danny Kaye in the "Choreography" number in *White Christmas*

an effete dancemaster with beret and British accent who sings about how kicks are out and old-time real dancing has now been replaced by "choreography." In the midst of the mayhem, Vera-Ellen's legs suddenly appear at the top of the screen as she is lowered slowly from above. Brascia and Vera-Ellen do a strenuous balletic routine and Kaye fortunately disappears offstage for much of it, only to return doing absurd steps to emphasize the point of his song. A routine with Vera-Ellen and Kaye parodying modern dance ideas would have been truly funny and exciting to see here, but Kaye is left to jump and flail about wildly à la Jerry Lewis, and the opportunity is missed.

The final Vera-Ellen featured number is a brief jitterbug routine to "Abraham" with John Brascia. The Berlin song was brought back from the original *Holiday Inn* movie. The frenzied dancing and her pitifully frail condition brings worry to the viewer concerning her stamina, but she gets through it with gusto. Of particular moment is the one close-up as she claps her hands and whirls around in a circle with her partner, her eyes brilliant and flashing and her smile enticing as she appears almost demonically energized. It is a dancer still in love with dancing and enjoying this moment. Unfortunately, it would be one of her final screen dance moments.

White Christmas had already become a holiday classic long before Vera-Ellen's death and it is the film for which she is best known. Regarding its annual television exposure, she commented: "I don't watch, but it's nice to know it's there."

By this time she was known as the actress with the smallest waist in Hollywood and her thinness was truly becoming alarming as she began to age prematurely.

Vera-Ellen is noticeably thin in the "Mandy" costume in *White Christmas*.

Yet at the time she seemed not to notice or be bothered by this and she could not or would not put on much-needed weight. Some critics also began to note that she was starting to look too thin. Dorothy Manners of *The Los Angeles Examiner* commented:

> Although she insists it's delightful dancing when you're light, some viewers of both *Call Me Madam* and *White Christmas* are inclined to believe she has carried slimness to the point of skinniness.

These comments were echoed by Philip Scheuer in *The Los Angeles Times*. Vera-Ellen finally commented on this growing criticism and defended herself:

> Men don't like you too thin. One must think of the whistles and such! And I have gained a few pounds since *White Christmas*.

For *White Christmas* she worked enormously hard, rising at 6 a.m. to get on set by 8:30 so she could practice until 6 p.m. each day:

Vera-Ellen with Richard Gully

I lose an average of five pounds per dance routine. Next to being a longshoreman, being a dancer on the screen is the hardest physical job in the world.

A.C. Lyles remembers her punishing routine:

Edith Head did her wardrobe for *White Christmas* and Vera-Ellen worked so hard on that picture that as the pic progressed Edith had to revamp the wardrobe by continuing to take her costumes in because she lost a lot of weight.

Vera-Ellen was disappointed that she wasn't getting enough work, especially from MGM and that her hits were coming from loanouts, thanks to her guardian angels Irving Berlin and Robert Alton. The dreadful state of the Hollywood musical saddened her terribly. Although she had been in some of Hollywood's most successful and charming Technicolor musicals, she lamented her fate at the end of 1954:

One musical a year to be in isn't very many, isn't really enough because nobody sees those long months of keeping in shape in between pictures! It's like a painter painting and nobody to look at the work.

Dramatic actresses have the luxury of letting down between pictures, but not dancers.

She was still living in her small house with her mother at 4557 Camellia Avenue in North Hollywood (her former boyfriend Rory Calhoun's old home, built in 1941), in the area now known as Studio City because so many people from the studios live there. She was swimming hours every day, but in other people's pools since she didn't own one. The women did their own housework but they did hire a maid to come in once a week. Vera-Ellen would go out on dates but come home at night to mother, even at age 33.

She was contented with this but she was still interested in getting to the top and being a super achiever in every aspect of her life. In her mind, one way to get to the top in one's personal life was to become royalty. That is one reason she was fond of repeating the story of Princess Elizabeth recognizing her at her Command Performance. In addition, she especially enjoyed a visit by the King and Queen of Greece to the set of *White Christmas*. Several scenes were shot of them with Vera-Ellen but they never appeared in the final film. Still, she would report frequently and fondly that her film opportunities allowed her to meet royalty.

During this period she began dating a man named Richard Gully and confessed "I'd like to get married again, if the right man comes along." Vera-Ellen hated to cook and so dined out almost every night, almost always consuming steak or roast beef. Although she lived frugally, she loved clothes and bought new clothes constantly until they overflowed all her closets:

Clothes are my one luxury. People in Hollywood have long memories and I can't wear any one gown too frequently.

The clothes were generally custom designed for her in yellows and/or blues. Having learned to simplify her look from her Goldwyn Studio years she now proclaimed:

A profusion of gems doesn't do anything for a woman except perhaps give her a feeling of financial security.

Vera-Ellen was seen at the premiere of Judy Garland's long-awaited *A Star is Born* on September 29, 1954 at the RKO Pantages Theater. A kinescope survives of her being interviewed by Jack Carson for KTTV television in Los Angeles. On November 4 between acts of television's *Lux Video Theater* on NBC she was plugging *White Christmas*. She had no films lined up after that release but she was happy because suddenly, unexpectedly, in the summer of 1954 Vera-Ellen fell in love again and this time the romance was serious. Louella Parsons, the famed (or infamous) gossip columnist, announced on October 20, 1954 that Vera-Ellen was finally going to marry again, this time to Victor (Vic) Bennett Rothschild, a wealthy member of the famed banking family. He was apparently related to the English branch of the family barons, and represented royalty in the public mind even though most of his money came from owning and managing gas stations. Vic, still vibrant and active today at age 80 despite incipient Parkinson's Disease, enjoys telling the story of how his grandfather had been a Baron

The happy bride and groom, Vera-Ellen and Victor Rothschild on their wedding day.

in London, but had gambled away his money and title, causing shame to his family and an early death for his mother.

According to Vic, his father, then 15, left England in disgrace and came by freighter to the east coast of America to start a new life. Vic's father must have had a colorful time in the New World for he was 69 years old when Vic was born in America. Vic's father allegedly married six or seven times, and died while Vic was just three. After the death of Vic's mother eight years later, Vic was raised in California by his much older brother Harry. Vic admits that the story has "a lot of gaps" but believes that it is essentially true. He says that he was the youngest of four children and that Harry had to take over control of the family at age 19.

Despite being related to the Rothschilds, Vic and his siblings grew up poor with barely enough to eat. His father became incapacitated and soon died. Harry, who had just begun to study at the University of Southern California, had to quit and support the family in Hawthorne, California, south of Los Angeles. He took a job driving gasoline from the refinery to the gas stations and soon realized that if he could find a way to purchase a refinery he could earn a great deal of money. Through his work he learned of a refinery which was in a ruinous state and which could be obtained cheaply. He read library books about how to manage and repair refinery equipment and he was able to convince a few investors to back him. Soon he had another refinery at Santa Fe Springs near Los Angeles and he had become an independent entrepreneur of staggering wealth. Once he purchased, repaired and maintained the refineries, money began to pour in and Harry found himself a millionaire in a short period of time and was able to buy out his partners.

Young Vic went to work for Harry but this was interrupted by a stint in the army with the paratroopers of the 11th Airborne Division in the Philippines and at Okinawa in World War II. After a few landings the war suddenly ended with the surrender of the Japanese after the atomic bombs were dropped at Hiroshima and Nagasaki. Vic was one of the first soldiers into Tokyo as an occupying force. Upon his return from the war he was given considerable responsibility with Harry, focusing on Harry's line of half a dozen service stations and five oil well drilling rigs in the Los Angeles and Bakersfield area. Although Harry was a genius at business and petroleum engineering, he never found success in his personal life. Constantly working and devising new ways to grow rich and improve his facilities, he neglected his family life and married five times, twice to the same woman. All the marriages ended in divorce and after his independent businesses failed in the mid 1980s when new national laws failed to protect the independent entrepreneur in the oil business, Harry spent his later years in a depressed, lonely state. But Vic was eternally grateful to him for giving him the opportunity to make good. Such chance led him into the company of the rich and famous.

Vic remembers how he met Vera-Ellen:

> Bob (Robert) Stack's wife had invited me and Vera to their house to play tennis with them and Vera liked to play and we started dating right away. Nothing serious at first, but then I got ill with the flu and she came around to see me and she was so kind as she was always to everyone. And our serious relationship grew out of that visit.

Vic was handsome and dashing, and had an eye for beautiful, slim and sophisticated blondes. He was a smooth talker and could be very persuasive and charming when pursuing a lady who interested him. A social animal too, he enjoyed being around celebrities, parties and drinking, but he could also be extraordinarily attentive and complimentary. Vera-Ellen told Louella:

Vera-Ellen models a bridal gown for husband-to-be.

We are shopping for an engagement ring and we are going to be married soon. I don't believe in long engagements. I knew this was it as soon as I met Victor, but I haven't even told my studio yet. I wanted you to be the first to know. The day Victor asked me to marry him was the day after *White Christmas* opened in New York. Mr. Y. Frank Freeman called me to tell me about my fine notices, and it just seemed that everything good happened to me that day.

Vera-Ellen was truly happy and excited about the new marriage and began to put on weight again so that she was looking healthier than she had in two years. She had fallen hard for her beau. Their engagement was announced only two weeks after their first meeting and the marriage announced only three months later. She posed radiantly for the United Press International in Santa Monica as they looked at their marriage license; he however looked somber and uncomfortable in the camera's eye. But on November 19, 1954 at St. Paul's First Lutheran Church in the San Fernando Valley,

Vera-Ellen's mother Alma Rohe poses with the happy couple.

they were married. To commemorate the occasion, the happy couple donated two perpetual flame lamps that are still in use in the church. Vic's brother Harry was the best man and his wife, M'Liss, was the matron of honor. An elegant champagne supper at a restaurant on Ventura Boulevard followed the ceremony. Vic was 31, actually two years younger than Vera-Ellen and it was his first marriage. He was a handsome, outgoing, redheaded oil executive, who worked with the United States Drilling Company in Pasadena.

Reportedly, Vera-Ellen was a heavy smoker but Vic detested cigarettes:

> I never knew she smoked and she never smoked around me. I was so sensitive to smoke too, so I would have smelled it on her breath or clothing if she had been doing it. If she had been a smoker she must have given it up without my knowing it.

The Magic and the Mystery   155

Victor and Vera-Ellen pose with Louella Parsons.

With this union Vera-Ellen had suddenly, instantly, become Hollywood and international royalty as part of one of the world's most famous and richest families. She now had a family crest with the name Rothschild, taken from the red shield on the house in the German Jewish ghetto in Frankfurt where the family originally lived. Mayer Rothschild founded the famous Rothschild banking dynasty in the later part of the 18th century. Through his five sons he spread the power and influence of his firm all over Europe, opening branches in London, Naples, Paris and Vienna as well as the main center in Frankfurt. Profiting during wartime when fighting princes needed their loans, munitions and supply connections, the family invested heavily in the Industrial Revolution and for almost 200 years was a major force in world economics and politics. And Mayer Rothschild's grandson had become the first Jew in the British Parliament. It was extraordinary that Vera-Ellen, so concerned about her Lutheran religion, should marry into one of the most important Jewish families in history.

After the festivities, the honeymooning couple was off for a week to Palm Springs and the exclusive Racquet Club, then on to brother Harry's 87-foot Rothschild family yacht (*V Westlake*) for a honeymoon cruise in Mexican waters that included a stop at Acapulco and was to last until New Year's Day. They first lived at 1451 Miller Way in Los Angeles and then moved to Pasadena, living on Aramingo Drive. With the move to Pasadena her name regularly appeared in society columns recording her comings and goings. Soon they would move to a beautiful gated home on Outpost Cove Drive with a long curving driveway high up in the Hollywood Hills overlooking all of Hollywood. Vic says that he got along beautifully with Alma Rohe but some of Vera-Ellen's family members and friends felt he was star-struck and were appalled that he was already intimating that he would like to become Vera-Ellen's manager. Nonetheless, they were happy that she had fallen head over heels in love.

And Vera-Ellen had dreamed of not only being a star but of really living like a star or a princess. Her life had become just like her roles in *Call Me Madam* or *Happy Go Lovely*. Suddenly, she was fantastically rich and living a real Cinderella story with a wonderful, handsome dream millionaire. It seemed incredible, the fulfillment of all her dreams, the beginning of a wonderful new life, especially when coupled with her role in a highly successful "A" picture like *White Christmas* that had garnered fabulous reviews. She had cried with joy at her good fortune at the candlelight wedding, causing

Victor helps Vera-Ellen keep in shape on the deck of their yacht in this publicity photo.

her mascara to run and Vic to smile. She had needed time to compose herself before greeting her guests. Vera-Ellen looked beautiful on that happy night in a high-necked gown of pearl satin with a bodice of champagne jersey, a tiny wreath of white roses on her head, pearl satin pumps and pearl kid gloves. The hat was designed by Rex, the gown by Amelia Gray. Apparently nobody noticed that she had put down her age on the marriage license as 31, a compromise between her "studio age" of 28 and her real age of 33 (and a way of not being older than her husband).

And MGM, which had all but forgotten about her, suddenly made the most of its publicity releases for its dancing star who was shown hanging all over her new husband. The studio still claimed she was only 28 and now also insisted that she had never been married before. Bob Hightower had been conveniently forgotten by MGM although Vera-Ellen admitted the marriage to interviewers. Her good friend Marie Windsor was delighted for her, partly because she too was engaged and would marry within one month. Their husbands later became good friends. Both ladies began turning their thoughts toward having a family.

It seemed that Vera-Ellen's star was on the rise again and MGM announced she would star in two forthcoming musicals: *Athena* and *Hit the Deck*. In the end she once again lost the first role to Jane Powell, but the film proved to be a thundering dud about health faddists, which, oddly enough, Vera-Ellen and her mother actually were in real life. *Hit the Deck* was an ensemble film and Vera-Ellen lost that part to the bouncy Debbie Reynolds. That movie was sparked by some spirited dancing in a funhouse set by Debbie and the talented former gymnast Russ Tamblyn. When all was said and done neither film made much money. Another announced film for her was to be called *Night Time Girl,* possibly a musical. It never got off the drawing board.

Once again dismayed over her lack of work, Vera-Ellen left MGM when her contract ran out in 1955. Vic remembers that they were both well aware that the old-fashioned MGM musical was going out of style and not making money as in the old days. She began the year on January 2 as a guest on NBC radio's *Nutrilite Show*, a variety show hosted by Jack Benny's popular comic tenor Dennis Day. She was offered the RKO low-budget Western *Tennessee's Partner,* but decided against it, thinking it too much of a comedown after *White Christmas*. During her years at MGM she often refused offers for Broadway, nightclubs and for television roles that were forbidden without studio approval. So her fortune at MGM paralleled that at Goldwyn—she spent most of her time on the shelf, not being allowed by studio executives to use her prodigious talent. At this time of unemployment she became something of a homebody, slowly redecorating the interior of her home. For a time, happy with her husband, she began to put on weight and look much healthier.

Though she was now free to try television, she had always been doubtful about developing an act for Las Vegas. Early in 1954 she had stated:

> I prefer movies to a Broadway show and as for night spots such as
> Las Vegas, getting an act together is very expensive for a dancer—
> three months of rehearsals with boys, lavish sets and all the rest.
> After so many beautiful pictures, an audience would feel let down if
> you didn't put on a comparable production.

And yet, without many other options other than retirement to devote herself to her new husband, she decided within a year to star in a dancing revue in Las Vegas, not only because the entire show was built around her but also because she was paid $15,000 for four weeks with the show. This princely sum set a record for the time, plus there was an option for another four weeks. On May 23, 1955 Vera-Ellen opened at the fabulous Dunes Hotel as the star of what may have been the greatest musical extravaganza put on there up to that time. Producer Alfred Gottesman wanted to introduce Broadway-style productions to Las Vegas with the new Dunes so he put together a cast of 60 to create *The Magic Carpet Revue, New York-Paris-Paradise.*

Robert Nesbitt directed and staged the 1-hour 45-minute extravaganza in the Arabian Room and the opening night had a few glitches, notably the problem of production number singers who moved about the stage and were unable to be picked up by the

Vera-Ellen in her Las Vegas extravaganza

stationary microphones. As an additional selling point, almost-nude chorus girls paraded about in lavish production numbers surrounding Vera-Ellen. It was a combination of Broadway, a Las Vegas floor show and the Ziegfeld Follies. There were 33 dancers under the direction of Bernard Pearce and gorgeous sets by Furth Ullman. There were comedic acrobats, a slapstick ventriloquist, singers of popular music and opera, and erotic specialty dances, but the entire evening was built around Vera-Ellen, who tapped and did ballet and sung, happily undubbed, and wore gorgeous costumes by Hollywood's famed designer Howard Shoup. Critics not only praised her dancing but also loved her singing and song presentation. Her routines were based on those

Vera-Ellen behind the scenes in Las Vegas

developed for her by Robert Alton. She did partnered dances with friend John Brascia, who was also given solo dancing opportunities. The Jaye Rubinoff Orchestra was cited for its superb playing. This production was one of the great triumphs of Vera-Ellen's career. Those who saw her in the Revue remember her as being sensational.

Unfortunately the show was an experiment which was virtually doomed to fail. It cost $80,000 for its first night, and although subsequent performances would cost much less, the extravaganza had to be paid for from the profits made in the casino each night. After a while, as the novelty of the show wore off, it was canceled in favor of the less expensive and more sure-fire draws such as Frank Sinatra and Tony Martin. Nonetheless, it was a personal triumph for Vera-Ellen, who proved that she was as spectacular headlining a show in person as she was in the movies, and that there had been no need to dub her voice in films when she could charm crowds in live performances.

While the sexy show was gaining strong notices, a "blonde" starlet named Jayne Mansfield received a great deal of press attention by lounging around the hotel pool in a revealing bathing suit. It was the first time that she began to draw major attention and she would soon become a rival to Marilyn Monroe.

By later in June 1955 the Las Vegas extravaganza had closed.

Though Vera-Ellen was a popular regular on the Los Angeles party circuit with her new husband, she now performed less and less often. She did an interview for *Art Linkletter's House Party* popular daytime television show. She danced on television's popular *Colgate Variety Hour* (the old *Colgate Comedy Hour* in a new format) in July 1955 and caused a sensation with her dazzling rendition of numbers she had performed in her Las Vegas spectacular at the Dunes Hotel, including a scintillating Apache dance. But her interests were turning more and more to her husband and home, even though her mother continued to push her to maintain her career. She wanted to devote herself to her second marriage, have a family and pursue her hobbies that by this time included tennis, swimming, riding, sailing and drawing in charcoal. At last she appeared truly happy.

But rumors began to surface that there were problems in her marriage. Vera-Ellen was of course set in her ways and increasingly concerned about her appearance and her career. Vic was said to have a roving eye for gorgeous thin blondes, but he insists to this day that he never was unfaithful during either of his marriages. Now 80 years old, he is divorced from his second wife Ingela and is about to marry for the third time.

Vera-Ellen began 1956 by guesting on *The Perry Como Show* on February 18 on NBC. The variety show was one of primetime's highest-rated programs. The program was a salute to the new science fiction movie *Forbidden Planet* and featured its stars

The Las Vegas show was a personal triumph for Vera-Ellen.

Robby the Robot and Anne Francis. Also performing was a varied cast that included ventriloquist Paul Winchell, actor Henry Fonda and the now legendary black pop group The Platters doing their current number one hit "The Great Pretender." The program survives and is notable for providing Vera-Ellen an opportunity to do sketch comedy. Perry Como introduces her no fewer than four times, calling her "Vera Allen" each time so that her name was never correctly pronounced during the entire evening. Como includes among her famous great dancing partners not only Donald O'Connor, Gene Kelly and Fred Astaire but also Danny Kaye.

The comedy sketch involves two jaded cowpokes Fonda and Como, who saunter into a saloon in the old west looking for excitement. There they find the good-hearted

IT'S A HIGHLAND FLING
OF LOVE AND LAUGHTER

IN CINEMASCOPE
AND
COLOR DELUXE
TO FILL THE SCREEN
WITH THE BEAUTY
OF THE HIGHLANDS

'WEE'
Jeannie
STARRING
VERA ELLEN as
Jeannie MacLean, with
TONY MARTIN, ROBERT FLEMYNG

Anne Francis singing "Bird in a Gilded Cage," definitively showing why she never had any other offers for singing parts. Vera-Ellen plays a dancehall floozy in cahoots as a card cheater with a gambler named Crooked Pete. She tips him information by writing the cards of other players on her own forehead in lipstick. The sketch is dreadfully executed with a full five-second dead halt with total silence as Fonda and Como miss their entrance cue. Nobody emerges unscathed from this dreadful and overlong bit. Even Robby the Robot appears with a Stetson hat on his head—it's that desperate.

Vera-Ellen manages a feeble soft shoe dance with Como in another sequence and dances with Como's choreographer Louis Da Pron. Both do a passable partnered ballet but they are unrehearsed, the stage is too small and they fail to perform their movements with anything approaching coordinated precision. Television dance was clearly not suited to Vera-Ellen if this number is any indication. She has not room to express the sort of fluid and complete movement she is noted for and there is not time to match her partner. Instead, he seems clearly to be following her movements and staying in the background, the reverse of a typical Vera-Ellen partnered dance. In any case, the result is remarkably unmemorable.

After a two-year hiatus from the screen, she returned to work in 1956 in a modest British musical called *Let's Be Happy*, with handsome singing star Tony Martin who had been popular for decades. Husband Vic accompanied her on the shoot. The film, released in 1957, was shot in Technicolor and Cinemascope, although it is only commercially available in a 16mm print today. The available print has deteriorated to the point where the opening credits have been chopped off and the color is so altered to red that it is advertised as a black-and-white print. The film was based on a play called *Jeannie* by Aimée Stuart and was to have been given that title until just before it was

IT'S A HIGHLAND FLING OF LOVE AND LAUGHTER

IN CINEMASCOPE AND COLOR DELUXE TO FILL THE SCREEN WITH THE BEAUTY

'WEE' Jeannie

STARRING
VERA ELLEN as
Jeannie MacLean, with
TONY MARTIN, ROBERT FLEMYN(

released by Allied Artists, a small company that had grown out of the low-budget company Monogram Pictures of the 1930s. Since musicals were in short supply and Vera-Ellen had left MGM and could not get film work of significance in the States, this seemed to be a rare opportunity. Again, her singing was to be dubbed and one of the enduring mysteries of Hollywood is who did it because nobody seems to know and there seems no record of it anywhere.

The story was a romantic comedy with some dramatic overtones and a few musical numbers so she could use her acting skills as well as her dance talent. She was happy to be reunited with her devoted Romanian producer and friend Marcel Hellman of Criterion Productions, who had supervised her previous British musical film, the surprisingly successful *Happy Go Lovely*, and who remained a big fan. He had given her a standing invitation that whenever she wanted to make another movie in England he would produce it, build the film around her and treat her as a star. He first offered her the project under the name of *Miss Morgan,* which she rejected. However, after several years and many offers to Vera-Ellen, he finally obtained her consent. It was now to be called *Wee Jeannie* but the title was soon changed to *Jeannie* and then at the last minute to *Let's Be Happy*. It would be a remake of the film *Jeannie* that Hellman had made 15 years earlier as a successful starring vehicle for the British actress Barbara Mullen. The earlier film had been released in America as *Girl in Distress* and won the praise of famed critic James Agee. It was the story of a cute Scottish old maid who travels to Vienna but the story was revamped and tailored for Vera-Ellen. Despite her concerns about returning to England, she was happy to do the picture:

The Magic and the Mystery

The farm girl Jeannie (Vera-Ellen) meets the debonair Mr. Smith (Tony Martin) on her way to Paris in *Let's Be Happy*.

> I had more dialogue in it than I ever had before. I like to dance but I'm less interested in just being a dancer. I want to do some dramatic stories in television. Or situation comedies.

In *Let's Be Happy* she played a prim and proper, naive and unsophisticated girl from Heatherdale, Vermont with a strong desire to visit Scotland to learn more about her family heritage. When her grandfather John MacLean, a native of Loch Lomond, dies and leaves the 28-year-old Jeannie MacLean (Vera-Ellen at age 35) $4,952 found hidden within the family house, she decides to spend it on the trip. The role is not unlike her role in *The Belle of New York* except that once she leaves the farm and arrives at the airport she is totally helpless. Desperately in need of someone to look after her on a flight to Paris, the first leg of her trip, she runs into a well-off business-man, Stanley Smith (Tony Martin) of Boise, Idaho, on his way to Paris to sell an idea for a new and better washing machine to a man named Fielding.

En route, she is constantly under the protective eye of the handsome, debonair Mr. Smith; Tony Martin pioneered this sort of successful playboy-with-a-roving-eye role that later was made so popular in films by Dean Martin. Once in Paris, Jeannie will take the train and boat to Edinburgh, Scotland in time for the festival (the same festival that provided the backdrop for her earlier British film *Happy Go Lovely*). When they arrive in the City of Lights, Mr. Smith discovers that, by a happy coincidence, Fielding has gone on holiday to Edinburgh. So once again Mr. Smith and Jeannie find them-selves together, this time on the train. Jeannie is unable to figure out how to get meals for herself or to find suitable accommodations in Scotland without his help and she

Even in a film as mediocre as *Let's Be Happy*, Vera-Ellen's sweetness shines through.

begins to fall in love with him. However, she sees that he has a roving eye. He picks up a saucy French model named Helene (nicely played by Zena Marshall), lies and breaks his date with Jeannie, and goes out on the town with the model.

Meanwhile Jeannie is romanced by an unscrupulous, penniless Scottish Lord (Robert Flemyng) who owns a castle in Loch Lomond that he can only afford to keep by renting it to tourists. Learning she has inherited money and thinking she is a rich American, he sweeps the impressionable girl off her feet and proposes marriage. During their courtship, Jeannie goes to the ballet and fantasizes that she is the ballerina. This scene has absolutely nothing to do with the rest of the film but does provide an opportunity for Vera-Ellen to dance.

In the meantime the devious Lord actually falls in love with her. When he learns that she too is nearly penniless he is already smitten and decides to marry her anyway. But she rejects him and, disgusted, returns home to her farm. Her girlfriend Sadie Whitelaw (Helen Horton) finds Jeannie isn't the same naive girl she was before her trip. In the meantime Smith realizes he loves her after all and he hurries to Vermont to woo her once again, promising to mend his ways forever. They sing "Let's Be Happy" and the film ends.

The sorry state of the available print makes assessing this film difficult, but Vera-Ellen does dance beautifully and most flexibly in the short dance sequences. In the first one she seems to float across the Cinemascope screen in airy lightness. She darts about the courtyard of her farmhouse in a plaid shirt and jeans as children dance around her and she sings "Going to Scotland." The scene is particularly delightful. The costumes are rudimentary, and the set simple with farmhouse and picket fence, but nothing else is needed. In another delightful moment, she falls in love with Mr. Smith and dances

The Magic and the Mystery

Vera-Ellen in the "Card Ballet" in *Let's Be Happy*

around the furniture in her hotel room in what the credits call "The Pyjama Dance." As choreographed by Pauline Grant, who worked with Vera-Ellen on her previous British film, it is brief but builds up a momentum of exuberance and joy until she dances near her window and sees Tony Martin stepping out with the French model after breaking their date, Suddenly, her world comes crashing down, not only because she is in love with him but also because she cannot tolerate a liar. This collision of happiness and tragedy is well played and well orchestrated and is one of the film's genuine highlights.

The ballerina fantasy sequence, based on an idea conceived and designed by Olga Lehmann and known as the "Card Ballet," features Vera-Ellen as personifications of the Queens of all four suites—Clubs, Diamonds, Spades and Hearts. Working with a group of male dancers dressed as "Jacks," she performs a ballet that involves several male-assisted somersaults, including one that ends in a nice split. She does several leg walkovers (leaping over the outstretched leg of her partner) and is finally caught in a deluge of falling cards. The routine is attractive but too short and a bit difficult to understand, yet the dancing is of high quality.

Even in Cinemascope, Vera-Ellen looks painfully thin. In the close-ups she no longer looks like the 30 years she now admits to, much less the 28 years of her character. Tony Martin was in a similar situation. Already in his 40s, he was playing a character of only 36 years. In one absurd sequence he guesses Jeannie's age as 22 and she replies in a manner that could have been taken from her real life: "A woman's allowed to take a slice off her age. It's understood!"

A big problem with *Let's Be Happy* is that this romantic comedy has almost no comedy, unlike Vera-Ellen's earlier British film. The story is nothing more than the voyage of a naive girl from the farm into the real world of air travel and hotel accommodations, finding romance *en route*. The minor sub-plot involving the Lord trying to woo her is almost incidental and is not developed as either drama or comedy. A good bit of screen time is spent, or rather filled up, touring Edinburgh. Unfortunately, if this film is any witness, Edinburgh is not one of the world's most dynamically visual cities. The script by Diana Morgan has none of Val Guest's charming and funny comedy that set *Happy Go Lovely* above the run of British musicals. Here, the funniest gag involves two fat men trying to pass each other in a train corridor, a joke that was tired in 1938 when Alfred Hitchcock used it in England in *The Lady Vanishes*. Director Henry Levin was brought from America but fails to inject the film with interesting visuals or much pacing, genuine drama or conflict. The characters have little depth as written, the production values are second-rate and everything falls flat.

The songs in *Let's Be Happy* by Nicholas Brodzsky and Paul Francis Webster are quite bland and easily forgotten. The staging of the dances is not up to the levels of Fox or MGM to which Vera-Ellen had become accustomed, but at least the producer respects her and has made her the true star around which the plot revolves. Tony Martin is an effective, handsome leading man and his singing is pleasant. Yet in this era of Elvis Presley and Pat Boone, his songs seem antiquated and the film resembles a throwback or a farewell to the Hollywood musical of the '40s and early '50s. In England Tony Martin and Vera-Ellen were still major stars. In Hollywood shifting public taste had made them poor bets for movies. Neither ever starred in another film.

The film has plenty of problems. Vera-Ellen's character is particularly poorly written. Everything Jeannie sees elicits a "Gosh" or "Gee whiz!", and her naiveté, innocence and primness border on the just plain dumb and silly. When she is about to go under a hair dryer for the first time, she actually asks if it will explode. When she is angry, she holds her feelings in and says to herself: "Isn't that the pink limit?" Vera-Ellen tries her best with the dialogue she is given, but the flat staging of her scenes does little to help. Moreover, throughout the first part of the film she is dressed in rustic, frumpy clothes that contribute to the overall drabness of the atmosphere. Her transformation in Scotland into an elegantly dressed lady of the world does not work because she seems too thin and frail at this point in her career to successfully carry it off. Still her expressive facial reactions to Martin's lines and singing are quite good and she once again is able to create a true character portrayal out of the thinnest of material. It is clear that with good direction she could still carry and anchor a film, but she requires better direction and a better vehicle than this.

The British press didn't think much of the film. *The Monthly Film Bulletin* justifiably found it "laborious" and "tricked out with production numbers which are for the most part vulgar in conception and undistinguished in execution." They added: "Success still eludes the Anglo-American musical." But *Variety* said it was "a gay, lively musical" where Vera-Ellen "gets her opportunity to shine when she visualizes herself in the shoes of a prima ballerina in an enchanting Ballet of Cards." *The New York Times* lamented that Vera-Ellen was "given little to do in the way of singing or dancing." Yet even in a film as mediocre as this, Vera-Ellen's sweetness shines through. In the opening ballet the viewer can feel her love of children and she seems believable as a young lady with high moral and ethical standards, a kind and gentle nature, a desire to pursue an objective to the limit, and a desperate need to be protected. Maybe that's because that is how she really was.

Vera-Ellen promoted her film in 1957 by being introduced from the audience on the Ed Sullivan television show and by appearing on the television game show *I've Got a Secret*, hosted by Bill Cullen, who was a long-time admirer. Her "secret" was that she was wearing an outfit made from suits owned by Bill Cullen and panelist/actor Henry Morgan. At the time of release of her last film Vera-Ellen stated:

> My role in the picture *Jeannie* was such a joy. It called for a diversity
> of dancing and costumes. I danced barefoot, in high heels, low heels,
> ballet slippers, and the costumes were lovely.

She hoped to follow this film with a prominent role in the musical *Les Girls* with Gene Kelly and Kay Kendall but again this hope quickly evaporated, especially after *Let's Be Happy* faded quickly upon release.

In May 1957, she was still having difficulty keeping weight on and her husband, who liked thin women, noticed no problems:

> I didn't notice anything unusual. She liked to be as light as possible
> when dancing. Normally she weighed about 108 and when she danced
> she wanted to be at a lighter weight, under 100 pounds. I thought this
> was perfectly normal. She worked out all the time because she had to
> stay in shape for her parts. She was easy to live with and apart from
> not liking high collars and liking to elevate your feet to improve
> circulation, as many people do, I saw nothing out of the ordinary.

She reported that her doctor had been advising her and she had worked out a strict diet, yet it still sounded like a formula for losing more weight, like something her mother would have handed her in the 1920s:

> Eat proper, healthful food that will build your body, not bloat it. Be
> sure to eat three meals a day and at regular hours. Favor all natural
> sweets instead of sugar. Eat dates, raisins, figs and prunes. Keep a jar
> of honey handy and have a teaspoon every time you begin to feel
> tired. For breakfast drink orange juice, eat a raw egg and some honey.
> Use a mixer to get the right blend. Olympic athletes use this prepara-
> tion. Try coconut milk and wheat germ for a mid-afternoon snack.
> Have a potato at least every other day and eat the skin. Do light
> exercises every day. Take a brisk walk daily and breathe deeply. I
> know this sounds like a reducing routine but you'd be surprised how
> it builds up your weight and curves.

Chapter Eight
The Machine Wears Out

1957 was not a banner year for movie musicals. The decline of this venerable Hollywood tradition forced Vera-Ellen off the screen and she was reportedly extremely depressed about the problem. Furthermore, MGM had lost faith in her and never felt that she was enough of a dramatic actress to bridge the gap to dramatic roles. Billy Grady, the critically important casting chief of MGM, was among her non-supporters and is reported to have blocked her from getting a number of roles. He is on record as stating: "She wasn't enough of an actress to follow a dance star like Ginger Rogers and play straight roles."

Yet she kept busy. She made her dramatic television debut opposite Robert Sterling on March 20, 1957 in an episode of Ford Theater entitled *The Man Across the Hall*, a delightful half-hour comedy which afforded her the only light comedic television acting role she ever had. She portrayed a Betty Furness–type spokeswoman for an appliance company. The most fun came at the beginning of the piece, which still survives, as she sings the praises of a new refrigerator that simply won't open no matter what she does.

On May 20th, 1957 she was reunited with her old friend Ray Bolger with whom she had performed on Broadway in *By Jupiter*. Now both were on the down side of their careers. Bolger, 53, had a short-lived television variety series, *Washington Square,* that failed to get real support from NBC.

The network changed its airtime almost every week, and it often ran every two or three weeks instead of weekly, both sure ways to kill a new show by making it difficult to find and not promoting it. This was all the stranger because the program was telecast in color. For a time it aired on Sunday afternoons. Fortunately, a video of the segment on which Vera-Ellen guest-starred survives and seeing it at once brings both delight and great sadness to her followers. In the program Ray Bolger tried his best to blend quality entertainment of the Ed Sullivan variety into a theme show format. On this evening the format was a trip around the world, inspired by the release of Mike Todd's blockbuster movie *Around the World in 80 Days*. Vera-Ellen is on hand in every scene, playing herself traveling around the world with Bolger and Mr. Edmund Carp (veteran character come-

Vera-Ellen on TV's *Masquerade Party* in 1958

The Magic and the Mystery

Vera-Ellen made several live television appearances in the 1950s.

dian Richard Haydn), a fastidious and idiotic travel agent. On the way they visit France, Italy and Spain and encounter singers, dancers and novelty acts ranging from Italian/ American singer Kay Armen to Spanish flamenco dancer Jose Greco.

The live program suffers from a woeful lack of rehcarsal that gives the numbers a ragged quality, and the stage is too small and doesn't allow full movement of the dancers. One chorus member inadvertently strikes a microphone producing muffled sounds and several lines are incorrect, but the show goes on. In an opening sequence Vera-Ellen does a solo with the dance group, The Martins. She is at the train station singing and dancing to "Gonna Get Away," but her singing is prerecorded and drowned out by a strong chorus. Her dancing outfit is modest with flaring skirt. Her neck is at all times covered with a scarf. She was 36 when this was filmed but she seems years older and dangerously emaciated. Her lightness and agility, so apparent in *The Belle of New York* just five years earlier, are still at work, but at the end of her brief dance feature she finds herself some distance from the knee of the dancer she is intended to light on and she fairly stumbles over to her mark. The crowd of people on the stage and closeness of the sets make it impossible for her to dance with full extension because she must be on the lookout for her camera marks, scenery and people. The lack of adequate preparation time shows and must have been very unsatisfying to a perfectionist like Vera-Ellen.

In her acting scenes with Bolger, they discuss the next stops on their trip. Vera-Ellen watchers will note that she is constantly, nervously concerned with making sure that her neck is covered with her scarf. But a charming number follows as they decide they can find all they want out of life just "Ten Minutes from Here." Bolger and Vera-Ellen do a comic dance, in which he moves with his herky-jerky, hopping and skipping style shaking his upper torso. Vera-Ellen, the supremely versatile partnered dancer, matches him step for step and shakes her upper body in a delightful parody of his movements. Given a little more rehearsal time, this number could have been a classic dance in a feature film and remains a true Vera-Ellen highlight, rescued from oblivion and made available by the nostalgic folks at Video Yesteryear.

Near the end of the program Bolger and Vera-Ellen do a romantic and old-fashioned Astaire-Rogers type dance to *April in Paris*, the title of Bolger's starring film with Doris Day five years earlier. It is fascinating to watch these old pros who have clearly not had time to rehearse more than five or six times try to bluff their way through the steps. At one point she twirls and he is to catch her hand delicately. They miss and exchange a glance that for a split second seems to say: "Oh, my God. Now what do we do!" But they struggle on. She slides down his arm onto the floor but the slide is rough and she nearly falls. Throughout the routine, Vera-Ellen is forced to keep a close watch that she doesn't crash into the curtain. It is at once horrible and yet given the rehearsal time involved it is amazing that they would risk such a complicated number. This is clearly not MGM but the forgiving viewer will enjoy here a rough version of what, given more time, would have been a beautiful number. Bolger worked very hard to try to bring high quality to each episode of his television show but despite his efforts, his network had no faith in him or his concept and the show never was given a chance to find an audience. Even if it had been renewed, it is doubtful that Bolger could have survived the punishing weekly or two-week schedule despite having kept himself in extraordinary physical shape throughout his long career.

With movie work becoming more and more scarce, Vera-Ellen did what fading stars often do. She resorted to second-tier road shows. On September 1, 1958 she made her first and only professional appearance back in Ohio, starring in *Best Foot Forward* doing summer stock at the Cincinnati Summer Playhouse. On November 22, 1958, Vera-Ellen was still performing, dancing to "Shall We Dance" on the Thanksgiving *Perry Como Show* and singing with her own voice. The hugely popular program also featured on that night Dorothy Collins, the singer from television's *Your Hit Parade*, famous Warner Bros. film composer Harry Warren, and pop star Jimmie Rogers, famous for tunes such as *Honeycomb* and *Kisses Sweeter Than Wine*. It would be the

Vera-Ellen as a snowman on *Masquerade Party* **in 1958**

biggest audience Vera-Ellen would ever have on television. Como enjoyed having her as a guest but never could say her name correctly, confusing her with the elderly character actress of radio and television Vera Allen. In 1958 she also did several television commercials, one for Lustre-Crème Shampoo and another for a hair dye firm. On February 15, 1959, Vera-Ellen also appeared on *The Dinah Shore Chevy Show* doing a sensual dance to the popular theme from the television private eye show *Peter Gunn*, written by Henry Mancini, and flying in on wires like Peter Pan. Other guests included droll comic George Gobel, composer Andre Previn and Craig Stevens, who portrayed Peter Gunn on the popular television show.

Donald O'Connor remembers that shortly after this time Vera-Ellen gave up performing on television:

> I can't remember what show it was but she was doing a number and the act before her was using real vegetables or something and made the floor slick and when she did her number she slipped and fell but got up again and finished the number. She was so embarrassed and it was live TV. That was the reason she stopped doing television, I know for a fact. She always worked to make everything perfect.

On April 6, 1959, Vera-Ellen attended the Academy Awards ceremony at the Pantages Theater and again caused quite a stir, wearing a form-fitting gold lame sheath which was the talk of the evening. Her comment on her dress was "Why not? It's the way Oscar himself dresses." So far as is known, Vera-Ellen's last scheduled television appearance was a guest spot on *The Chevy Show*, to be hosted on November 10, 1959 by her former co-star Tony Martin and additional guest stars comedians Joan Davis and Red Buttons and singer Nat King Cole. Newspaper ads were taken out to announce the production featuring a photo of the two stars, but Vera-Ellen and Joan Davis did not appear due to the Asian flu. Red Buttons pulled out of the show allegedly due to a weak script. The choreographer was Eugene Loring but Vera-Ellen never got to work with him.

With television out of the question and no movies to look forward to, Vera-Ellen found the work drying up even more and the glamour of the old days was gone. It just wasn't the time for musicals anymore and soon she couldn't see the point of going on with it and retired. At 37 it was becoming increasingly difficult to maintain her perfect Olympian form year round when the jobs weren't stimulating enough. Her close friend, Paramount producer A.C. Lyles, reported that she still received but declined a number of offers to do stage musicals, including Las Vegas appearances, but she had had enough.

Vera-Ellen:

According to *Variety*'s Vera-Ellen obituary, she made one final film, the British suspense thriller *Web of Evidence*, but upon investigation this turns out to be an error, a confusion with the actress Vera Miles who starred in the film.

Vera-Ellen's performing credits, so far as is known, end in 1959, a year in which the Hollywood musical all but died and she had aged and was much too emaciated to play dancing movie leads or ingenue roles on television. And even if she were still able, dancing leads in movies were becoming rare indeed.

At this point Vera-Ellen's reclusive private life becomes increasingly difficult to document. Surprisingly, her mother became

Vera-Ellen still maintained her dance practice even while pregnant.

less active in their Lutheran church, letting her membership lapse in October 1961, but the reason is unknown. In November 1962 eyewitnesses report a particularly strange episode. When Vera-Ellen and husband Vic were in Palm Springs celebrating their eighth wedding anniversary, Vic was observed paying an inordinate amount of attention to a female guest at the restaurant. The waitress thought that Vic was married to the guest and brought the cake to her, at which point Vera-Ellen became so upset and enraged that she immediately left the table and drove all the way back to Los Angeles despite being many months pregnant. Eventually, the situation was patched up but according to director George Sidney the marriage showed signs of strain such as this well before the arrival of their child, due to Vic's persistent womanizing, a statement that Vic vigorously denies.

On March 3, 1963, at age 42 after nine years of marriage, Vera-Ellen gave birth to her daughter, Victoria Ellen, sometimes written Victoria-Ellen, who was the love of her life. Her friend Marie Windsor, who had married when Vera-Ellen married, also had a child within one month of this. But little Victoria died on June 20, 1963 (some sources give June 22) at the age of just over three months. The child had been left in the care of Alma, while Vic and Vera were away. She was at a dance class and Vic was in his office in Pasadena. Vera returned first to find that the child was dead and, according to Vic, she phoned him the news and he drove "a hundred miles an hour" to his home. Alma Rohe was completely distraught. Somebody had called for emergency help but attempts

Vera-Ellen happily poses with her tiny daughter Victoria-Ellen.

to revive the child were too late. Vera-Ellen had run to a neighbor's house in her initial distress but the neighbor's teenage son was home alone and had no idea what to do. As the reality of the moment sunk in, she phoned Marie Windsor to pour out her grief. Death was reportedly caused by infant crib death, now known as Sudden Infant Death Syndrome or SIDS. Her close friend A.C. Lyles recalled these painful times:

> She had always wanted a family and the loss of her baby seemed to take the life out of her. She was never the same after that. It really traumatized her and I don't think she ever got over it... I talked about the death of the baby as little as possible and she didn't say too much to me about it... A couple of times it came up and she got so emotional about it that I just didn't want to get into it and once in a while she would say something about the baby and I would try to get her off the subject.

Cousin Fred Maurer added:

> She kind of changed after that. It was a terrible blow to lose a child she'd had so late in life. I know her mother was heartbroken.

Vera-Ellen:

The strain on her marriage became more severe after the child's death. A rupture may also have occurred between Alma Rohe and Vic. Alma would later tell friends: "Victor blamed me for the child's death and he still does."

But Vic strongly denies this:

> I never blamed her mother for the baby's death. We always got along very well. There was no question of foul play and I talked to the doctor at the time who said that it was a death by natural causes, that the lungs had filled up with fluid and the baby had suffocated.

In July 1963, Vera-Ellen let her membership in the Lutheran church lapse after Victoria's death, and she never renewed it.

Ugly rumors circulated through Beverly Hills and the Hollywood community (and still persist) that Alma Rohe had killed the child or had inadvertently or accidentally caused its death. It was said that Vic had started these rumors but he denies this. Another rumor prevalent at the time stated that Vera-Ellen had become temporarily insane, grabbed the child, and took it into the nursery and refused to come out until the police and firemen broke down her door and physically removed the child from her arms. People who visited Vera-Ellen soon after the event, however, do not recall seeing broken doors in the house, and this story has not been substantiated. The truth appears to be that she became desperately upset, as anyone would under the circumstances, phoned her husband and soon phoned Marie Windsor to pour out her grief. And it took a very long time for her to do anything about altering the nursery room.

Instead of taking charge of the situation, which had so devastated Vera, Vic seemed to distance himself from it. He appears to have had little to do with the burial of the child and, until we informed him in 2003, did not know that the baby had been cremated, but did remember that the funeral took place with the casket closed. A surprising recent revelation from the cemetery records now suggests that Victoria was buried full body, not cremated, in an unmarked grave in the plot reserved for Vera-Ellen and her mother. Vera-Ellen may have intended to commemorate the child with a headstone but perhaps she couldn't face it. It still has not been done to this day. Says Vic:

> I am embarrassed to say that I did not know that the baby was buried without a headstone. I thought that had been arranged but if you say so I guess it is true. I think Vera just did not want to deal with the death and because it was a reminder of all the pain it caused her.

Recent research on SIDS suggests that fewer babies actually die of it than originally believed. The term is often used as a catch-all employed when the actual cause of an infant's death is unknown. Vera-Ellen had the child late in life at age 42, and this alone would increase the risk of problems in a newly born infant. Vera-Ellen was also extraordinarily thin and, as will be shown below, apparently suffered from Obsessive-Compulsive Disorder and anorexia nervosa. Physical manifestations of the latter illness frequently include disruption of the menstrual cycle and disturbance of hormonal levels. For several reasons, the infant may not have been as healthy as she might have

Vera-Ellen's Outpost Cove home, taken in 1965

been if she had been born to a younger, healthier woman. The child therefore may have had a number of problems that brought about the condition known medically as "a failure to thrive." Moreover, the use of any of Alma's unusual health or diet formulae on the child would surely have weakened her further. Given Vera-Ellen's natural propensity toward self criticism, she may have blamed herself for the child's death and been tormented by thoughts such as "if I had only...." for some time, even years.

After the death of Victoria, Vera-Ellen aged considerably. It is difficult to know if this was the result of genetic predisposition, prolonged grief or the result of punishing treatment she had inflicted upon her body by keeping herself trained to a fever pitch for so long. The years of excessive beef consumption, chain smoking, and her curious diet, which usually consisted in this period of roast beef and overripe fruit, cannot have helped and anorexia nervosa may have been a major culprit in debilitating her. Several close friends believe that she had a complete nervous breakdown after the death of the child and that she took a long time to recover from it. Friends say that Vic was just not the sort of man to deal with this situation or recognize that she needed professional help. He never kept a picture of the baby for posterity and did not know that one existed until he saw the first edition of this book. During the good times, Vic had found Vera to be charming, refined and very easy to live with, but he was not prepared to cope with this situation.

As arthritis, depression, high blood pressure, possible anorexia and premature aging racked her body, Vera-Ellen now became more and more withdrawn from the public, wishing to hide her deteriorating appearance and protect her image, although she did maintain contact with a few close friends. Her marriage began to fall apart, as so often happens in the case of the death of an only child, complicated by an omnipresent mother who was involved in it. As psychologist Rosarie Hartmeyer has commented:

The sadness never leaves and it permeates the house and can destroy the marriage. One partner may be able to put it behind him but the other may not be able to. Staying in the house and seeing the nursery, you get to thinking you are to blame. The marital relationship can easily break apart amid the grief.

On September 15, 1966, perhaps a little more than three years after the death of baby Victoria, Vic, her husband of almost 12 years sued for divorce claiming extreme cruelty and that she had inflicted mental suffering on him causing "pain, anguish and humiliation." In the hotly contested divorce settlement, Vera-Ellen got their lovely hillside home in Hollywood's Outpost Cove with its beautiful swimming pool. Quite soon Vic remarried. He had met a beautiful woman in her 20s named Ingela even before his divorce from Vera and lost no time in pursuing her, even though the young lady too was just divorced. Ingela and Vic ran off to Las Vegas and got married and Vera was all the more stunned since she had known Ingela and her ex-husband socially. Now Vic was really gone forever, suddenly married to a woman whom Vera thought was just an acquaintance of theirs.

About this period in Vera-Ellen's life, psychologist Rosarie Hartmeyer writes:

> Regarding the death of her child it would not be uncommon for her to feel guilt, particularly since she was out at a social occasion when the child died. She would always wonder if she could have made a difference if she had been home caring for the child. Not marking the child's grave may indicate lack of self esteem and a desire not to face the death of the child. After her marriage broke up she must have lived a very lonely life, complicated by financial woes.

By this time Vera-Ellen was scarcely news anymore and her divorce notice in *The Los Angeles Citizen-News* only merited three scant paragraphs. After this she ceased to be covered in the newspapers at all and disappeared from public and media view. A.C. Lyles recalls:

> This second divorce was another terrible blow. It was a very bitter divorce. I never saw her do or say anything that was humiliating or harming to her husband like he said in his complaint. She did complain a lot about the bitterness of the divorce and she would say "how am I ever going to afford the lawyers to fight him." I tried constantly to get her out of the house and she would say that maybe she would come over but she really was becoming more and more of a recluse.

Vera-Ellen was seldom seen at public affairs after this. The collapse of her second marriage, the death of her child, the waning of the film musical and studio indifference had hurt her deeply. Vera remained attentive, loving and supportive to her family, including her mother, aunt and cousin. She saw her mother regularly and she maintained her interest in dancing by taking lessons right up to the end of her life, with support from friend and instructor Michael Panaieff. But she never danced in public again.

Dance director George Sidney, who was neither a friend nor admirer of Vera-Ellen, recalled this later stage of her life bluntly:

> Vera-Ellen thought she was responsible for the baby's death. She went off the deep end emotionally. She really went nuts. After the baby died she would speak to people as if the baby were still alive. She became unpredictable and stranger and stranger.

Along with the chaos and heartbreak of her personal life, she found her arthritis worsening, making it impossible for her to dance professionally even if she had chosen to. The ailment gradually affected even her ability to walk normally, a bitter blow for someone used to performing incredibly difficult movements with the greatest of ease and flexibility. She continued taking dance classes, mostly to regain enough flexibility so she could walk and perform simple movements with less pain and because dancing was her life. Swimming in the heated pool also provided some relief.

In the middle and later 1960s, television talk show host Mike Douglas, a long-time Vera-Ellen fan, acting after being prompted by her friend Bill Dennington, wanted to get her to go on his show and reminisce about her wonderful film work. When his show moved from Philadelphia to Los Angeles in 1978 he reportedly was still hopeful. Having vowed now to close the door to entertainment offers, she turned down his requests, saying: "I just don't think I would have anything interesting to say."

But the truth was she was concerned about her appearance. With her physical condition deteriorating, she preferred for the public to remember her the way she was in her movies. Like Dietrich and Garbo, she wanted to protect her image for posterity. She stated that she just "wasn't up to the person she once was" and wasn't "in good enough condition" to appear in the media. Since she always was a person able to divide her life into rigid compartments, she simply shut the iron door on the entertainment business part of her life forever.

In 1969, Alma Rohe, who was still living in the house on Camellia Avenue, confided to her neighbor Edith Swartz that she was worried about her daughter. Edith's daughter Pamela Stackel was a young lady then and remembers visiting Vera-Ellen's Outpost Cove home with her mother and Alma. Pamela wanted to meet Vera-Ellen, the vivacious star of stage and screen, but when she got there she found most of the big home closed up and most of the furniture under dust covers. And despite having a lovely tea service that was visible to her guests, Vera-Ellen served the tea from an old thermos. She seemed distracted, her conversation trailed off and didn't always make sense, and she continually looked around as if she heard something that no one else could hear.

According to Pamela, Alma told her mother later that Vera might have been imagining that she heard the baby crying or that she thought someone was following her. Pamela also recalls the strange and vacant look in Vera-Ellen's eyes and her subdued attitude that was "not at all the vivacious woman I had seen on the screen." Ironically, Pamela and her husband Rob now live in the Camellia Avenue house once occupied by Alma Rohe and Vera-Ellen.

Vera-Ellen posed by her pool for friend Bill Dennington.

After all that she had been through, it is possible that Vera-Ellen suffered occasional bouts of extreme depression. She lacked the finances to obtain proper mental health care (and she was possibly concerned about the stigma of doing so), so she may have struggled with her mother's help through some periods when she was not feeling up to par. But such episodes as this one are definitely *not* typical of her later life. Her behavior on this particular day may even have been the result of strong medication she was taking for arthritis. Others who knew her throughout her last 20 years report that

The Magic and the Mystery   179

she normally was lucid and sharp, and not prone to self-pity or morose fantasy. Yet even they note her negative reaction when she was allowed to dwell on the subject of the baby for an extended period.

Consenting to a rare interview in 1971, she reminisced about her varied career:

> I don't think I'm missing too much not being active. They don't make as many musicals today. All musicals have to be blockbusters, and how many of them are doing well? I frankly can't see myself in the type of message film that's coming out. The whole business is different today.

Reflecting on the various media in which she performed she stated:

> Films are the best medium for a dancer. You can have unlimited space, and you can preserve what you do. Television gives you great exposure. The theater can be a rough experience, in that you have to do the same routine every night for the run of the play, but it's a good proving ground... Moviemaking for me has always been hard work and fun. It's nice to be remembered and rediscovered.

Toward the end of 1971, Vera-Ellen was still getting occasional offers to return to work. Broadway was riding a nostalgia craze with the revival of the hit 1925 musical *No, No, Nanette*, starring 1930s icon Ruby Keeler and Helen Gallagher and bringing back the ancient stage and film choreographer Busby Berkeley to assist in the production. Vera-Ellen was offered either of the principal parts for one of the road shows of the production, which was to travel in 1972. She thought about it but turned it down. She did not want her public to remember her as an older woman who didn't look her best and she wasn't sure she could measure up to the quality of dancing she had done before. She preferred to have people remember her the way she looked in *White Christmas*, but did at least briefly entertain the thought of being rediscovered.

But rediscovery was not to happen in her lifetime. In 1972, the definitive history of *The MGM Stock Company* was written by James Robert Parish and Ronald L. Bowers. The work included chapters on dozens upon dozens of the actors and actresses who had been contracted to MGM whether they were superstars, character actors or minor blips. It included chapters on such obscure MGM entities as Ann Richards, Sara Haden, Cecilia Parker and Susan Peters but no chapter on Vera-Ellen. It was another cruel slap in the face. About the only mention of her work in that 800-plus page opus is the statement that in *On the Town* the "labored ballet dancing of Kelly and Vera-Ellen in this Leonard Bernstein musical is less impressive with passing years...." This negative assessment and near complete neglect of her brilliant and critically praised work seems so insensitive and cruel. Could it really be that in the opinion of those authors all her hard work at MGM had amounted to nothing?

During this period she continued to go to dancing classes but was otherwise increasingly withdrawn. She was forgotten by Hollywood critics, film historians and ex-husbands (although fan letters continued to pour in) and more and more unable to deal alone with life's continued hard knocks. She struggled on putting up a happy front but some friends saw through the façade and realized that she was keeping her physical and mental pain locked deep inside.

It must have seemed incredibly strange to her that a life devoted to a serious diet of health foods and constant maintenance of the body should lead to a condition where she was unable to move without pain. Cousin Fred Maurer reports:

> To help keep the arthritis from developing even faster she worked out regularly at a studio right up until her death. She also was a believer in herbal medicines which her mother encouraged her to take to combat the arthritis. She was in much pain for at least 10 to 15 years prior to her death.

In her family the women normally lived into their later 80s but already her health was failing her. In 1954 when she was 33 she had stated:

> I'll probably go on limbering up at the gym bar when I'm 80 — and that's a frightening thought.

She would barely make it to 60.

Her mother urged her repeatedly in the early '70s to sell the small house on Camellia Avenue and let her move into the Outpost Cove house so they could take care of each other. But Vera-Ellen had worked so hard for years to get to the top that she insisted on maintaining her own life and lifestyle. She held firm that she had to live by herself so her mother stayed at the small North Hollywood home. When her mother became unable to fend for herself, Vera-Ellen put her in a nursing home and visited her regularly.

Vera-Ellen still stayed in touch with some of her friends in Norwood and nearby Mount Adam, especially old Harry Hessler, her original dancing teacher who died in 1977. Hessler's nephew Herman Hessler reported:

Vera-Ellen and Doris Day reminisce at a Hollywood party.

> Uncle Harry died...[in his late 90s] and he was still spry. He would go out to visit Vera-Ellen in Hollywood every couple of years and always said she was wonderful and had never changed. He said that despite all her fame, she still treated him like she did when she was a young kid. He also taught Doris Day. They were both wonderful dancers, my uncle told me, but he didn't have much to say about Doris later on.

The Magic and the Mystery

His last visit, as warm an occasion as ever, was in 1973 when he was 89. Another close Norwood friend, and former colleague of Vera-Ellen and Doris Day at Hessler's Dance Studio, Katherine Ralston, kept in touch until the mid-1970s when her husband suffered a stroke and she failed to keep up the correspondence. After Katherine Ralston had become engaged to Norwoodite Paul Murphy and he was stationed in California in the Navy at the end of World War II, Vera-Ellen and her mother had welcomed him and his Navy buddies on weekends at their California home. The Murphys kept a lifelong scrapbook on their famous friend that Katherine maintains devotedly to this day. She hopes to present her vast collection of material in another Vera-Ellen tribute book.

In 1974 the major reunion of the surviving MGM stars was held for the premiere of *That's Entertainment!* Vera-Ellen was conspicuous by her absence. Perhaps because she refused to attend, nothing of her work at MGM was included by the film's producers. MGM's failure to include even one tiny clip of her work there hurt her deeply, especially since she had been told that the "Slaughter on Tenth Avenue" sequence was going to be used. She was suffering a great deal from her illnesses, and she did not want her public to see her in a deteriorated physical condition after she had been the model of beauty, health and perfection all her professional career. She absolutely did not want people asking what had happened to Vera-Ellen. Cousin Fred Maurer reports:

> After she retired from film she became more reclusive because she was in a lot of pain from her arthritis and felt that she didn't look presentable. If she did go out she would wear heavy facial makeup so that people wouldn't see the pain in her face.

She struggled on one day at a time and her money began to run out despite the small alimony payments from Vic. She held her head high, kept up appearances and asked only to be respected and left alone. With her few close friends such as Bill Dennington she seldom talked about her career and made it a point never to say anything bad about anyone. When *That's Entertainment, Part II* came out in 1976 once again no footage of Vera-Ellen was included, even though she had been informed that "Slaughter on Tenth Avenue" was going to be in it since it had been bumped from the first film. This time she was truly devastated and her many friends at the Panaieff dance studio tried to comfort her, as they all felt outraged by this oversight which appeared deliberate. Unwilling to say a mean word about anyone, she told a close friend at the time:

That's okay. I had fun, but it was sure hard work. I was kind of hoping they'd use Fred and I from *Belle* or Gene and I doing "Slaughter"
but I guess they had too much footage already.

By the time MGM got around to including footage of Vera-Ellen in their 1985
That's Dancing! and in *That's Entertainment! III* (1994) she was long dead.

1976 photos show that Vera-Ellen at 54 already looked like an old woman with
stooped shoulders, bent knees and tiny fragile arms and wrists. Arthritis was greatly
bothering her neck, perhaps the result of a dancing accident many years before but
when she would go out with friends she would try hard to maintain her perfect posture.
She was not a wretched recluse as has been commonly thought at the end of her life.
She did have friends and seemed to still enjoy going out with them occasionally. The
dance classes brought her daily joy and she was known to phone friends and talk for
long stretches, often with a fine sense of humor and knowledge of world politics, and
she always had great concern for everyone's lives and health despite her own deteriorating condition. Bill Dennington talked with her regularly throughout this period and
occasionally visited her:

> She wasn't that unhappy as many people think during this time and
> she looked very well when I would see her and I didn't notice wrinkles.
> I thought she seemed terrific. Whenever we would go out she would
> eat a lot and she was aware that people thought she was too thin and
> would ask me to be sure and tell people "what a good appetite I
> have." She still had her nice, dry sense of humor and she loved to
> drink vodka on the rocks and she loved to laugh.

Offers to appear or perform still came in. Bill Dennington remembers speaking to
her about the fact that director Brian De Palma reportedly wanted her for a cameo
dancing role in *The Fury*, a fantasy thriller with Kirk Douglas, and there was talk she
would be reunited in it with Donald O'Connor. She did not take the role.

Nonetheless, life was not yet through kicking Vera-Ellen around. In 1977, the *National Enquirer* began to harass and stalk her but she refused to grant them an interview. Having gotten wind of her daily dance class routine, their reporters entered
Panaieff's trying to get information about her but were ordered to leave. Trying to
interview a waitress a few doors away at a local restaurant they were also stonewalled
by people trying to protect Vera-Ellen. Undaunted, they tracked her down by waiting in
a car by Panaieff's and shot some brutal and humiliating photographs of her. Described
by the *Enquirer* as being 51 (when in fact she was 56 but still old beyond her years), the
merciless paper ran photographs of her puffy, fallen face and skeletal body next to
images of her at her most glamorous in 1952 during the making of *The Belle of New
York*. She was still wearing a high-necked dress and one could still see her lovely lips
and the turned up nose, but her veins were protruding from her arms and she was very
thin. *The National Enquirer* failed to report that she had been seriously ill for some
time, traumatized by the collapse of her marriage and death of her only child, riddled
with crippling arthritis and a number of other illnesses. They also had not given her
time to make herself up properly so that she looked better, but rather sought to capture

Vera-Ellen with Bill Dennington

her at her very worst. This was a cruel, unnecessary indignation and it hurt her terribly. It was a low point in journalism even for *The Enquirer*. She had worked so hard to maintain her dignity and now it was shattered. A bitter yet still defiant Vera-Ellen reportedly told the *Enquirer*:

> I'm retired. I stopped when I was ahead. I don't need my work any
> more, and I don't need the applause.

When her cousin and friend Fred Maurer saw the piece he was infuriated and offended "to the depths of my soul." Bill Dennington called it an outrage:

> It was so disgusting. She guarded her image so carefully and wanted
> to stay the way she was in the movies for her fans. She had retired
> and wanted a little privacy. It was so horrible.

Circa 1977, when Betty Garrett staged a theater benefit to help their mutual choreographer friend Michael Panaieff replace his dancing studio floor after a fire, Vera-Ellen made a rare public appearance. Panaieff Studio was a well-known ballet school in Hollywood on La Brea Boulevard where many retired dancers were known to gather, among them the great John Brascia, Vera-Ellen's film dancing partner and friend. Attracted by her respect for Mr. Panaieff (with whom she had been taking dancing lessons long after her career ended), her love of dancing, and her awareness of the importance of proper facilities for dancers, she came to the benefit and there were the expected whispers among the attendees: "Look. That's Vera-Ellen!" It was terribly hard for her

Vera-Ellen:

to appear and added a sort of *Sunset Boulevard* aspect to the proceedings, but dancing was her life and in this one case she could not compartmentalize things away. She hated to mingle with the entertainment world again but she went. It would be the last time she would appear at such an event.

She would occasionally stop to chat with neighbors at her mailbox, among them Jo Dennis, her neighbor from 1972 to 1981, who remembers that she was "proud that she was still limber enough to lift her leg straight up against the wall. She must have been, because one time she did this for my husband, on her car!"

Several times in the later 1970s, including once in 1978, Vera-Ellen's lovely home was robbed and she lost a consider-

Vera-Ellen poses on the rooftop of the Panaieff Studio building.

able amount of jewelry including an inscribed pin from Fred Astaire and a gift from Gene Kelly. It caused her severe (and understandable) paranoia and fed her desire to hide away from contemporary life as much as possible. She had to pinch her pennies and was not able to hire guards or install an expensive protection system. She had gardeners and pool people working at the house and she suspected that some of the workers may have been casing the house and setting it up for robbery but nothing could be proved. This fear made her increasingly reluctant to carry out much-needed house repairs and when her roof began to leak she resorted to using pots and pans to catch the water. She also feared that repair people, seeing a woman living alone in a sumptuous home, would overcharge her for repairs and create problems where there weren't any, just to gouge her. She felt trapped within a deteriorating environment, and keeping up appearances was becoming very difficult. Her car, a 1965 Cadillac, was getting old and was expensive to service on a limited income.

She could have sold the house and moved into the smaller one, giving a boost to her financial situation, but she had reached a certain station in life and she wanted to maintain that level. She had pride in reaching the heights—the beautiful home, the Cadillac, the giant pool, the prestige neighborhood, the view over the city. Having all this meant to her that she was still "someone" in Hollywood so she hung onto it to the end. Unfortunately, the house was falling down all around her and springing leaks she could not afford to repair. She stopped inviting people to see her at her home. She did not try to raise money for herself by going on talk shows or "remember me" fan gath-

The Magic and the Mystery

erings and she never complained publicly about her lot. She had been raised to go forward with life and make the best of things and not whine. That was her strong, small-town Midwestern upbringing coming to the fore. She was determined to keep her dignity and status. The pool was not only a status symbol but functional, for she kept its temperature at 98 degrees to help with her painful arthritis.

During this period, Vera-Ellen was walking in her den when she forgot about a few glossy photographs of herself she was keeping on the floor to send to fans. She slipped on them and fell hard on her hip, injuring herself severely and requiring the use of a walker for some months. When she went to visit her mother, Alma shouted: "You're disgusting. Get away from me. I don't want to see you like this." Apparently she wanted to keep in her mind the image of her famous dancing daughter in the prime of her career and wasn't ready to abandon the fame she enjoyed vicariously through her daughter. She wasn't even glad to see her or appreciative of her care. To be sure, Alma, despite her size, could be very difficult. Even late in her life, Vera-Ellen still called Alma "mommy" at times. This latest rejection was such a tremendous shock to her that she confided her pain to several friends, something she rarely did. Vera-Ellen resolved to try to protect her image for her fans as best she could and there is little doubt she was also doing it to please her mother.

Unfortunately, adversity was still not through with Vera-Ellen. While returning home from a dancing class in 1979, she stopped at the nearby restaurant frequented by the dancers and her purse was stolen. Since she carried everything important to her in her purse due to fear of her home being robbed, it was a devastating loss and she was despondent for weeks. In the purse was her mother's engagement ring and an alimony check from Vic. Nothing was ever recovered and it took a great effort for her to cancel all the credit cards and get new ones. She lamented the fact that a lady could no longer go out in daylight in safety but at least she was able to call Vic and get another alimony check sent right away.

About this time Vera-Ellen's mother Alma began to decline rapidly and became senile to the point that she sometimes could not recognize her daughter and she had to be put into a convalescent home, which became another major expense. In addition she maintained Alma's home as if her mother was going to return to it—it was not rented out and Alma's personal effects were untouched. A gardener was retained and the utilities continued to be paid. Perhaps keeping the house the way it always was when her mother was in it provided a measure of security in her life, as if things might return to the way they were. Vera-Ellen checked on the house every Sunday, picked up the mail and visited her mother. Still, the absence of an occupant for the house attracted attention and it was broken into three times, possibly by neighborhood teens, and small thefts occurred. Each time Vera-Ellen fixed the damage and had the locks changed but the constant expenses made it impossible for her to adequately maintain her own home, and the installation of air conditioning, which she truly wanted, was impossible under the circumstances.

In 1980 when she was 59, Vera-Ellen ran into old friend, Lee Graham of *Hollywood Studio Magazine*, at the supermarket and then again at the night post office. They used to play tennis, ride and visit with each other regularly. He remembers that she said her mother was still alive at 87 and was living in a nursing home that Vera-Ellen provided for and still visited regularly. Vera-Ellen was still taking dancing classes, and using the exercise to relieve her arthritis agonies, for by now she was in serious, constant pain and rapidly deteriorating health. She was living alone quietly at her home on Outpost Cove Drive, Hollywood, out of the limelight. Graham wrote an article about this encounter for *Hollywood Studio Magazine* but it was not published until April 1980, By then Alma Rohe had died on February 18, 1980 at the age of 88.

The loss of Alma was another difficult blow for Vera-Ellen for, although she had to battle constantly to remain independent from her quietly strong-willed mother, Mommy had always been there for her and loved her deeply in her own way. In fact, Vera-Ellen had become much like her mother—a food faddist, set in her ways, driven for success, deeply religious, excessively neat and regimented, and concerned with keeping up appearances. Without her mother, she now felt increasingly alone. And there wasn't much money left either.

Much of her time was spent in her home now. In the kitchen she would cook up batches of vegetables to freeze in serving containers. She lived mostly in the dining room with its exceptionally long table where she would put newspapers and mail. Significant amounts of fan mail continued to pour in. She did her bookkeeping here, writing her checks, listening to the radio and keeping up on current events and politics. Her telephone was here and here she also ate, retiring to her den at night to watch television. Her bedroom was used only to sleep. Conversations with friends usually ran to what vitamins they were taking and whether or not they were steaming vegetables.

She had all but completely shut her ex-husband Vic out of her life, except for the alimony checks. She was becoming increasingly addled and easily confused. In her home were racks of barely used clothing, lovely cottons, linens and silks, and there were blouses left in cleaning bags but, instead, she wore the same five or six outfits every week until they were threadbare and she was having the cleaners mend them.

A.C. Lyles often called and tried to help:

> Near the end I used to call and say come over to the commissary, over to the studio, and have lunch with me or do you want to catch a movie or something and she really became reclusive then.

Early in 1981 the American Film Institute saluted Fred Astaire with their Lifetime Achievement Award, and Vera-Ellen, in very bad shape from battling a variety of illnesses, was invited to attend but once again refused. Perhaps in retaliation for her no-show, she was completely cut out of the Fred Astaire compilation footage and was deeply hurt by this. Footage from *The Belle of New York* was prepared but deleted. Astaire was reportedly not pleased about the slight to Vera-Ellen also, and told Hermes Pan, his dear friend and co-choreographer, that he loved dancing with her. But Astaire never expressed regret or contacted her and Vera-Ellen told a close friend at this time: "I never hear from the old stars."

One "old star" who admired her and did take the time to call was Eleanor Powell. Ellie, as she was known to friends, was a deeply religious woman who was concerned about Vera-Ellen and believed her to have been "a great dancer and one of the most versatile, a terrific triple-threat (tap, ballet, specialty dancing)." The former stars talked for a very long time and Vera-Ellen was thrilled at this rare courtesy extended to her.

Living alone and in constant pain, she became more and more confined to her home. In her last interview, given March 26th, 1981, accompanied by a photo in *The Los Angeles Times*, she reported amazingly that she was still going to Michael Panaieff's dancing classes daily:

> I still go every day. It's part of my life. It's good for me physically, mentally and everything. I try to stay a little limber. You can't expect to do such strenuous things to the body as I did, year after year, without some wear and tear. Even a machine wears out.

Old habits die hard. Vera-Ellen still followed her strict diet until the end of her life.

Neighbors such as Jo Dennis remember the daily routine of Vera-Ellen driving to the Panaieff dance class and then getting out of her white convertible to get her mail, always wearing on her way home her leotard and tights, which bagged because she was so thin. George Sidney recalls: "After her career ended she took lessons from the Russian Panaieff and he would tell her what he wanted her to do but she'd do what she wanted to do instead — points and high kicks."

The dance classes represented her connection with dance, which was her life. She felt that no matter what happened to her during the rest of the day, everything would be all right if she could just get to Panaieff's, even if she was literally almost crawling there, and find her same place at the bar. It became a ritual and an obsession, in sickness and in health, 'til death do her part. During the last year of her life, she seemed determined to emaciate herself further and continued dieting, barely eating at all. At Panaieff's she was seen with Saran Wrap wrapped around her body under her leotard and wool sweaters piled around her. She also wore woolen leg covers up to her thighs and a towel around her hips so that by the time she had finished her workout she was dripping wet when she came into the dressing room. Whenever friends would try to suggest that she was sweating too much she would ignore them and change the subject.

During this time fans would occasionally track her down and want to meet her. She was always gracious and polite if approached but always shy and retiring. Some of her long-time friends tried to protect her during her final days, among them especially the pianist at Panaieff's for over 30 years, Phebe Stanton. Since Phebe was single and lived alone, she understood Vera-Ellen's hard life and tried to make her final days easier whenever possible. But even with her few close friends she remained a private person, not revealing much about herself and preferring to talk about their lives. Despite frequent invitations she wanted to be left alone and found her energy declining daily. Her fan mail, which she always tried to answer through the years, began to pile up in her home. Friends kept urging her to put on weight but she would just smile and ignore them.

Vera-Ellen:

One of Vera-Ellen's long-time friends after her show business days, Bill Dennington, spent time with her near the end and spoke to her regularly by phone from Philadelphia. Bill had first met her in 1967 and was quickly invited to her home where they spent five hours together. From then on they kept in touch and in her later years he usually spoke with her once a month. Whenever he visited Los Angeles they would go to dinner or she would have a small party with friends in her home:

> When my parents celebrated their 50th anniversary, she not only sent flowers, but called them on the telephone. That's the special kind of lady she was.

At one point, Vera-Ellen called Bill and asked that he not stop by and see her, no doubt because she felt so poorly and didn't look well enough to present herself in public, but soon after she phoned him back and apologized, saying "how could I not want to see you, dear Bill. Please forgive me." Bill last saw Vera-Ellen on August 7, 1981 after having spent the evening of August 5 at her home. They had a three-hour lunch at Butterfields on Sunset Boulevard and although she was obviously very ill, she had just been to the dance studio to work out on the bar and allowed Bill to take photographs, probably the last photos of her. The following day, August 8, Bill and Vera-Ellen spoke on the phone before he went on with his trip. She was still driving the car every day to the dance class and continued to do so until August 11. There were no buses for her to take in this area and a taxi was just too expensive.

By this point in her life, Vera-Ellen was using thick pancake makeup and overstated mascara, the result of making herself up at home under strong theatrical lights as if she were still performing. It would have been suitable for a stage performance, perhaps, but it gave her face a slightly orange hue at times when she went too far with it. Her eyelashes appeared beaded and although friends at Panaieff's found it bizarre, no one wanted to offer criticism. And during this period, suffering severely from arthritis, she went reluctantly to the doctor for help with a growing knot she felt at the base of her neck. It was diagnosed as cancerous and spreading dangerously through her system. It was hardly a surprise to her as she realized she was declining rapidly. Bill Dennington notes:

> She knew even before the diagnosis that she had cancer. She knew. She just didn't want to go to doctors. She hated to go to doctors. She was, I think, getting more and more interested in Christian Scientist ideas in this period.

Former husband Vic Rothschild reports:

> When married to me she did not believe in going to doctors. She was a Seventh Day Adventist. She also didn't believe in complaining about things.

Not wanting to prolong her agony and thinking about friends who had suffered a long painful death from cancer, she decided against surgery and simply chose to face the end with as much dignity as she could for however long she had left.

Neighbor Jo Dennis remembers that near the end another neighbor would regularly bring her paper, which had been tossed in the steep driveway up to her garage. But Jo remembers one day, probably August 21, when the neighbor noticed something wrong:

> The neighbor called to say that the papers had been piling up but that her car was in the garage. He and I decided to enter the house and look for her. The house was spooky—it looked as though it had been abandoned for many years. We called for her, and finally she came out from the bedroom, looking dazed and like a living skeleton. She said that she had cancer but that she didn't want to go to a hospital.
>
> Another neighbor and I brought her meals and gave her some basic care for several days. Even then she refused anything sweet, claiming that it was not good for her diet! Because we had noticed in the kitchen that she had numerous pharmacy bags that had never been opened, all seeming to contain identical items, such as pancake makeup, we went through the house looking for sleeping pills that she may also have accumulated, as we were afraid she might either deliberately or accidentally overdose. I went through her phone book and found the name of her lawyer and called her. The lawyer told me that Vera-Ellen was dying of cancer and that her affairs were in order....
>
> The last time that I went to check on her a group of three women were there—I don't remember their names, but I found out later that they were well-known women from old show business days [one was actress Joan Caulfield]. They were trying to convince Vera-Ellen to go to the hospital.... She finally agreed, and the paramedics were called....
>
> I received permission from her relatives... to go through the fan mail and return it, as many of the letters were recent and contained photos, which I thought people would want back. When we went through the house to gather collectible stuff, we were shocked to discover that Vera-Ellen had kept the baby crib and some other baby things in a closet of what had been the baby's room.
>
> People have said that Vera-Ellen never quite recovered from the crib death, and maybe that was true.

After lapsing into a semi-coma for several days, Vera-Ellen died of cancer on August 30, 1981 at the UCLA Medical Center at age 60 but at the time of her death, she was, according to *Variety*, suffering also from arthritis, anorexia and high blood pressure. She never knew that at this time a beautiful new book called *The Hollywood Musical* was appearing in bookstores and the book jacket featured a gorgeous color portrait of Fred Astaire and Vera-Ellen dancing in the clouds in *The Belle of New York*. Ann Miller sent flowers to the hospital but Vera-Ellen never saw them either. Spending her last four days of life in an oxygen mask, she had dwindled to just 73 pounds. The hospital room quickly filled with flowers and there were visitors such as actress Jan Sterling, who rushed over when she realized Vera-Ellen might not have anyone to be

with her. Tragically, late on the night of her death, Vera-Ellen was alone in the hospital, and she summoned a nurse to help her place a phone call to her beloved friend A.C. Lyles who remembers the moment:

> I really don't know if she was talking to me and wanting to tell me something and I don't know exactly what it was because she was so weak I really couldn't hear. I didn't want to tire her by continually asking "what did you say, what did you say?" And the next morning I decided to go by the hospital—she was near where I was living—and I learned she had died.

He never learned what she was trying to say to him at the end.

The Magic and the Mystery   191

Chapter Nine
Anorexia Nervosa

Many authors have claimed that Vera-Ellen suffered from anorexia nervosa and bulimia during her career. Fred Astaire's biographer Larry Billman wrote of her in 1997:

> Obsessive about her performances and her weight, she would turn out to be one of Hollywood's first recorded cases of bulimia.

Statements like these, derived from *Variety*'s obituary of her and tabloid articles at the time of her death, are often accepted today in other publications without being examined or questioned. In documenting Vera-Ellen's alleged condition it is necessary to review the evidence as to whether or not she had either or both of these illnesses, and if she had them, to determine why or how she contracted them.

This investigation suffers from two problems. First, it is not possible to talk to Vera-Ellen to assess her feelings (but sufferers are often unwilling to recognize their affliction or to discuss it publicly anyway) and, second, proper assessment or diagnosis should be made by a physician or psychiatrist specializing in the disorder. Yet it is possible, in consultation with such doctors, to reach conclusions about her condition based on her own statements about her personal feelings and comments about her by her friends and family. The result is an educated guess — and nothing more than that — about what may have happened to Vera-Ellen. These conclusions need to be tested by further evidence.

It seems probable that she developed anorexia nervosa but there is no evidence for bulimia. Before discussing the relationship of these two diseases to her, however, some preliminary remarks about them are in order. The reasons behind the poor health and subsequent death of Vera-Ellen, and other celebrities such as Karen Carpenter, have not been fully understood by the general public. Sufferers of anorexia nervosa or bulimia often endure ridicule and may be treated as if they were freaks because these diseases seem so odd and absurd to non-sufferers. However, sufferers are not crazy people but rather tragic victims often lacking the power to understand that they have an illness. They may not even be able to save their own lives without help and support. They are not unintelligent either, but rather are normally among our most creative and brightest citizens.

Since sufferers of anorexia frequently wither away slowly, tabloid newspapers and magazines had a field day with stars such as Vera-Ellen and Karen Carpenter. *The Enquirer* did an unpardonable thing in comparing pictures of a gravely ill Vera-Ellen near the end of her life with glamour pictures of her taken during her *The Belle of New York* period. They did this purely for the shock value of showing how far Vera-Ellen had declined physically from the height of her career when she had been a great beauty. This brazen publicity stunt was all the more reprehensible because Vera-Ellen, through no fault of her own, was likely suffering from an extremely serious and sometimes fatal illness that afflicts a broad section of the population. She also became ill at a time

A very thin Vera-Ellen with husband Victor (center) at a party in 1962

before anorexia nervosa was widely recognized and treatment was commonly available. She had no reason to think that there was anything wrong and never underwent medical treatment for anorexia nervosa. A.C. Lyles points out: "Nobody knew what anorexia was in those days. We didn't know much about eating disorders."

Today both disorders can be treated, usually but not always successfully (the failure rate/death rate is circa 6 percent, according to one survey) by specialized teams of psychiatrists, dietitians and physicians. But in Vera-Ellen's day such an affliction in a performer or artist would not have been recognized. It would have been dismissed as over-sensitivity or artistic temperament, a general lack in the person of an ability to keep weight on or a reaction to excessive rehearsing. And, since Vera-Ellen's mother Alma was petite and slender, and her maternal grandmother and grandfather extremely small, her thinness was thought to be hereditary. As late as 1974 doctors were still puzzling over a phenomenon usually referred to as "self-starvation," for the term anorexia nervosa hadn't yet joined the vernacular.

Only in the last 25 years have doctors learned a considerable amount about anorexia and bulimia nervosa. Anorexia nervosa is a psychological disorder, a psychoneurosis and a phobia of being fat and having a distorted, bloated or generally misshapen body. When sufferers view themselves in a mirror, they see themselves as fatter than they actually are, with a perpetual need to slenderize and to alter their physical appearance. A related illness, bulimia nervosa, is a mental disorder that frequently involves eating,

The Magic and the Mystery   193

Vera-Ellen's illness may have started in her school days.

sometimes binge eating, and vomiting out of great concern over weight and body shape. The two disorders frequently occur together and may be intertwined. Often with bulimia the sufferer may keep his or her normal weight and not become emaciated.

Not every woman with anorexia has the same psychological and physical makeup but a profile has been developed over the years that suggests who typical sufferers might be. The disease is most common among young girls, even as young as 8 in recent years, as the age of onset seems to be getting lower and lower. Girls in their teens and early 20s are highly susceptible, particularly those from upper middle class to upper class families or families with parents who stress high goals and standards for their children.

The "why" of this self-induced disorder is not easy to explain and may vary from sufferer to sufferer. Sociocultural pressure to achieve (or not disappoint parents) is often a dominant factor. The behavior might begin after a disparaging comment is made to a young girl about her appearance or abilities, or it might result from difficulty in fitting into a social situation because of perceived failings in one's appearance. Somehow the mind decides that control over one's life and perhaps even the favor of friends and acquaintances can be achieved through excessive diet and manipulation of the body. The affliction changes from being psychopathological to physiopathological when the disorder moves from the mind to the body as the sufferer begins to mold her body to the image she seeks.

The fact that Vera-Ellen exhibited most of the characteristics typical for anorexia nervosa is attested through her own statements or descriptions of her by others. Yet she was also an atypical sufferer in that she did not come from a wealthy or upper middle class family but from one with a less than average income after the Depression hit. It is difficult to know when the illness may have started in her case, but it is possible that it began as early as her days in Norwood Elementary School when she was so short that she had difficulties fitting in and being treated as an equal. She required a special stool to be as tall as the class, for example, and had a speech impediment with regard to the letter "s." Close friends may not have realized her problems since she would have internalized them. Her desire to exceed everyone else in everything also fits the profile. Most women with anorexia are excellent students with a desire to take the toughest classes and do superior work. Vera-Ellen's contemporaries considered her to be the best student in the history of the school. Her mediocre marks in physical education only caused her to redouble her efforts to exceed in that area. All of this is typical, if very early, behavior that can eventually lead to anorexia.

Her obsession in her middle teens with manipulating her body in order to make herself taller and her daily diet rituals during her pre-teen and teen years may have been major contributing factors to the illness. Her belief that she could make herself acceptable by slimming down and stretching out and that she was actually growing one-half inch each year (she claimed this even when she was 32) are all typical reactions. So is her obsessive neatness and her fastidious care (just like her mother) about not only food but various aspects of daily life, especially her clothing. She was devastated when her wardrobe was criticized because she always paid careful attention to her clothes, designing many outfits herself with ankle-length skirts and off the shoulder bodices, usually in blue and yellow dotted with something red. Her makeup preferences were a deep red lipstick and lots of mascara and she always liked to drape scarves around her neck or wear high-necked collars. Later on, when she was in her 30s, she developed a mannerism of tugging at her scarf when she was nervous to make sure it covered her neck as she appears to have become very sensitive about the appearance of her neck. Everything had to be done exactly the way she wanted it, everything in its place and orderly. Nightgowns needed to be blue with lace trimming and could not be worn with any trace of wrinkles. Her perfume was always Blue Hour.

Also symptomatic might have been her obsessive attempts to alter her facial appearance by holding her cheeks in with her fingers for long periods of time so she could achieve a sunken-cheek, model-like appearance. She also sought to alter her appearance by standing on her head repeatedly and changing her voice timbre. Her genuine belief in her ability to metamorphose her body from ugly duckling to sexy glamour girl, while continually claiming "I'm no glamour girl," would also seem typical of the illness. This reshaping regime was reinforced by improvements she saw in her career after these changes were made so that she felt rewarded. The extreme pressure from her studio MGM may have contributed strongly to her problems since the executives insisted that she maintain herself in a thin, highly energized state. She likened herself to a machine, waiting for work, obsessive about letting up for even a moment. She was well known to friends for having an iron resolve about the way things had to be done (as did her mother) and she would stick to her program no matter what. Insecure, sweet, ambitious and eager to please, she would resort to any measure to achieve the look her studio desired and the success expected of her by her mother.

The inability to grow up and leave the home coupled with an excessive need to please one or both parents is also typical of women with anorexia. Vera-Ellen never really left home in the sense that her mother lived very near her or with her for almost her entire life, except for the period of her marriage to Robert Hightower. Moreover, throughout this period she remained strongly influenced by and attentive to her mother and always spelled mother with a capital M or called her mommy.

Vera-Ellen was able to remain a child, at least in the mind of her public, for an extended period by removing five years from her age when she arrived in Hollywood. The 23-year-old young lady was presented as if she were 18, still a young girl. This retardation of maturity may also have contributed to the emergence of the illness, for a person believed to be 18 then was treated differently by others from one of 23 years.

The Magic and the Mystery

Vera-Ellen and Marie Windsor in 1953

Low self-esteem and insecurity are other common factors in the illness. Vera-Ellen, despite her considerable intellectual gifts, constantly referred to herself as a low-brow. Her reclusiveness (already noticeable in childhood due to concern about her tiny frame) and her constant need to please by laughing at everything people said that was even slightly amusing may also relate to the illness. She hated to talk to people on the telephone, except for close friends or men she was dating, and whenever possible she wrote letters to avoid phone use. She spent considerable time worrying about the way she looked, which often caused her to be late for everything that wasn't a dancing assignment.

Women with anorexia are often extremely kind and sensitive toward other people while being self-deprecating, traits that fully describe Vera-Ellen. Her compulsions to buy gifts for everyone and be attentive to everyone's needs all the time were ways she attempted to gain approval. Her dissatisfaction with her own dancing, necessitating endless rehearsal and provoking self-deprecating remarks (such as references to herself as a "goof"), was well known. Her close friend in Hollywood, the late actress Marie Windsor, recalled to us in August 1998, shortly before her death:

> My strongest memory of Vera-Ellen is that she was a truly wonderful person. She was very thoughtful and sensitive and was always buying gifts for her friends. We had a very close relationship.
>
> Some time way before we both got pregnant in 1962 we were doing celebrity guest appearances together in Mexico City. Julie Bishop, the actress, was with us and someone else and we appeared at a circus. There was trouble with the plane, a delay, and it was December 11th, my birthday.
>
> Finally, we were told to board the plane and Vera could not be found and they paged and paged her and finally told us they would have to leave without her and finally she made it. I was so angry. She was always late and I was so mad and I said "where were you" and she had been out buying presents for my birthday! And that's the kind of person she was.

Other good friends recall her always sending or bringing them gifts, remembering their birthdays or even their parents' birthdays or anniversaries. The passing of someone else's parent usually brought flowers sent by her with a thoughtful card. Cousin Fred Maurer remembers:

> When we'd come to visit her, she was so wonderful to us. She would turn herself inside out for you. She was such a kind and wonderful person.

Sometimes this extremely kind behavior is the result of intense fear of being rejected, a supersensitive fear of criticism. An extremely kind act toward her could also trigger a supersensitive reaction. She was quite easily and often reduced to tears by a kind thought on her behalf, as if she were surprised that anyone would think her important enough to make a fuss. Of course it is difficult to know how much of her behavior was triggered by her presumed illness and how much was the result of the fact that she was an extremely sweet, sensitive, nice person.

Symptoms of anorexia can stay dormant for some time, then suddenly reemerge or emerge in a fuller manner when triggered. After her husband Robert Hightower left for military service and she became a star on Broadway, she became excessively thin and felt the emotional difficulty of having to excel every day. That is one reason why she preferred film work, where a mistake could be corrected and she did not have to perform live. Once she got to Hollywood, and away from daily live performances, her weight quickly returned.

The traits of severe dieting and renewed body manipulation are next seen in her with the termination of her Goldwyn contract and her sudden period of unemployment. She used this time to retrain or "reshape" herself in order to avoid being washed up at 26 or 27. This was a period of major stress as she began to fear that the faith and dedication of her mother toward her career might not become fully justified.

When she got her MGM contract in 1948 the studio made it plain to her that they were dissatisfied with her body shape, the over-muscular look of her upper thighs in particular, and that she would have to slim down considerably. Samuel Goldwyn approved of her muscular legs and 20th Century Fox never complained but to be an MGM star required a taller, sleeker look, more in the manner of their rising young ballerina/dramatic actress Cyd Charisse. In order to metamorphose, Vera-Ellen went on a punishing, severe diet. At MGM she was forced to compete for roles against the most beautiful and talented women in the world. Equally traumatic was the unimaginable pressure of dancing in a film with a living legend and exacting partners such as Fred Astaire or Gene Kelly, which she was soon assigned. Kelly in particular was known for driving his partners into the ground with hard work and criticism. She wanted to look her best and, Debbie Reynolds reminds us, she was constantly told her best wasn't good enough.

Women with anorexia often have an ultra-strict dietary regimen. As we have seen, Vera-Ellen's mother Alma was what used to be known as a "food faddist" and insisted that her daughter stay on the strictest of diets from the time she was a tiny child. So Vera-Ellen grew up following tightly prescribed, ultra-peculiar dietary regimens. When an adult, she ate adequate protein and micro-nutrients but ate little else. Her extreme particularity about foods is a common trait among women with anorexia. During her early MGM years Vera-Ellen drank a lot of milk and peppermint tea and ate wheat germ, raw sun-dried fruits, and no processed sugar (honey was substituted). Her obsession with meat (she would mention at times that she would like to be a big game hunter) was well known. She ate a lot of steak, and at the time meat was considered extremely healthful as a source of protein that would not put on body fat. This idea was commonly embraced by dancers in particular. In those days it was thought that bread and pasta would bloat and should especially be avoided by dancers, but now they are often advised that glycogen from pasta and bread is stored in the liver and can provide energy during a performance.

In a time when health foods were considered odd (as late as 1954 they were still depicted as a goofy, eccentric fad in films such as *Athena*), Vera-Ellen was way ahead of her time. But she simply did not have all the data for healthy eating choices available today, particularly information linking excessive beef consumption and heart disease, and she was susceptible, as her mother had been, to dietary quackery. In her day there was a widespread belief that still exists among many dancers that excessive protein in the diet contributes markedly to strength and endurance. Vera-Ellen followed this notion religiously and believed that it was effective. She tried to do the right thing for her body based on available wisdom and for a while it seemed to work:

> I'm very healthy and a person's health depends a great deal on what they eat, so I must be on the right track.

Unfortunately, she wasn't.

Women with anorexia frequently seek to be superwomen and super achievers, often to please their parents. In school they are usually extremely quiet even though they are at the top of the class academically. The parents of such women may deliberately or inadvertently put extreme pressure on the youngster to succeed. In Vera-Ellen's

Vera-Ellen displaying her typical daily routine for a publicity shot.

case her mother was fond of telling everyone she had dreamed of her daughter's great success even before she had given birth to her, a rare example of inadvertent pressure being exerted on a child still in the womb. So Vera-Ellen was expected, indeed prophesied, to become the greatest female dancer of her generation, the ultimate dancing superwoman, which amazingly she accomplished, playing the American superwoman in *On the Town*. Cousin Fred Maurer notes: "Perfection in her dancing was the most important thing to her."

An odd combination of extreme friendliness and reclusiveness may occur in women with anorexia, as it did in Vera-Ellen's case. Desperately needing to be loved and liked by all, such women seem to have easy-going natures. Vera-Ellen was loved by her

The Magic and the Mystery

friends and certainly by fans with whom she spent enormous amounts of time corresponding and even occasionally visiting in their homes. At the same time her awkwardness and reclusiveness on movie sets at rehearsals are well documented, so much so that the casts of *On the Town, Happy Go Lovely* and *The Belle of New York* did not always know what to make of her.

Vera-Ellen's reclusiveness on the sets may have been in part a desire to avoid people she saw as rivals and competitors, even though she would not disparage such people to others. Most of her good friends were people either outside of the business, for example people in her old hometown, or people in other aspects of the business who were not competing with her for parts, such as Marie Windsor, Rock Hudson or A.C. Lyles. She talked of keeping her body trained like a machine to avoid losing ground to younger competitors trying to take her place. Her competitors or colleagues skilled in dancing often viewed her as odd and reclusive while friends outside the orbit of her power frequently referred to her as the kindest, gentlest, sweetest, warmest person in the world. She was, on the other hand, close to Donald O'Connor, her dancing partner in *Call Me Madam,* whom she greatly admired, but even he never really got to know her away from work. Her cousin Fred Maurer, who was close to her from the time she was 10 years old, still felt distanced from her and made this observation about her nature:

> She was a highly moral individual and a very, very private person. Everyone and everything was kept compartmentalized in her life. She did not make a lot of social friends at work and that may be part of the reason it is hard to track down now people who knew her socially. If you were a relative, she would write to you or speak with you about certain things but not about the movies. If you were a fan she would communicate other things. If you were a Hollywood friend she would talk about Hollywood things. She kept the different aspects of her life completely separated and didn't talk across the different areas and kept each area private.

One may question whether or not her mother was evil and drove her into her condition. The answer is that she was not evil but may in fact have led her daughter to her condition inadvertently. Women with anorexia most often are the children of parents who want a better life for their offspring and who were themselves goal-oriented high achievers. Sometimes the parents may have failed at their own goals and try to achieve them through their offspring. Alma Rohe was a proud parent and enjoyed basking in her daughter's fame and letting people know she was the mother of a star, rather than the wife of an unemployed piano tuner. Even after Vera-Ellen retired Alma tried repeatedly to get her to stay at least somewhat in the limelight. Since her mother had sacrificed so much to help her career, Vera-Ellen felt a strong sense of obligation to her. They were very close and yet there were tensions too. Vera-Ellen felt that her mother was trying to control her life too much and trying to stay too close to her all the time. Alma tried repeatedly to move in with her daughter, but Vera-Ellen held firm about maintaining her own private life and having her mother at arm's length.

Alma had directed her daughter's life from the time she was a child. She was responsible for the removal of five years of Vera-Ellen's life through age falsification. She made up the story about her pre-birth "vision" of her daughter's superstardom and tried to control her to a significant degree right up to the end of both of their lives, but there was enormous genuine affection between the two of them as well. The pressure on the little girl to become a superstar was terrific and helped create a climate of dependency and insecurity where anorexia could flourish. Despite her mother's desire for the limelight, Vera-Ellen's parents were as Fred Maurer puts it "kindly, wonderful, loving people with deeply ingrained Christian principles." There is every reason to believe that they only wanted the very best for their daughter and loved her very much while at the same time Alma maintained definite ideas about what her daughter should become.

Since the disease wasn't recognized in Vera-Ellen's time, her mother probably had no idea that Vera-Ellen had such a serious problem. Nobody in the family knew anything about anorexia and her cousin, with whom she was quite close, says it was, to his knowledge, never discussed or thought about at any time in her life. Her close friends had no clue and had never heard of the disease either until the very end of her life. They felt that she was so skinny and frail because her mother was tiny and frail. However, Alma Rohe did know that Vera-Ellen had become delusional at times and still did not insist that she get professional help. She may have been afraid of the stigma of having her daughter see a psychiatrist or risk being institutionalized; she wanted her to remain Vera-Ellen, the star.

A typical desire of the woman with anorexia as well as the individual with Obsessive-Compulsive Disorder (OCD), about which more will be said shortly, is to fill each moment with activity, including constant study and self-improvement with the underlying insecurity and belief that she is inferior. Such individuals may seem to be in perpetual motion, feeling life more deeply and intensely than the average person. This profile certainly fit Vera-Ellen who was a mass of energy, always pursuing something new to its ultimate limit. Making a movie about Spain required intensive Spanish. A knitting scene required a course in the fine points of knitting. In the early '50s Vera-Ellen continued to fill every moment with activity. She studied tap, ballet, modern dancing and drama whenever she was free, and also took French lessons and dabbled in oil painting although she had a strong aversion to the odor of turpentine. She took dancing lessons up to the very end of her life. But this attitude, this desire to excel at so many things and particularly anything that might be important for her career, infuses every moment of her screen time with excellence. She was incapable of doing a frame of film or a dance step or a transition from one step to another step that wasn't studied and honest.

Women with anorexia make difficult wives and may not choose the best husbands for themselves, due to poor self image, and her two failed marriages (particularly the second) may have been due at least partly to her behavior. Her obsession with being a superwoman generally would not have been welcomed by most males in those days. Many affected women seek to be thin, smart, independent wives and mothers who are also extremely successful in their careers. They also often may need to dominate the relationship with the male, if not overtly then psychologically, in small ways. Her declaration that she was constantly reminding her first husband that she earned more than

MGM put tremendous pressure on Vera-Ellen to maintain her hourglass figure.

he did seems otherwise odd unless put in the context of a woman with anorexia. Rendering the male impotent in the relationship through such insults would not lead to marital bliss, especially in the 1940s. We know less about the details of her second marriage except that initially it seems to have been a happy one, despite numerous rumors of infidelity denied by the husband. Vic Rothschild was good friends with Marie Windsor's husband Jack and the foursome would holiday together in places such as Mexico City and they were often tennis partners or attended tournaments together. It wasn't until the death of Vera-Ellen's child in 1963 that the second marriage fell apart irrevocably, and allegedly ended in bitter hostility, although Vic today only has kind things to say about Vera. In both marriages conflict between the males and Vera-Ellen's mother appears to have played a major role.

Women with anorexia are obsessive about their weight and overall appearance. Stories spread about Vera-Ellen's problems of this nature during her work in *On the Town*. There was tremendous pressure from the studio for her to keep that hourglass figure and that stunning 18- to 20-inch waist if she wanted to graduate to more mature parts and be a pinup girl. The cute, pudgy starlet and specialty dancer of the Goldwyn era had to disappear. In the opening sequence of *On the Town*, she is literally described as a superwoman but in order to achieve that part she had to become one: a sexy, domestic, glamorous, athletic, artistic, refined girl next door. At the time, Vera-Ellen echoed the studio line and commented:

> I used to be skinny when I was working on the stage. Then I gained weight after arriving here. It must have been the California climate. I've trimmed down since. When I gain weight there is the threat that I may grow muscle bound in my legs and I won't have that. I've learned that the best prevention is to raise your feet to a high level whenever you're not working. Even when I go to a picture theater, I rest my feet in my escort's lap.

By 1948 when she was working for MGM, she was voluptuous but never heavy and simply didn't need to reduce. Still, she didn't see it that way, largely because MGM kept the pressure on. They convinced her to watch her weight, and once she became convinced of something she would do it to the extreme even if it killed her. So in 1949 she was on a diet of meat, especially steak, and she said she drank two quarts of fruit juice every day and had a breakfast of black coffee, half a grapefruit and at least one box of strawberries (frozen, if they were out of season). Friends say she ate less than this. And she remained determined to get her weight down and keep it down.

In 1981, after Vera-Ellen's death, Gene Kelly would recall:

> We were all worried about her at MGM. She was so frail, and worked so hard, that she always lost weight during a big production number. She drove herself so relentlessly that sometimes her legs had to be packed with ice between scenes.

She also began the curious practice of wrapping her legs up in Saran Wrap or its equivalent after performing, trying to get her weight down by making herself sweat and comply with studio desires to maintain what the critics called her "whistle-bait figure." This practice used to be common among dancers, is still occasionally done, and can be seen periodically advertised today on television and in catalogs. Special plastic or rubberized wraps were worn commonly to achieve spot reduction particularly of the hips and thighs. Vera-Ellen could have seen ads for products like these in popular film magazines such as *Photoplay* when she was growing up in the early 1930s in Ohio. In every issue she could see Dr. Jeanne P.H. Walter, 389 Fifth Ave., New York advertising her "flesh colored rubber ankle bands" that could be used "to obtain slender ankles and calves." The alleged doctor also claimed that these bands would "support and shape the ankles while reducing them." In fact *Photoplay* and other magazines were full of ads encouraging young girls to reshape and remake their bodies from top to bottom. There was the "Nose Adjuster," Nancy Lee's Miracle Cream to rub on your body and make you more slender, and the National Developer that young ladies wrapped around themselves to increase their bust size. Today reputable doctors place no faith in these techniques and it is considered dangerous to wrap plastic or rubber around the legs because this practice would impede circulation and ventilation. The use of fads and extreme diet practices like these, plus a desire to create an overall lightness of being, are consistent with symptoms manifested by individuals suffering from anorexia nervosa.

Vera-Ellen applied certain "treatments" to restrict her own actions, such as speaking to everyone in an extra-low voice because her voice coach Marie Bryant wanted her to improve her sound quality. Co-stars in *On the Town* found that she didn't quite fit in as one of the gang and that her voice-lowering "treatment" made her seem odd and snooty. They had been in the limelight a lot longer and to them she seemed to be playing the movie star a bit too much in real life and it didn't suit her. She also seemed strangely concerned about her bone structure and facial appearance. In 1998, she was described by Betty Garrett who appeared with her in *Words and Music* and *On the Town*:

> She was darling sweet and dedicated and yet a strange gal. She did little socialization and had an obsession about her weight. When I knew her she was determined to lose weight and there was no necessity for her to diet. She worked hard all day. And she got so thin. I think now that she may have been suffering from anorexia. She was obsessed with her bone structure and kept trying to change herself somehow. She was different from the person I remember on the stage from *Connecticut Yankee*.

Vera-Ellen told a number of friends how Ann Miller called her "Vera-Girl" and how much she admired Miller for the extraordinary extra taps she could generate: "Annie always amazed me. I sometimes wondered where all that sound came from."

But Ann Miller told us that Vera-Ellen was "not someone I got to know well during the filming of *On the Town* and we didn't socialize after work." Debbie Reynolds recalled how badly MGM treated Vera-Ellen when they told her she had to make a lighter weight while they were filming *Words and Music:*

> Vera-Ellen was told that she was too fat, that her top thighs were too heavy. No matter how she exercised, the fat remained. Vera-Ellen was never fat, but she was insecure and wanted to please so she believed them which was the worst thing she could have done. She cut way back on her food intake. After that she drank coffee all day and ate only a steak and a vegetable at night. Her legs became absolutely angular. That regimen started her on the road to deeper, more intractable psychological problems. Her life eventually turned into a tragedy, and the diet killed her.

Vera-Ellen:

While Debbie Reynolds' assessment of Vera-Ellen's life is oversimplified, none-theless the constant pressure from MGM between 1948 and 1950 to slim down may have done real harm. Already insecure and impressionable, Vera-Ellen desperately wanted to be a success as a dancing actress; it was what she lived for. After being cut from Goldwyn's roster, she knew that MGM was not only her big chance with the most important studio in the world for musicals, but it was probably also her last chance. She would either be a hit at MGM or vanish into obscurity and all her mother's efforts would be for nothing. Her body reshaping coupled with fervent prayer had worked before when she was a child, she believed, and she was willing to sacrifice whatever it took to achieve her goal. She was driven to stranger and stranger practices and an obsession with slimming. But she believed that MGM was giving her good advice which would make her a superwoman and superstar. This of course was the same studio (at the same time) that drove Judy Garland into film after film until she resorted to habit-forming pills to get through each day and eventually collapsed, during the shooting of *The Pirate* in 1948 with Gene Kelly.

Between 1948 and 1952 Vera-Ellen became one of MGM's most popular pinup girls. She appeared in photos all over the world — on cards, in Sunday supplements and movie magazines in poses that combined her wholesome girl-next-door look with an emphasis on her beautiful legs and 18- to 20-inch waist. There were photos in swim-suits, with dogs, with cannons, on piles of books, in a ballerina mode, but almost always with the same emphases. The constant photography sessions required that she maintain her best appearance at all times.

In addition, she was increasingly concerned about rivals like Sally Forrest who was actually used as a threat by the studio if Vera-Ellen didn't accede to their wishes. An even bigger threat was Cyd Charisse, the beautiful ballerina who was making a name for herself in dramatic roles such as *Tension* (1950) with Richard Basehart. But she never said bad things about her or became visibly envious. She just resolved to work harder to make herself better. She worried too about her circulation, insisting on elevating her legs as much as possible. Debbie Reynolds recalls seeing her in the hair-dressing salon at MGM: "Vera-Ellen would be sitting with her legs up, but never with her feet crossed at the ankle because it hurt circulation."

She worried increasingly about her pudgy cheeks and the general look of her face since she had gotten word that she was considered too round-faced to be a true MGM glamour girl. She wanted to be sexy and have sunken cheeks and set out on a program of body morphing to accomplish it, much as she believed she had made herself grow when she was a little girl. On the set of *The Belle of New York*, a puzzled Fred Astaire marveled at her peculiar behavior and ideas about her appearance:

> She was doing this (fingers indenting cheeks) all day long. She'd bend over to let the blood flow to her head. She had certain ideas about how she wanted her face to look. I thought she looked pretty good. She was very thin. I liked that... I'm not too good at lifting heavy women.

Her inability to fit in, her increasing tendency to be reclusive and her single-mindedness about doing her work and not worrying about making and maintaining necessary contacts in the business caused her to lose parts. She doesn't seem to have

The Magic and the Mystery

grasped this important, and some would say all-important, aspect of show business. She commented in August 1950:

> Too many actresses worry about contacts in furthering their careers. Don't fuss, do your job, and keep working to improve. If you get to be the best, the producers will use you.

But as she got thinner and thinner and aged rapidly she found herself working on projects of less and less quality. Sufferers of anorexia nervosa will frequently not be aware of their illness or they will deny that they are ill, but they usually maintain an obsession with "thinness." The condition is particularly common among dancers needing to maintain an ideal weight to the point where they may be measured with calipers, tape measures and rulers to see if they are complying with ideal statistics and comparing well to charts and scales of ideal height and weight ratios. Anorexia often leads to a gaunt, emaciated look as the search for thinness starves the body (the haggard look of singer Karen Carpenter in her later days would serve as a typical example). The illness can trigger a look of premature aging. This appears to begin with Vera-Ellen after the tremendous failure of her most important starring vehicle *The Belle of New York*. The change in her appearance between 1952 and 1953 is marked and severe.

Change of location can be another disruptive factor for the woman with anorexia. When Vera-Ellen went to England and was cut off from friends and her usual diet, especially meat, all she had left to fall back on was her obsessive work ethic. Everyone on the film felt she was rehearsing way beyond what was reasonable and she spent a great deal of time alone; she was described by the screenwriter as "a real loner." At this point her condition worsened and she dropped to a dangerously low weight and does not look well in the film. The unhappy period in England coupled with the pressure from being neglected for film roles once again by her studio MGM debilitated her.

Once back in familiar surroundings in America, Vera-Ellen gained weight and looked her most stunningly beautiful at age 31 in the film *The Belle of New York*. Everything was riding on this picture and it was her first real co-starring role in a film for a major American studio. The film seemed so promising, especially given the quality of the personnel working on it. How could Fred Astaire make a money-losing musical? And the great producer Arthur Freed had made it his pet project. But it was a bomb, and Vera-Ellen was devastated. Her weight dropped significantly after this film. She began to lose her youthful beauty and body tone, and by 1953 the physical deterioration seemed to be accelerating sharply. Despite some healthier time in 1954 and 1955 when she kept weight on after her second marriage, by 1957 she looked as if she were a frighteningly frail 45 years old when she was only 36.

During the filming of *White Christmas*, her last major film, her obsessive work ethic and odd diet caused severe weight loss, as A.C. Lyles remembers:

> She was very careful about her diet and she always thought that she danced better when she was thinner. You know when she first came to Hollywood the pictures she made with Danny Kaye over at Goldwyn show her face was rounder and she weighed more than she ever did.

Vera-Ellen is very thin in the British film *Let's Be Happy*.

Obviously, a body forced to exist with anorexia nervosa for a long period of time eventually breaks down with all sorts of ailments that can include extreme bouts of depression; reclusiveness; heart, abdominal, kidney, liver and brain problems; hormonal and electrolytic problems; and anemia. Some scholars think hypothalamus dysfunction in the brain is a major factor present in anorexia nervosa. In any case, when the *National Enquirer* so shamefully photographed her on the street in 1977 she was suffering from a variety of disorders that were no doubt mystifying to her as well.

When Vera-Ellen reached her 40s her body broke down increasingly and by the time she was in her early 50s she looked like an old woman. Since women in her family normally lived very long lives, this was most unusual and might be attributed to anorexia along with the other illnesses she had developed. One physician has suggested that the excessive consumption of red meat and lack of a well-rounded diet may have contributed to a number of her ailments.

Dr. John Bailey, a specialist in the treatment of ADHD (Attention Deficit/Hyperactivity Disorder) studied our text in an attempt to explain the complex phenomenon that was Vera-Ellen. He is convinced that she was not suffering primarily from anorexia nervosa but rather from a psychological/psychiatric condition known as OCD (Obsessive-Compulsive Disorder). One of the many sub-types of OCD is BDD (Body Dysmorphic Disorder) wherein the sufferer becomes obsessed with the thought that something is wrong with her body, leading often to anorexia nervosa or reduced appetite due to the nervous condition of OCD. This condition is, according to Dr. Bailey, frequently inherited, possibly from her mother who had such unusual dietary habits and a desire to be so obsessively particular, orderly and neat. Dr. Bailey believes that

The picture of beauty, innocence and health — Vera-Ellen as her fans will always remember her.

there is strong evidence that Vera-Ellen suffered also from ADHD in that she was such a Type A personality from the very start of her life with a huge drive and tremendous energy to succeed. ADHD is often associated with late growth spurts due to delayed long-bone growth, a desire to accomplish everything within a given area in order to create a complete set, and an absence of the fear of heights. Such sufferers are often stubborn about their opinions and, oddly, late for everything that isn't essential to them. They have terrible anxieties about annoying things touching their skin, especially chokers or high-necked clothes; if they wear something over their necks it must be very carefully selected.

The OCD sufferer is a perfectionist who must study and learn all the time while constantly putting herself down and filling each moment with activity to avoid the boring. They are always in a search mode looking for something to do and can only rest when totally exhausted. Such individuals usually have a high IQ and show vivacious flashing eyes when performing their specialties and many are attracted to careers in film and communication.

Rosarie Hartmeyer, former Assistant Chief Psychologist for Kaiser Permanente Health Plan of Northern California, also assessed Vera-Ellen's condition from the facts presented in this biography. She reached a conclusion similar to that of Dr. Bailey, the OCD diagnosis, despite the fact that the two doctors have never contacted each other. While neither doctor can be certain what vitamin supplements Vera-Ellen was taking throughout her life, Dr. Hartmeyer notes that, nonetheless, Vera-Ellen's peculiar and poor diet in childhood and as an adult was certain to affect her mental health:

> As an adult it is clear that she was malnourished. She avoided breads, pasta, and potatoes and ate red meat with a limited amount of vegetables and fruits. The foods she avoided are essential because they are rich in B vitamins essential to healthy nervous system function. With such a deprivation of B-6 and B-12 her nervous system was depleted possibly causing eventual temporary memory loss, auditory and visual distortions, irregular sleep and energy production patterns in the body. This is typical of an extreme alcoholic. Lack of folic acid could also have caused problems with conception, healthy pregnancy and a healthy infant.

She notes that her anorexia later in life was more likely a result of her Obsessive-Compulsive Disorder and a thiamin deficiency in the brain. Her need to be in constant motion doing everything to perfection may have hidden her ability to feel pain, sadness or anger at her mother. Dancing until her feet bled was not normal behavior. She seemed incapable of reacting or feeling, but rather just moved on to the next available thing, whatever it was. In her later years she was in need of a psychiatrist plus serious medical counseling about her diet. Also she had a problem with low self esteem which eventually became dementia as she sought to cover up her past life. In addition her painful illnesses in middle age were the result of her bad diet, dance injuries and joint overuse. At the end of her life, Dr. Hartmeyer observes, she was increasingly in denial of the painful realities she had to face and the suffering she had endured. Dr. Hartmeyer adds:

> She exhibited reclusiveness and narcissism. When she had a film out she was not reclusive and she reveled in being a star. When she wasn't the star of the moment she receded as if in shame. She overly reacted to criticism. When a critic criticized her dress and style, she turned herself into a glamorous woman. There was no middle ground for her.

Whatever the answer to the mystery that was Vera-Ellen, we find that by the time she was middle-aged she ended up with much more than her share of life's dark side when all of her physical, psychological and psychophysical problems came home to roost. These problems, along with the death of a child, two divorces, the loss of her highly influential mother, and the development of severe arthritis, high blood pressure and cancer, led to a tragic ending for this talented star.

The Magic and the Mystery

Chapter Ten
The Magic Lives On

What then was Vera-Ellen really like? Hers was a complex personality. She loved to be the center of attention and to spend hours talking with reporters or answering fan mail. There was a strong ego there, a need to be Miss Popularity and a desire even to become Hollywood royalty that she subsequently fulfilled by marrying a Rothschild, keeping Pomeranian dogs, driving a Cadillac, deliberately lowering her voice for effect and dressing in the finest outfits.

But she was still the simple, kind and religious Midwestern girl from Norwood, who never changed at all to her friends. She was always happy to see old friends when they came out to Hollywood and remained a "good talker and easy to be with." And she was so kind and dear to her Hollywood circle of friends. Actress Celeste Holm, who co-starred with her twice, said: "Few girls can equal Vera-Ellen in talent, intellect, and downright sweetness of character." She was, in short, different things to different people who filled the varied compartments of her life.

Many mysteries remain. Her striving for perfection that pushed her to the top seems to have brought with it the psychoneurotic disorder and the physical disability that ultimately destroyed her career. But if she had been more able to control her obsessive drives would she still have become Vera-Ellen, the premier screen dancer of her day? She was considered friendly and outgoing by those who knew her well and yet others reported that she was easy to know and be with only if she wanted to be with you. Some others said she was strange and a real loner. Are all these people talking about the same woman? Was she really all these things at the same time and how much of her persona was occasioned by her illness? Only Vera-Ellen knew what she was really like and yet she may have suffered from disorders that distorted her perception of herself and the world around her to the point that even she was probably unable to understand herself.

Her pursuit of an almost spiritual lightness of being on the dance floor, her quest for the perfect form and the perfect dance, led her to create astonishingly beautiful dancing. Yet, ironically, that same quest emaciated her and robbed her

Little Vera loved being the center of attention.

of her beauty, costing her the opportunity to sustain her career and achieve many of her goals. As she aged prematurely, studios would not use her, so she was dragged down the ladder from movies to television to summer stock at the end. Her reputation for oddness too, especially in the later stages of her career, and her lack of networking skills, did not provide the opportunities needed for her to sustain a thriving career. For a time she had the marriage to Victor Rothschild to depend on and did not need to work but that too slowly ebbed away. She did not have the support of enough people in her profession with the power and will to look after her best interests. She could count on Michael Panaieff, A.C. Lyles and Marie Windsor in Hollywood and people like Bill Dennington in Philadelphia but there were few others.

Vera-Ellen left her husband Victor one dollar in her will.

And yet, with it all, she has left behind a body of work, each frame of filmed dance revealing an unsurpassed perfection achievable only by one who was totally driven and devoted to her work. Her life is at once a horror story, a tragedy, a monument to dedication, a legacy of the highest form of art by one of America's true superwomen.

Vera-Ellen had made her will on April 16, 1951 leaving her money to her mother. On June 15, 1956 she inserted a codicil, adding Victor Rothchild's name to her will and leaving him one dollar, stating that all of her property before her marriage was "my own separate property." Since her husband had been wealthy she preferred, in the event of her mother's death, to leave it to her aunt Julia Maurer and then to Julia's descendants. The codicil is written in her careful, meticulous, calligraphic and elegant hand.

The estate finally reverted to her only known surviving relative, Julia's son and Vera-Ellen's cousin Fred Maurer, with whom she had always been very close. Their relationship developed partly because they were both only children and they always seemed to understand each other well. When she died she was not rich by Hollywood standards, especially for someone married to a Rothschild, but due to her real estate holdings and small payments from Vic she was not destitute. It is unclear if she had signed a prenuptial agreement, did not wish to take much divorce settlement money from her husband, or simply could not afford to fight him and his attorneys. Her total

The Magic and the Mystery

net worth was $755,060.88, mostly due to the value of the house at 7269 Outpost Cove Drive that was valued at $500,000. Her personal property was valued at only $135,000 and she had an income from properties annually of $10,000. In the will, even though her real name was Vera Ellen Rohe Rothschild, she retained the hyphen.

Fred Maurer reported that Vera-Ellen had kept all of Victoria's baby clothes, even her cloth diapers up to the end and George Sidney noted that he believed that "the grave of Victoria had no marker because she never accepted the baby's death."

She was cremated and buried next to the unmarked grave of her daughter Victoria Ellen Rothschild and her mother Alma Catherine Rohe at Glen Haven Memorial Park, San Fernando, California. Her father was also buried there, in Grave H, Plot 170, Section IV, a different area. Her tombstone, which was purchased and erected by Fred Maurer in 1982, reads only "Vera-Ellen," her stage name with no last name. It includes the hyphen and features a lovely image of her dancing, which was created by her niece Mary Maurer, now an art director for the Sony Corporation. There is no mention that she was a Rothschild or even a Rohe. Fred Maurer arranged that a bouquet of flowers was placed at Vera-Ellen's grave every Memorial Day and he said that this would continue "for as long as I live." He remained true to his word until his death on July 6, 2001.

The memorial service for Vera-Ellen was held at Westwood Memorial Park and Mortuary and, since she left no final instructions, her dear friend and producer A.C. Lyles finally got to produce something with Vera-Ellen. He handled the arrangements for her final curtain, her memorial service, personally arranging a proper sendoff with contributions made in her name to the Actors' Fund:

> Driving over for this I was thinking about Vera dancing and I thought it would be nice for the eulogy to be something like the wonderful stage show where everyone steps out and says something and steps back. So I said this was going to be like *A Chorus Line* and I want each of you to step out and say something. Instead of talking about yourself we'll talk about Vera, and a lot of people got up and told wonderful stories about her.
>
> Ah, I've given a lot of eulogies and done a lot of services for well-known people in our business but it was that service that made me realize what a very beloved and extremely respected lady she was.

A Seventh Day Adventist minister conducted the service, rather an oddity since Vera-Ellen was raised a strict Lutheran. When we talked to A.C. Lyles in August 1998 he remembered his dear departed friend and his thoughts on that sad day in 1981:

> She was one of the most wonderful people I have ever known. She loved life and was such a great friend and companion. I still have a picture of her I have hanging here in my office at Paramount. She was so nice and enthusiastic with everyone, especially with her fans always. She was such a dear, kind person. She had a sweetness not only in her face but in her soul. I miss her very much even now and I

Vera-Ellen's gravesite, with marker erected in 1982 by Fred Maurer and designed by Fred's daughter.

am so pleased that something is being written to honor her talent and memory. I know she would have loved to be thought about again but, bless her heart, I don't think she would understand people being this devoted to her.

Cesar Romero attended the service. He had co-starred with her in *Carnival in Costa Rica* and *Happy Go Lovely*, and Stefanie Powers came too, and of course her beloved friend Marie Windsor. Even Victor Rothschild, her ex-husband, attended and sent a large wreath in the shape of a heart like the hearts Vera-Ellen collected for almost all of her life. The gaudiness of the wreath and its inscription, "from Rothschild and family," offended some of the attendees who knew how quickly Vic had remarried. For a time his second marriage was successful and produced three children, all who seem to adore their father. But this marriage too ended in divorce. Another old friend, Betty Lynn, best known as Don Knott's girlfriend on *The Andy Griffith Show*, came too. But there was not one star or director there from MGM.

Betty Lynn recently told us: "Vera-Ellen was every bit as sweet in real life as she was on the screen. She was always smiling, very happy and very charming." Friend Richard Gully commented at the service: "She was a wonderful person. There was not a mean bone in her body." George Sidney, who was not at the funeral service, has stated: "She was personable and very dedicated to her craft. Almost everyone liked her, but her work always came first." Stefanie Powers, who attended dance classes at Panaieff's when she was in town and had the time, reminded everyone at the funeral that Vera-Ellen was loved by the dance class regulars and that "Vera's place in class will always be hers." This referred to her habit of always going to the same place at the bar. For several weeks after Vera-Ellen died, no one took her place at the bar as a gesture of respect.

The Magic and the Mystery

With her death Vera-Ellen became big national news all over again. Unfortunately tabloid obituaries sensationalized her tragic end and emphasized how she had gone from being "a female Fred Astaire" to "a sad recluse." They stressed the contrast between her terrible last years of "tragedy and heartbreak" and how she had only "lived happily ever after at the end of her spectacular Hollywood musicals."

Nor did things go well for efforts to preserve Vera-Ellen's memory after her death. When cousin Fred Maurer and his wife came to California to take possession of the memorabilia stored in boxes in her garage, they found that mice had eaten most everything. Almost everything that she had been saving, precious souvenirs of her career, had to be thrown away. Still, two boxes of clippings, magazine articles and the like survived and were sent to Fred's daughter in California. Neighbor Jo Dennis had also been given a substantial collection of Vera-Ellen's material and Caren Frenzel, a long-time fan and memorabilia collector, had been given additional material from the collection during a visit to Vera-Ellen's cousins in Minnesota. Still another group of recovered material was given to the Academy of Motion Picture Arts and Sciences after her death.

There were also complications resulting from the will handled by Grace Smith of the Actor's Fund. According to California law a house cannot be left vacant for long stretches of time without someone in control of the premises. Fred Maurer reported that before he was notified and could take possession of the house some time went by, and Debbie Reynolds was reportedly using the home for a time. He added Ms. Reynolds received two of Vera-Ellen's beautiful film costumes from the Maurers for exhibit in a museum she was planning to preserve the memory of Hollywood stars. A dispute arose about the transfer of the house and, whatever transpired, there was ill feeling on the part of the Maurers toward Ms. Reynolds. Attempts have been made to clarify this situation, but Ms. Reynolds would not return any phone calls regarding the costumes or the house.

The facts, as recalled by Mark Maurer, Fred's son, seem to be that a woman named Shirley Kelly was named executor of the estate. She was the oldest daughter of Toddy Maurer's sister and was someone whom the family could trust in Los Angeles. However, Shirley was starstruck and overwhelmed at first by someone of the magnitude of Ms. Reynolds, who obtained permission from Shirley to occupy the house legally. While there Ms. Reynolds allegedly put up a troupe of dancers associated with her. From this point the story gets difficult to sort out. At least one of the dancers allegedly had four dogs who defecated and urinated in the house, and, in addition, the carpet was ripped out and accusations were made by the Maurer family that items belonging to Vera-Ellen had been taken without permission. The Realtor had difficulty showing the house because of the dogs and the dancers were reportedly not eager to leave. In any case, things did not go easily for Vera-Ellen's estate after her death. It was as if the dark cloud that seemed to follow her about in key moments of her personal life simply went right on after she was in her grave.

The Maurers sold the Outpost Cove house for $340,000 but soon after the new owner, production designer Anthony Sabotino, moved in, the owner of a flat-roofed house which already existed in front of Vera-Ellen's home decided to raise its roof, blocking a good part of the beautiful view of Hollywood. The Outpost Cove area was soon awash with fighting neighbors as a third neighbor claimed that the flat-roofed house owner was secretly cutting down the tops of her trees to improve *his* view. The only good result of this situation was that Vera-Ellen had not lived to see the final crowning indignity of losing some of her vast panorama.

Not long after Vera-Ellen's death, former co-star Donald O'Connor starred with Chita Rivera in a Broadway sequel to the original *Bye Bye Birdie* entitled *Bring Back Birdie*. While performing a song entitled "Middle Age Blues" in which he lamented growing older, he sang the line "Vera-Ellen, where'd you go?"

If there is one bright spot in the tragic end to the life of Vera-Ellen, it is that her influence lives on within her own family, for her niece and nephew, Fred and Toddy Maurer's children, have continued the family tradition within the entertainment field, not in front of the footlights but behind the scenes. Mary Maurer is proud of her roots. She started working in the business not long after she arrived in Hollywood to help her dad sort through Vera's archives. She spent many hours salvaging aging tattered photo clippings and yellowed memorabilia and in so doing got to know much more about the life of her famous second cousin and to wish that she could have known her better in person.

Not long that visit with her father, Mary began to think seriously about her own future and decided to move permanently to California and attend Art Center College of Design in Pasadena. Soon after her graduation in 1987 she started working in the music business and is now an award–winning senior art director currently employed by Sony Music Entertainment in Santa Monica. Mary has been nominated for a Grammy and her work included in the permanent collection of the Library of Congress. She has worked on music packaging for such artists as Shawn Colvin, Gloria Estefan, Neil Diamond, Carlos Santana and soundtracks such as *The Titanic, The Divine Secrets of the Ya Ya Sisterhood, Maid in Manhattan* and *The Sopranos*. Her work has been published by the major sources of web graphics and communications arts. Mary now lives in Los Angeles with her fiance, a motion picture editor, only a few miles from Vera-Ellen's beautiful home. And Vera-Ellen had one final lasting influence on her niece — Mary loves to dance and takes all kinds of dance lessons in her spare time. She adds:

> Although I was only a young girl when I met her, Vera changed the course of my life, one step at a time. She is the reason I'm here in California today.

Mary's brother Mark Maurer was also greatly influenced by his encounters with Vera-Ellen:

> My first memory of Vera's house is from 1965, my first visit to California. I was very young and the house was one of grandeur: a fountain, the pool and her daughter Victoria's room, virtually unchanged since her death, full of toys and even candy.

Mark returned to Los Angeles in the winter of 1982 after Vera-Ellen's death to house-sit at the Studio City house but soon moved into the home on Outpost Cove Drive in the Hollywood Hills. He was shocked at what he found.

Although the house itself was in poor condition due to her reclusive, secretive lifestyle, the pool and view were fantastic. It was a Minnesota boy's dream come true to live in the Hollywood Hills! I had such a great time living in her house, entertaining and enjoying the energy. I drove her white Coupe de Ville convertible and had the greatest summer of my life.

In 1983, when Mark's father Fred sold the home to production designer Anthony Sabotino to satisfy the state taxes, the designer took a shine to young Mark. While Sabotino transformed the home into a beautiful home once again, although more stark and simplified in design, he offered Mark a position working in a small scenery shop for theatrical shows and plays. Mark decided to attend UCLA to obtain an MS degree in Kinesiology.

Influenced by his famous cousin and exposed to the Hollywood lifestyle, Mark decided to enter the entertainment field from the inside and use his newly made connections to advance his career:

> For the last 10 years I have been working for CBS doing lighting and electronics. I have worked on shows such as *David Letterman* and countless game shows including *The Price is Right, Wheel of Fortune, Pyramid* and *Hollywood Squares*. I have also worked on the *Survivor* finales, several CBS soap operas and, for the past two years, the Miss America Pageant in Atlantic City.

Mark is married and he and wife Katie have a two-year-old son (Tate) and a daughter (Anneliese) on the way. Living in Valencia in a lovely new home, he remembers fondly the days spent in Vera-Ellen's home:

> Her legacy is the reason I now live here in California and am so completely happy. Although I was only five years old when I visited her, I have memories of her as a stylish woman who ultimately changed my life.

Throughout the 1980s Vera-Ellen was remembered as a Hollywood legend, not for her dancing accomplishments or film career, but for being the mysterious recluse with anorexia who supposedly went to pieces when her baby died and lived alone for years in the Hollywood Hills. This is clearly an exaggeration of her final years, which were nowhere near as dark and weird as Hollywood writers want to paint them. Unfortunately, dwelling on her eccentricities obscured appreciation of her accomplishments. Few remember the amazing talent she had or how much she contributed to the American musical on stage and screen. When she was alive and in financial and medical difficulty no group honored her or publicly recognized her accomplishments, and in death she became the tragic fodder for tabloids. Said Toddy Maurer, wife of Vera-Ellen's cousin:

She didn't deserve all the rough things that happened to her at the end. She was always so kind to people in need and so caring about others.

Finally, now, over 20 years after her death, there is a renewed interest in Vera-Ellen that rises at the end of every year when *White Christmas* is shown all over America. A.C. Lyles also honored her memory with a generous tribute:

> In 1995 I sponsored her name for the Walk of Fame on Hollywood Boulevard. There was a large turnout of people who adore her and her star is on the east side of the Boulevard at LaBrea at the merging of two intersections.

Her lifelong friend in Norwood, Ohio, Katherine Ralstin Murphy has been receiving call after call from Vera-Ellen aficionados who all find their way to her. She said in August 1998:

> Why is there all this sudden renewal of interest in Vera-Ellen now and why didn't any of you do something for her while she was alive?

In any case, the magic of Vera-Ellen lives on. She put her life and soul into her dancing and it is all there waiting on film for a whole new generation to discover. Fred Astaire perhaps put it most succinctly:

> She was a real accomplished dancer, that girl. Ballet, tap dancing, anything you wanted to do.

And at her funeral, her long-time friend Marie Windsor spoke: "As long as film exists, she will not be forgotten."

For those of us who remember Vera-Ellen for her still unappreciated artistic genius, Marie's words resonate deeply in our hearts.

Vera-Ellen in 1945

Vera-Ellen:

Epilogue

Before undertaking research for this book, I had always thought that the celluloid fairy-tale princess named Vera-Ellen had married royalty and lived happily ever after. I never knew the real story of her difficult life and I only wish I could have staged a retrospective in her honor while she was alive, and had her cousin Fred Maurer convince her to come and let us honor her. We would have given her our university's Distinguished Lifetime Achievement Award in the Humanities and she would have seen that her life's work really did amount to something important. But at least at the University of Arizona, once a year, there is a Vera-Ellen day in our "Art History of the Cinema" class where circa 350 students learn about her life and, more importantly, view clips from her films, studying her unique artistry. Still, it is so sad she didn't live to see herself a featured part of a university scholarly curriculum, right there next to Alfred Hitchcock, Fred Astaire, Ginger Rogers and Gene Kelly. I bet she would have liked that and would have modestly said "I don't understand why you are doing this."

Television and especially networks such as *Turner Classic Movies*, *American Movie Classics* and the *America One Network* with their periodic revivals of Vera-Ellen classics such as *Words and Music*, *Three Little Words*, *White Christmas*, *Happy Go Lovely*, *The Belle of New York* and *On the Town* have made a whole new generation ask: "Who was that amazingly talented Vera-Ellen and whatever happened to her?"

On August 26, 1998, just a few days before the 17th anniversary of Vera-Ellen's death, one of her most enduring fans, Bob Johnston of San Francisco flew down to visit her gravesite at Glen Haven Memorial Park, San Fernando, California,. He went to lay flowers on her grave for the both of us, and to photograph it for this tribute book. His account of his experience speaks volumes about how quickly our society forgets its most special people:

> It was about a two-hour drive from John Wayne Airport, David, so if you go, definitely fly into Ontario. I had called in advance the week before to confirm Glen Haven's operating hours (Sunday 9-4:30) and the fact that Vera-Ellen was interred there. That done, all should have gone smoothly. It didn't.
>
> I arrived just at 2 p.m. When I drove up to the memorial park headquarters there was a young woman standing on the steps as if she were waiting for someone — it turned out she was expecting her ride home. She asked if she could help and I told her I was there to see and photograph Vera-Ellen's grave for her biography. She didn't recognize the name and said she was sorry but the office was closed. Since her boss had left early she had been told that she could leave early too. I stood there wondering what to say or do as panic set in. I told her I'd called in advance and that I'd made the trip all the way from San Francisco on the strength of my assurance they would be open.
>
> Fortunately, she kindly took pity on me and agreed to reopen the office and find me the grave location that they had refused to give

out over the telephone. After fifteen minutes of looking without any luck she admitted that their records were in a mess. We tried the names Vera-Ellen and Vera-Ellen Rohe. Finally, when she was about to call it quits, I asked her to try one more combination: Vera-Ellen Rothschild. Our luck quickly changed for there were the locator cards — three of them.

The young lady marked down the grave locations while I scrambled to record as much off the cards as I could, for she refused to let me Xerox them. That done, she handed me a vague map of the memorial park, locked up and left. An hour followed of laborious searching grave after grave in the nearly 100 degree heat and I was about to give up when I spied a maintenance worker.

He spoke mostly Spanish but between my broken Spanish and his broken English we communicated and 15 minutes later he led me to her grave site. Finally! He apologized for the unkempt condition of the cemetery — apparently he was waiting for a cooler day to mow the grass. But there were the graves! I was exhausted and thirsty but I got the photographs and beat a retreat to my air-conditioned rental car.

I guess it was then that it hit me — an overwhelming sense of melancholy. I remembered seeing in the window of the office some kind of legal document. From the little I could read it seemed the cemetery was being sued over the management of the maintenance endowment fund. Sure, from a distance, the place looked okay but close up the gravesites were poorly maintained. And it struck me funny that the memorial park is such a very long way from anywhere she lived. But there was Vera-Ellen, or rather, Grave B, Plot 188, close by her mother's marker over Grave D, Plot 188. Protected between them was just an empty, weedy, grassy area where the records say her daughter had been interred, but there was no memorial marking the passing of little Victoria E. Rothschild. I can't really explain it but somehow, David, I think you'll understand when I tell you that I felt like I wanted to cry. I didn't sleep well Sunday night.

Vera-Ellen's marker is simple but with an elegance that typified her. The simple granite stone reads: Vera-Ellen 1921-1981. At the upper left was a silhouette etching of a woman dancing. Fred Maurer had it set up. It was actually made from a photograph of Vera-Ellen dancing and designed by her niece Mary Maurer. Otherwise there was nothing to give even a hint of who she was.

Forgive me for carrying on about this but I felt you, more than anyone else, would understand. For some reason I'm still a bit upset about how forlorn I felt at the grave, how sad that she had outlived so many who were important to her in life. I was upset at how she seemed now to have been cast away where only the most diligent searcher could find her. A part of me was very glad to have found her, to be able to say a prayer at her gravesite that somehow in her afterlife she

Vera-Ellen:

had found the true happiness she sought in life. But another part of me wasn't so sure about the whole experience and all I could think was the saying "Earth to earth, ashes to ashes, dust to dust." Thank heavens for her movies and the book, for without them time would surely erase her memory completely.

Vera-Ellen portrait 1946

Vera-Ellen:

Bibliography

Agee, James, *Agee on Film* (New York, 2000)

Arnheim, Daniel D., *Dance Injuries: Their Prevention and Care* (St. Louis, 1980)

Astaire, Fred, *Steps in Time* (New York, 1959)

Billman, Larry, *Fred Astaire—A Bio-Bibliography* (London, 1997)

Billman, Larry, *Film Choreographers and Dance Directors* (Jefferson, North Carolina, 1997)

Blum, Daniel, *Great Stars of the American Stage* (New York, 1952)

Boyko, Angela, "Vera-Ellen," *Angela's World Internet Website*

Brand, Harry, Press Releases from 20th Century Fox

Carroll, Harrison, "Film Dancer Star Vera-Ellen Admits Marriage on Rocks," *Los Angeles Herald Express,* 2-13-46

Carter, Joyce, "Is Her Love Life Jinxed?" *Photoplay,* 44, September 1953, 53, 83-84

Clooney, Nick, "Stories of Stars and Other Mail," *Cincinnati Post*, 9-23-96

Connolly, Mike, "Impertinent Interview," *Photoplay*, 3-52

Curtis, Connee, "You Can't Stump Vera," *Modern Screen,* 2-45

Day, Doris, "Your Toes Know," *Hollywood Reporter,* 10-30-50

Ellen, Vera, "Leave Him to the Girls," *Modern Screen,* August, 1953, 75

Flinn, John C., "Biography—Vera-Ellen," *Allied Artists Press Release,* 11-56

Ford, Eve, "The Lady's in Love," *Photoplay*, 42, December, 1952, 74-75

Fordin, Hugh, *M-G-M's Greatest Musicals: The Arthur Freed Unit* (New York, 1975)

Frazzella, Joe, "Vera-Ellen," *Films in Review,* 46 no. 3-4, March, 1995

George, Dee, "Dancing Star Enjoys Wadena's Weather," *Lakes Alive,* Nov./Dec. 2000, 62, 63

Gottfried, Martin, *Nobody's Fool: The Lives of Danny Kaye* (New York, 1994)

Graham, Lee, *Hollywood Studio Magazine,* 4-80

Graham, Lee, *Hollywood Studio Magazine,* 11-81

Granger, Stewart, *Sparks Fly Upward* (New York, 1981)

Green, Stanley, and Burt Goldblatt, *Starring Fred Astaire* (New York, 1973)

Hall, Prunella, "Screen Gossip," *Boston Post*, 7-6-46

Heffernan, Harold, "Goldwyn Rubs His Hands Over Ohio Girl Dancing Find, 21," *Cleveland Plain Dealer,* 7-7-46

Hopper, Hedda, "Vera-Ellen and Hightower Separation Rumor Confirmed," *Los Angeles Times,* 2-14-46

Hopper, Hedda, "Hedda Hopper," *Los Angeles Times* 5-6-52

Hopper, Hedda, "Sprightly Vera-Ellen Travels Fast Pace to Keep Her Energy," *Los Angeles Times,* 7-5-53

Hopper, Hedda, "Vera-Ellen Will Be Wed to Rothschild," *Los Angeles Times*, 10-20-54

Hudson, Rock and Sara Davidson, *Rock Hudson: His Story* (New York, 1986)

Manners, Dorothy, "Wisp of Love Eludes Star," *Los Angeles Examiner,* 3-1-53

Manners, Dorothy, "They Eat Well but Toes Hurt, Vera-Ellen Says of Dancers," *Los Angeles Examiner,* 5-2-54

Manners, Dorothy, "Vera Diets—to Gain!" *Los Angeles Examiner,* 5-19-57

Marill, Alvin H.*, Samuel Goldwyn Presents* (New York, 1976)

McClay, Howard, "Howard McClay," *Los Angeles Daily News,* 3-9-52

McPherson, Jim, "Always on Her Toes," *Movie Scrapbook*, 11-21-1993

Morley, Sheridan and Ruth Leon, *Gene Kelly: A Celebration* (London, 1996)

Motion Picture Academy of Arts and Sciences Margaret Herrick Library Vera-Ellen Collection

Oderman, Stuart, "Vera-Ellen," *Film Fan Monthly*, 1-9 (cover story)

Oppenheimer, Jerry and Jack Vitek, *The Idol: Rock Hudson* (New York, 1986)

Parish, James Robert, *The Cinema of Edward G. Robinson* (South Brunswick, 1972)

Parish, James Robert, and Ronald L. Bowers, *The MGM Stock Company* (New York, 1972)

Parsons, Louella, "Dancer Vera Ellen to Wed V. Rothschild," *Los Angeles Examiner,* 10-20-54

Quinlan, David (editor), *The Film Lover's Companion* (New York, 1997)

Ragan, David, "Tragedy of Miss Twinkletoes," *Globe,* 10-27-81

Ragan, David, *Movie Stars of the '40s* (New York, 1985) 214, 215

Reynolds, Debbie, *Debbie: My Life* (New York, 1988)

Roberts, Caren, "Vera-Ellen: Belle of Broadway." *Hollywood Studio Magazine*, 16/3, February 1983, 28-29

Rohe, Vera-Ellen, "Last Will and Testament," 4-16-51 (codicil 6-15-56)

Schallert, Edwin, "Vera-Ellen Gets Chance at Comedy," *Los Angeles Times,* 9-25-49

Scheuer, Philip E., "Vera-Ellen's Dancing Partners Range from Astaire to Crosby," *Los Angeles Times,* 10-23-54

Scott, John L., "The Hyphen Puts Best Dancing Toes Forward," *Los Angeles Times*, 9-2-45

Scott, John L., "Vera-Ellen Compares Musical Filming 'Comforts' in U.S. To British Trials," *Los Angeles Times*, 8-26-51

Sennett, Ted, Ted Sennett's *On-Screen/Off-Screen Movie Guide* (New York, 1993)

Shaw, Len G., "Vera-Ellen Recalls When Her Act Was Washed Out," *Detroit Free Press,* 9-13-46

Short, Ernest, *Fifty Years of Vaudeville* (Westport, 1978)

Silverman, Stephen M., *Dancing on the Ceiling: Stanley Donen and His Movies* (New York, 1996)

Skolsky, Sidney, "Hollywood is My Beat," *Hollywood Citizen-News*, 10-14-54

Skolsky, Sidney, "Hollywood is My Beat," *Hollywood Citizen-News*, 12-15-49

Smith, L. Allan, "Lady Bountiful," *Circle of Stars* (Winter, 1953)

Stalling, Penny, *Flesh and Fantasy* (New York, 1978)

Thomas, Tony, *The Films of Gene Kelly* (New York, 1991)

Townsend, Dorothy, "Vera-Ellen, 55, Ex-Star of Movie Musicals, Dies," *Los Angeles Times*, 9-2-81

Vera-Ellen, "The Role I Liked Best..." *Saturday Evening Post*, 11-10-51

Vera-Ellen, "Why I Pray," *Motion Picture Magazine* February, 1951, 45, 55

20th Century Fox Press Releases for *Carnival in Costa Rica, Three Little Girls in Blue, Call Me Madam*

Wiley, Mason and Damien Bona, *Inside Oscar* (New York, 1987)

Wilson, Liza, "Candleflame Blonde," *Photoplay*, 39, May, 1951, 42, 113

Yudkoff, Alan, *Gene Kelly: A Life of Dance and Dreams* (New York, 1999)

Zorina, Vera, *Zorina* (New York, 1986)

—, "Eighth Lower," *Silhouette*, 13, 1935 (Norwood High School Yearbook)

—, "Tenth Lower" and "Choral Group," *Silhouette*, 14, 1936

—, "Girls Who Stop the Show," *Look,* Feb. 8, 1944, 54-61

—, "Vera-Ellen, Husband Part," *Los Angeles Examiner*, 2-14-46

—, "Film Starlet Sues Dancer Husband," *Los Angeles Herald*, 7-10-46

—, "Dancer Sues Mate Abroad," *Los Angeles Examiner*, 7-11-46

—, "Vera-Ellen, Film Dancer, Asks Divorce," *Los Angeles Times,* 7-12-46

—, "Dancer Asks Divorce Though Love Professed," *Los Angeles Times*, 7-13-46

—, "Divorce Notice Sent Vera-Ellen's Mate" *Los Angeles Citizen-News*, 7-18-46

—, "Supple," *Long Beach Press Telegram*, 10-4-46

—, "Famous Toes Plus Frost Equals Story," *Los Angeles Times*, 1-14-46

—, "Dancer Gets Decree on Plea Husband Was Too Conceited," *Los Angeles Times*, 11-28-46

—, "Single Again," *Los Angeles Examiner,* 11-28-46

—, "3 Gobs and 3 Girls On the Town," *Screen Stories*, 1-50

—, "Meet 'The Hyphen,' *Photoplay,* 8-50

—, "So Happy She Cried," *Cincinnati Times-Star*, 2-16- 52

—, "Vera-Ellen is Vera-Nice," *Motion Picture Herald*, 4-26-52

—, "The Strange Case of Vera-Ellen," *Screen Life*, 9-53

—, "Wedding Day," *Los Angeles Citizen-News*, 11-19-54

—, "Vera-Ellen and Oilman to Wed Today," *Los Angeles Times*, 11-19-54

—, "Step With Cupid," *Los Angeles Examiner*, 11-19-54

—, "Dancer Vera-Ellen Wed to Victor Rothschild," *Los Angeles Times*, 11-20-54

—, "Vera-Ellen, Rothschild Wed by Candlelight," *Los Angeles Examiner*, 11-24-54

—, "Transition," *Newsweek,* 11-29-54

—, "Married," *Time*, 11-29-54

—, "Amateur Hour at the Garden," *NBC Chimes*, 1955, 16

—, "Playhouse Signs Vera," *Cincinnati Art and Music*, 6-8-58

—, "Vera-Ellen," *Current Biography*, February, 59

—, "Vera-Ellen," *Current Biography Yearbook*, 1959, 463

—, "Rothschild Claims Vera Was 'Cruel,' " *Los Angeles Citizen-News,* 9-15-66

—, "Obituaries," *Hollywood Reporter*, 9-1-81

—, "Obituaries," *Variety*, 9-1-81

—, "Vera-Ellen, Dancer in Movies," *New York Times*, 9-2-81

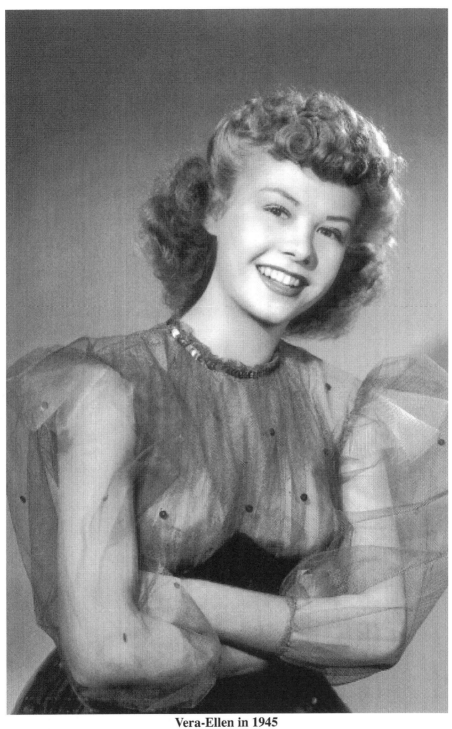

Vera-Ellen in 1945

Vera-Ellen:

Radio Credits

Major Bowes Original Amateur Hour (CBS)—January 21, 1937—She tap dances to "When You're Smiling."

Chesterfield Supper Club (NBC)—September 3, 1946—She gives an interview from the Miss America Pageant in Atlantic City. This may have been a show hosted by Perry Como.

Hi-Jinx (NBC)—September 9, 1946—Jinx Falkenberg interviews her about her dancing career.

Tony Awards (Mutual Broadcasting System)—March 28, 1948—Vera-Ellen joins Jessica Tandy, James Stewart, Henry Fonda and Basil Rathbone in interviews at the Second Annual Antoinette Perry Awards from the Grand Ballroom at the Waldorf-Astoria Hotel in New York City.

The Louella Parsons Show (ABC)—October 23, 1949—Gossip columnist Parsons interviews Rock Hudson and Vera-Ellen after their Mr. and Mrs. Oscar dress-up stunt.

Screen Writers Guild Annual Award Party (NBC)—February 5, 1950—Vera-Ellen performs a scene from *On the Town*.

MGM Musical Comedy Theater (Mutual Broadcasting System)—January 30, 1952 and repeated November 12, 1952—Vera-Ellen stars in a one-hour show called *Born to Dance*.

Martin and Lewis Show (NBC)—June 23, 1953—She is the sole guest star with Dean Martin and Jerry Lewis.

Bob Hope Show (NBC)—January 4-8, 1954—Vera-Ellen plays the Lady Editor of the Week on five consecutive broadcasts of Bob's 15-minute Monday to Friday program.

Bud's Bandwagon (Armed Forces Radio)—November 11, 1954—Bud Widom interviews Vera-Ellen and Danny Kaye at the Hollywood Premiere of *White Christmas*.

Nutrilite Show (NBC)—January 2, 1955—Dennis Day, popular singing tenor of *The Jack Benny Program* hosts a variety show with Vera-Ellen and Johnny Mercer as guests.

Vera-Ellen:

Television Credits

Toast of the Town—February 14, 1954 (CBS)—Ed Sullivan celebrates the 30th anniversary of MGM. Vera-Ellen participated in the opening production number.

Hollywood Premiere of A Star is Born—September 29, 1954—KTTV, Los Angeles. Vera-Ellen is interviewed by Jack Carson at the RKO Pantages Theater.

Lux Video Theater—November 4, 1954 (NBC)—Imperfect Lady was the program but Vera-Ellen was not in it, being instead interviewed between acts plugging *White Christmas.*

Colgate Variety Hour—June 13, 1955 (NBC)—Vera-Ellen performs an Apache dance. Charlton Heston hosts.

Art Linkletter's House Party–1955 (CBS)—date uncertain. Interview.

The Perry Como Show—Feb. 18, 1956 (NBC) 8 p.m. EST—guest star in special show saluting the release of the science fiction movie *Forbidden Planet*. Also appearing were Anne Francis and Robby the Robot (from the film), ventriloquist Paul Winchell with dummy Jerry Mahoney, actor Henry Fonda and famed black pop music group The Platters.

I've Got a Secret—May 22, 1957 (CBS)—Bill Cullen hosts Vera-Ellen as guest.

Art Linkletter's House Party—June 18, 1957 (CBS)—Interview.

Ford Theater—March 20, 1957 (ABC)—Vera-Ellen's only light comedy acting performance on television in "The Man Across the Hall" with Robert Sterling.

Washington Square—May 20, 1957 (NBC)—Vera-Ellen's only television color broadcast, dancing with host Ray Bolger.

Masquerade Party—1958 (month unknown, CBS or NBC)—Vera-Ellen guests as a snowman.

The Perry Como Show—November 22, 1958 (NBC)—Vera-Ellen dances to "Shall We Dance." Vera-Ellen's largest television audience exposure.

The Dinah Shore Chevy Show—February 15, 1959 (NBC)—Vera-Ellen's last known television or professional performance.

1945 studio portrait

Vera-Ellen:

Vera-Ellen Recordings

A Connecticut Yankee — cast recording may now be out of print. Show-Biz Records Album # 5601 A/B; AEI #1138

Deep in My Heart – Falling in Love With Love/You Took Advantage of Me (both songs cut from final print). MGM Composers Collection Laserdisc Set

Danny Kaye and Vera-Ellen in *White Christmas*

Vera-Ellen:

Filmography

Wonder Man (RKO, 1945)
Cast: Danny Kaye (Buzzy Bellew/Edwin Dingle); Virginia Mayo (Ellen Shanley); **Vera-Ellen** (Midge Mallon); Donald Woods (Monte Rossen); S.Z. Sakall (Schmidt); Allen Jenkins (Chimp); Edward Brophy (Torso); Steve Cochran (Ten-Grand Jackson); Otto Kurger (R.J. O'Brien); Richard Land; Natalie Schafer; Huntz Hall; Virginia Gilmore; Edward Gargan; Grant Mitchell; Giseal Werbiseck; Alice Mock; Mary Field; Aldo Franchetti; Maurice Cass; Luis Alberni; Noel Cravat; Nick Thompson; Nino Pipitone; Baldo Minuti; James Falvin; Jack Norton; Frank Orth; Charles Irwin; Cecil Cunningham; Eddie Dunn; Byron Foulger; Margie Stewart; Frank Melton; Barbara La Rene; Albert Ruiz; Willard Van Simons; Chester Clute; Eddie Kane; Ray Teal; Leon Belasco; Carol Haney; Ruth Valmy; Margie Stewart; Alma Carroll; Georiga Lange; Karen X. Gaylord; Mary Moore; Gloria Delson; Deannie Best; Mary Meade

Credits: Producer: Samuel Goldwyn; Director; H. Bruce Humberstone; Writers: Don Hartman, Melville Shavelson; Philip Rapp, Jack Jevne and Eddie Moran; Based on a Story by Arthur Sheekman; Cinematography: Victor Milner and William Snyder; Editor: Daniel Mandell; Music: Ray Heindorf; Music Director: Louis Forbes; Art Design: Ernst Fegte and McClure Capps; Special Effects: John P. Fulton; Set Design: Howard Bristol; Choregoraphy: John Wray; Academy Award Nominations for Best Score (Lou Forbes and Ray Heindorf); Best Song (David Rose and Leo Robin); Best Sound (Gordon Sawyer); Academy Award for Best Visual Effects, John Fulton and A.W. Johns; Technicolor, 98 minutes

The Kid from Brooklyn (RKO, 1946)
Cast: Danny Kaye (Burliegh Sullivan); Virginia Mayo (Polly Pringle); **Vera-Ellen** (Susie Sullivan); Walter Abel (Gabby Sloan); Eve Arden (Ann Westley); Steve Cochran (Speed MacFarlane); Lionel Stander (Spider Schultz); Fay Bainter (Mrs. E. Winthrop LeMoyne); Clarence Kolb (Wilbur Austin); Victor Cutler; Charles Cane; Jerome Cowan; Don Wilson; Knox Manning; Kay Thompson; Johnny Downs; Pierre Watkin; Frank Riggi; Karen X. Gaylor; Ruth Valmy; Shirley Ballard; Virginia Belmont; Betty Cargyle; Jean Cronin; Vonne Lester; Diana Mumby; Mary Simpson; Virginia Thorpe; Tyra Vaughn; Kismi Stefan; Betty Alexander; Martha Montgomery; Joyce MacKenzie; Helen Kimball; Jan Bryant; Donna Hamilton; Frank Moran; John Indrisano; Almeda Fowler; Snub Pollard; Robert Wade Chatterton; Torben Meyer; William Forrest; Jack Norton; Billy Nelson; Ralph Dunn; Billy Wayne; George Chandler; Betty Blythe; James Carlisle; Robert Strong; William Newell; Tom Quinn; Billy Bletcher; George Sherwood; Donald Kerr; Jack Roper; Steve Taylor; Al Hill; Jay Easton; Syd Saylor; Eddie Hart; Eric Wilton; Alex Pollard; Billy Benedict; Mary Forbes; Hal K. Dawson; Dulce Daye; Jack Gargan; Lester Dorr; Jack Cheatham

Credits: Producer: Samuel Goldwyn; Director: Norman Z. McLeod; Writers: Don Hartman and Melville Shavelson; Based on the Screenplay by Grover Jones, Frank Butler and Richard Connell, From the Play *The Milky Way* by Lynn Root and Harry

A publicity portrait of Vera-Ellen from *The Kid From Brooklyn*

Vera-Ellen:

June Haver, Frank Latimore, Vera-Ellen and Charles Smith in *Three Little Girls in Blue*

Clork; Cinematography: Gregg Toland; Editor: Daniel Mandell; Music Director: Carmen Dragon; Art Design: Perry Ferguson and Stewart Chaney; Set Design: Howard Bristol; Choreography: Bernard Pearce; Technicolor; 114 minutes

Three Little Girls in Blue (Fox, 1946)
Cast: June Haver (Pam); George Montgomery (Van Damm Smith); Vivian Blaine (Liz); Celeste Holm (Miriam); **Vera-Ellen** (Myra); Frank Latimore (Steve); Charles Smith (Mike); Charles Halton (Hoskins); Ruby Dandridge (Mammy); Thurston Hall (Colonel); Clinton Rosemond; William Forrest, Jr.; Theresa Harris; Eddie Acuff; Al Murphy; Roger Neury; Coleen Gray; Smiki Whitfield; Jesse Graves; Don Garner

Credits: Producer: Mack Gordon; Director: H. Bruce Humberstone; Writers: Valentine Davies; Brown Holmes; Lynn Starling; Robert Ellis; Helen Logan; Based on the Play *Three Blind Mice* by Stephen Powys; Cinematography: Ernest Palmer; Editor: Barbara McLean; Music: Josef Myrow and Mack Gordon: Music Director: Alfred Newman; Art Design: Lyle Wheeler and Joseph C. Wright; Costumes: Bonnie Cashin; Choreography: Seymour Felix and Babe Pearce; Technicolor; 90 minutes

Carnival in Costa Rica (Fox, 1947)
Cast: Dick Haymes (Jeff Stephens); **Vera-Ellen** (Luisa Molina); Cesar Romero (Pepe Castro); Celeste Holm (Celeste); Anne Revere (Elsa Molina); J. Carroll Naish (Rico

The Magic and the Mystery   235

Celeste Holm, J. Carroll Naish and Vera-Ellen at the wrap party of *Carnival in Costa Rica*

Molina); Pedro de Cordoba (Mr. Castro); Barbara Whiting (Maria); Nestor Paiva (Father Rafael); Fritz Feld; Tommy Ivo; Mimi Aguglia; Lecuona Cuban Boys; Anna Demetrio; Severo Lopez; William Edmunds; Soledad Jiminez; Alfredo Sabato; Martin Garralaga

Credits: Producer: William A. Bacher; Director: Gregory Ratoff; Writers: John Larkin, Samuel Hoffenstein and Elizabeth Reinhardt; Cinematographer: Harry Jackson; Editor: William Reynolds: Music: Ernest Lecuona; Choreography: Leonide Massine; Songs: Al Stillman, Sunny Skylar, Harry Ruby and Ernesto Lecuona; Technicolor; 96 minutes

Three Little Words (MGM, 1950)
Cast: Fred Astaire (Bert Kalmar); Red Skelton (Harry Ruby); **Vera-Ellen** (Jessie Brown Kelmar); Arlene Dahl (Eileen Percy); Keenan Wynn (Charlie Kope); Gale Robbins (Terry Lordel); Gloria DeHaven (Mrs. Carter DeHaven); Phil Regan (Himself); Harry Shannon (Clanahan); Debbie Reynolds (Helen Kane); Paul Harvey (Al Masters); Carleton Carpenter (Dan Healy); George Metkovich; Harry Mendoza; Billy Gray; Pat Flaherty; Pierre Watkin; Syd Saylor; Elzie Emanuel; Sherry Hall; Pat Williams; Charles Wagenheim; Tony Taylor; Phyllis Kennedy; Donald Kerry; Beverly Michaels; Bert Davidson; William Tannen; George Sherwood; Harry Barris; Alex Gerry; Helen Kane; Anita Ellis

Frank Sinatra, Betty Garrett, Jules Munshin, Ann Miller, Gene Kelly and Vera-Ellen in *On the Town*

Credits: Producer: Jack Cummings; Director: Richard Thorpe; Writer: George Wells;: Cinematography: Harry Jackson; Editor: Ben Lewis; Music Director: Andre Previn; Art Design: Cedirc Gibbons and Urie McCleary; Choreography: Hermes Pan; Songs: Bert Kalmar and Harry Ruby; Academy Award Nomination for Best Score, Andre Previn; Technicolor; 102 minutes

On the Town (MGM, 1949)
Cast: Gene Kelly (Gabey); Frank Sinatra (Chip); Betty Garrett (Brunhilde Esterhazy); Ann Miller (Claire Huddesen); Jules Munshin (Ozzie); **Vera-Ellen** (Ivy Smith); Flo-

rence Bates (M. Dilyovska); Alice Pearce (Lucy Shmeeler); George Meader; Bern Hoffman; Lester Dorr; Bea Benaderet; Walter Baldwin; Don Brodie; Sid Melton; Robert B. Williams; Tom Dugan; Murray Alper; Hans Conried; Claire Carleton; Dick Wessel; William Phillips; Frank Hagny; Carol Haney; Eugene Borden; Judy Holliday

Credits: Producer: Arthur Freed; Directors: Gene Kelly and Stanley Donen; Writers: Adolph Green and Betty Comden: Based on the Musical Play by Betty Comden, Adolph Green and Leonard Bernstein; From the Ballet *Fancy Free* by Jerome Robbins; Cinematography: Harold Rosson; Editor: Ralph E. Winters; Music: Leonard Bernstein, Roger Edens, Saul Chaplin and Conrad Salinger; Music Director: Lennie Hayton and Roger Edens; Art Design: Cedric Gibbons and Jack Martin Smith; Special Effects: Warren Newcombe; Set Design: Edwin B. Willis and Jack D. Moore; Costumes: Helen Rose; Makeup: Jack Dawn; Choreography: Gene Kelly and Stanley Donen; Academy Award for Best Score, Roger Edens and Lennie Hayton; 98 minutes

Words and Music (MGM, 1948)
Cast: Perry Como (Eddie Lorrison Anders); Michey Rooney: Lorenz Hart; Ann Sothern (Joyce Harmon); Tom Drake (Richard Rodgers); Betty Garrett (Peggy Lorgan McNeil); Janet Leigh (Dorothy Feiner); Marshall Thompson (Herbert Fields); Jeanette Nolan (Mrs. Hart); Richard Quine (Ben Feiner); Clinton Sundberg; Harry Antrim; Ilka Gruning; Emory Parnell; Helen Spring; Edward Earle; Cyd Charisse; With Special Guest Appearances by: Judy Garland; June Allyson; Gene Kelly; **Vera-Ellen**; Mel Torme

Credits: Producer: Arthur Freed; Director: Norman Taurog; Writers: Fred Finklehoffe and Ben Feiner, Jr.; Based on a Story by Guy Bolton and Jean Holloway; Cinematography: Charles Rosher and Harry Stradling; Editors:Albert Akst and Ferris Webster; Music Director: Lennie Hayton; Art Design: Cedric Gibbons and Jack Martin Smith; Special Effects: Warren Newcombe; Set Design: Edwin B. Willis and Richard Pefferle; Costumes: Helen Rose and Valles; Makeup: Jack Dwan; Choregoraphy: Robert Alton; Technicolor; 119 minutes

Love Happy (UA, 1949)
Cast: Groucho Marx (Detective Sam Grunion); Harpo Marx; Chico Marx; Illona Massey (M. Egilichi); **Vera-Ellen** (Maggie Phillips); Marion Hutton (Bunny Dolan); Raymond Burr (Alphonse Zoto); Bruce Gordon (Hannibal Zoto); Melville Cooper (Throckmorton); Leon Belasco (Mr. Lyons); Paul Valentine (Mike Johnson); Eric Blore (Mackinaw); Marilyn Monroe (Grunion's Client)

Credits: Producer: Lester Cowan; Director: David Miller; Writers. Frank Tashlin and Mac Benoff; Based on a Story by Harpo Marx; Cinematography: William Mellor; Editors: Basil Wrangell and Al Joseph; Music Director: Paul J. Smith; Art Design: Gabriel Scognamillo; Special Effects: Howard Anderson; Choreography: Billy Daniel; Black and White; 91 minutes

Happy Go Lovely (RKO, 1951)
Cast: David Niven (B.G. Bruno); **Vera-Ellen** (Janet Jones); Cesar Romero (John Frost);

Bobby Howes (Charlie); Diana Hart (Mae); Sandra Dorne (Betty); Gordon Jackson (Paul Tracey); Barbara Couper (M. Amanda); Henry Hewitt (Dodds); Gladys Henson; Hugh Dempster; Joyce Carey; John Laurie; Wylie Watson; Kay Kendall; Joan Heal; Hector Ross; Ambrosine Phillpotts; Molly Urquhart; David Lober; Jonathon Lucas; Jack Billings; Douglas Scott and His Debonair Boys; Rolf Alexander; Ian Stuart; Leon Biedryski

Credits: Producer: Marcel Hellman; Director: H. Bruce Humberstone; Writers: Val Guest and Arthur Macrae; Based on a Story by F. Dammann and H. Rosenfeld; Cinematography: Erwin Hillier; Editor: Bert Bates; Music: Mischa Spoliansky; Music Director: Louis Levy; Art Design: John Howell; Choreography: Jack Billings and Pauline Grant; Songs: Mischa Spoliansky and Jack Fishman; Technicolor; 97 minutes

The Belle of New York (MGM, 1952)
Cast: Fred Astaire (Charlie Hill); **Vera-Ellen** (Angela Bonfils); Marjorie Main (Mrs. Phines Hill); Keenan Wynn (Max Ferris); Alice Pearce (Elsie Wilkins); Clinton Sundberg (Gilfred Spivak) Gale Robbins (Dixie McCoy); Lisa Ferraday (Frenchie); Henry Slate (Clancy); Carol Brewster, Meredith Leeds; Lyn Wilde; Buddy Roosevelt; Roger Davis; Dick Wessel; Percy Hilton; Tom Dugan

Credits: Producer: Arthur Freed; Director: Charles Walters; Writers: Robert O'Brien, Chester Erskine and Irving Elinson; Based on a Play by Hugh Morton; Cinematographer: Robert Planck; Editor: Albert Akst; Music Director: Adolph Deutsch; Art Designer: Cedric Gibbons and Jack Martin Smith; Set Design: Edwin B. Willis, Richard Pefferle; Costumes: Helen Rose and Gile Steele; Choreography: Robert Alton; Special Effects: Warren Newcombe and Irving G. Ries; Songs: Johnny Mercer, Harry Warren and Roger Edens; Technicolor; 82 minutes

Call Me Madam (Fox, 1953)
Cast: Ethel Merman (Mrs. Sally Adams); Donald O'Connor (Kenneth); **Vera-Ellen** (Princess Maria); George Sanders (Cosmo Constantine); Billy De Wolfe (Pemberton Maxwell); Helmut Dantine (Prince Hugo); Walter Slezak (Tantinnin); Steven Geray (Sebastian); Ludwig Stossel (Grand Duke); Lilia Skala (Grand Duchess); Charles Dingle (Senator Brockway); Emory Parnell (Senator Gallagher); Percy Helton (Senator Wilkins); Leon Belasco; Oscar Beregi, Jr.; Nestor Paiva; Sid Marion; Torben Meyer; Richard Garrick; Walter Woolf King; Olan Soule; John Wengraf; Fritz Feld; Erno Verebes; Hannelore Axman; Lal Chand Mehra

Credits: Producer: Sol C. Siegel; Director: Walter Lang; Writer Arthur Sheekman; Based on the Broadway Musical by Howard Lindsay and Russel Crouse; Cinematography: Leon Shamroy; Editor: Robert Simpson; Music: Irving Berlin; Music Director: Alfred newman; Art Design: Lyle Wheeler and John de Cuir; Special Effects: Ray Kellogg; Set Design: Walter M. Scott; Costumes: Irene Sharaff; Makeup: Ben Nye; Choreography: Robert Alton; Nominated for Academy Award for Best Score and Best Costume Design; Technicolor; 114 minutes

White Christmas

Big Leaguer (MGM, 1953)
Cast: Edward G. Robinson (John B. "Hans" Lobert); **Vera-Ellen** (Christy); Jeff Richards (Adam Polachuk); Richard Jaeckel (Bobby Bronson); William Campbell (Julie Davis); Carl Hubbell (Himself); Paul Langton (Brian McLennan); Lalo Rios (Chuy Agilar); Bill Crandall (Tippy Mitchell); Frank Ferguson (Wally Mitchell); John McKee (Dale Alexander); Mario Siletti (Mr. Polachuk); Al Campanis; Bob Trocolor; Tony Ravish

Credits: Producer: Matthew Rapf; Director: Robert Adrich; Writer: Herbert Baker; Based on a Story by John McNulty and Louis Morheim; Cinematography: William Mellor; Editor: Ben Lewis; Music: Alberto Colombo; Black and White; 70 minutes; unavailable on DVD or video

White Christmas (Paramount, 1954)
Cast: Bing Crosby (Bob Wallace); Danny Kaye (Phil Davis); Rosemary Clooney (Betty Haynes); **Vera-Ellen** (Judy Haynes); Dean Jagger (General Waverly); Mary Wickes (Emma); John Brascia (Joe); Anne Whitfield (Susan); Richard Shannon; Grady Sutton; Sig Runmann; Robert Crosson; Herb Vigran: Dick Keene; Johnny Grant; Gavin Gordon; Marcel de la Brosse; James Parnell; Percy Helton; Elizabeth Holmes; Barrie Chase; I. Stanford Jolley; George Chakiris; Mike Pat Donovan; Glen Cargyle; Lorraine Crawford; Joan Bayley; Les Clark; Ernest Flatt; Bea Allen

Credits: Producer: Robert Emmett Dolan; Director: Michael Curtiz; Writers: Norman Krasna, Norman Panama and Melvin Frank; Cinematography: Loyal Griggs; Editor: Frank Bracht; Music Director: Joseph J. Lilley; Art Design: Hal Pereira and Roland Anderson; Set Design: Sam Comer and Grace Gregory; Costumes: Edith Head; Choreography: Robert Alton; Academy Award Nomination for Best Song ("Count Your Blessings") by Irving Berlin; VistaVision, 120 minutes

Let's Be Happy (Allied Artists, 1957)
Cast: **Vera-Ellen** (Jeannie MacLean); Tony Martin (Stanley Smith); Robert Flemyng (Lord James MacNairn); Zena Marshall (Helene); Helen Horton (Sadie Whitelaw); Beckett Bould (Reverend MacDonald); Alfred Burke; Vernon Greeves; Richard Molinas; Eugene Deckers; Russell Waters; Paul Young; Peter Sinclair; Magda Miller; Brian Oulton; Guy Middleton; Katherine Kath; Charles Carson; Jock McKay; Michel Anthony; Jean Cadell; Gordon Jackson; Carl Duering; Molly Weir; Jameson Clark; Ewan Roberts

Credits: Producer: Marcel Hellman; Director: Henry Levin; Writer: Diana Morgan and Dorothy Cooper; Based on the Play *Jeannie* by Aimee Stuart; Cinematography: Erwin Hillier; Editor: E.B. Jarvis; Music: Nicholas Brodszky; Music Director: Louis Levy; Art Design: Terence Verity; Costumes: Anna Duse; Choreography: Pauline Grant and Alfred Rodrigues; aka '*Wee' Jeannie*; Technicolor; 107 minutes

That's Dancing! (MGM, 1985)
MGM musical clips of Vera-Ellen

That's Entertainment! III (MGM, 1994)
Vera-Ellen finally made the cut in scenes from *On the Town*.

Gene Kelly: Anatomy of a Dancer (TV, 2002)
Clips of Vera-Ellen and Gene Kelly

Vera-Ellen:

Vera-Ellen Websites on the Internet

Angela's Vera-Ellen Page (Angela Boyko)
    http://www.geocities.com/soho/4439/Vera_Ellen.html
Michael Day Vera-Ellen Website
    http://www.gorilla.net/~mikeday/veraellen/
The Vera-Ellen Shrine (Janine Gastineau)
    http://pw1.netcom.com/~budazach/Vera-Ellen.html

Vera-Ellen:

About the Author

David Soren is Regents' Professor of Classics at the University of Arizona and a Fellow of Great Britain's Royal Institute of International Affairs and the Johns Hopkins School of Advanced International Studies. He was named by *Esquire* magazine as one of their Outstanding Young Americans in the Field of Science and his archaeological discoveries in Classical Archaeology have been named among the 70 most important of the 20th century by Oxford University. Recently he was named an Honorary Italian Citizen for contributions to Italian archaeology. He is the author of 11 books and over 50 scholarly articles on art history, archaeology, film and dance, and was a former singing and dancing cast member on CBS' *Horn and Hardart Children's Hour*.

Vera-Ellen:

Index

A

Aldrich, Robert 139
Allyson, June 31
Alton, Robert
  30, 33, 39, 77, 78, 101, 117, 122, 126, 142, 144, 146, 150, 160
Anderson, John Murray 33
Anderson, Richard 136
Arden, Eve 31
Art Linkletter's House Party 160
Astaire, Fred 11, 29, 36, 37, 50, 56, 60, 79, 84, 92, 94, 103, 108, 112, 113,
  114, 115, 116, 118, 119, 121, 130, 161, 185, 187, 190, 192, 198, 205, 206, 214, 217, 219

B

Babbit, Margery Belcher 40
Bacher, William A. 62
Balanchine, George 45, 79
Band Wagon 37
Barstow, Richard 77
Belle of New York, The 9, 79, 99, 108, 113-120, 130, 134, 135, 141, 164, 171, 183,
  187, 190, 192, 200, 205, 206, 219
Belmore, Bertha 39
Berle, Milton 48, 75
Berlin, Irving 122, 125, 142, 144, 150
Bernstein, Leonard 83, 84, 180
Best Foot Forward 171
Big Leaguer 135, 138, 139, 140, 141, 142, 240
Billings, Jack 103, 105, 239
Blaine, Vivian 58, 92, 120, 235
Blair, Betsy 36
Bolger, Ray 11, 36, 37, 39, 44, 79, 118, 122, 129, 130, 169
Boswell, Eve 103
Brascia, John 142, 144, 147, 148, 160, 184
Bremer, Lucille 36
Burr, Raymond 90
By Jupiter 36, 37, 38, 45, 46, 47, 118, 169
Byfield, Ernie, Jr. 136

C

Caesar, Sid 37
Caesar's Hour 37
Cahn, Sammy 55
Calhoun, Rory 136, 151
Call Me Madam 30, 33, 122-138, 142, 149, 156, 200
Cantor, Eddie 48, 54
Carnival in Costa Rica 62-74, 213
Caron, Leslie 12, 83, 97
Carter, Janis 36
Casa Manana 28, 29, 30, 37, 77
Champion, Gower 40, 120
Champion, Marge 40, 120
Charisse, Cyd 11, 12, 55, 97, 109, 121, 133, 198, 205
Chatterton, Ruth 131
Chevy Show, The 172
Clooney, Rosemary 142, 145, 147
Cochran, Steve 54, 57
Colgate Variety Hour 160
Comden, Betty 72, 84
Connecticut Yankee, A 40, 41, 43, 44, 45, 47, 112, 204
Coyne, Jeanne 87
Crosby, Bing 142, 144, 147
Cullen, Bill 168
Curtis, Margaret 92
Curtiz, Michael 144

D

Da Pron, Louis 162
Dahl, Arlene 94
Daniel, Billy 91
Dantine, Helmut 125, 138
Day, Doris 16, 97, 112, 171, 181, 182
Day, Michael 8, 10, 63, 74
De Haven, Gloria 77
De Wolfe, Billy 124
Deep in My Heart 142, 231
Dennington, Bill 10, 135, 178, 179, 182, 183, 184, 189, 211
Dennis, Jo 10, 185, 188, 190, 214
Dennison, Terry 9, 10
Dixon, Lee 32
Donen, Stanley 84, 120
Doolittle, Jimmy 131
Dorsey, Tommy 68
Douglas, Mike 178

Drake, Tom 142
Du Barry Was a Lady 31
Dumke, Ralph 37

E

Eggert, Marta 32
Ellers, Dorothy 55
Ellis, Anita 95, 113
Evans, Joan 120

F

Falkenberg, Jinx 55, 61
Felix, Seymour 59
Fine, Sylvia 52
Flemyng, Robert 165
Ford Theater 169
Forrest, Sally 97, 98, 205
Fosse, Bob 120
Freed, Arthur 83, 113, 206
Freedley, Vinton 30
Friday, Pat 64

G

Gabor, Zsa Zsa 97
Gae, Nadine 39
Gallagher, Helen 180
Garrett, Betty 8, 40, 43, 84, 184, 204
Gershwin, Ira 120
Gibbons, Cedric 113
Gibbs, Georgia 115
Godfrey, Arthur 75
Goldwyn, Samuel 44, 45, 48, 71, 198
Gordon, Mack 58
Grable, Betty 49, 73, 77, 99, 122
Grady, Billy 169
Graham, Ronald 37
Granger, Farley 136
Grant, Pauline 103, 166
Grayson, Kathryn 40
Green, Adolph 72, 84
Guest, Val 8, 98, 100, 101, 103, 167
Gully, Richard 150, 151, 213

H

Hammerstein, Oscar 31
Haney, Carol 87
Happy Go Lovely 8, 58, 92-112 156, 163, 164, 167, 200, 213, 219
Hart, Lorenz 31, 33, 38, 41, 42, 45
Haver, June 58, 73, 77
Haydn, Richard 170
Haymes, Dick 62, 63, 68
Head, Edith 150
Hellman, Marcel 99, 163
Hepburn, Katharine 36
Hessler Dance Studio 16, 19, 22, 181, 182
Hessler, Harry 181
Hessler, Herman 181
Higher and Higher 31, 32, 33, 39, 45
Highland Fling, A 92
Hightower, Lewis 39, 40
Hightower, Robert 33, 34, 35, 39, 42, 46, 47, 68, 71, 135, 138, 157, 195, 197
Hightower, William 39
Holm, Celeste 59, 62, 69, 210
Hope, Bob 142, 143
Hopper, Hedda 71, 130
Hudson, Rock 98, 105, 134, 135, 136, 200
Hujer, Flower 39, 40
Humberstone, Bruce 58
Hutton, Betty 44, 77, 94
Hutton, June 50

I

I Am a Camera 142
I've Got a Secret 168

J

Jack Paar Show, The 46
Jaeckel, Richard 139
Johnston, Bob 8, 9, 219
Johnston, Johnny 115

K

Kalmar, Bert 94
Kalmus, Nathalie 59
Kaye, Danny 48, 52, 54, 56, 76, 92, 130, 142, 143, 146, 147, 148, 161, 206
Keel, Howard 40, 121, 139
Keeler, Ruby 32, 180

Kelly, Gene 11, 12, 30, 36, 57, 77-92, 103-105, 109, 120, 122, 129, 142, 161, 168, 185, 198, 203, 205, 219
Kelly, Shirley 214
Kern, Jerome 31
Kid from Brooklyn, The 44, 48, 54, 55, 56, 57, 58, 73, 94
King of Jazz 33

L

Laine, Frankie 55
Lane, Burton 120
Lang, Walter 125, 128
Latimore, Frank 59
Leave it to Me 30
Lecuona, Ernesto 62, 69
Let's Be Happy 162-168, 207
Levant, Oscar 37
Levin, Henry 167
Levine, J.D. 17
Lewis, Ted 27, 28
Lober, David 104
Louella Parsons 144, 151
Love Happy 89
Lucas, Jonathan 104, 105
Lux Video Theater 151
Lyles, A.C. 8, 53, 75, 78, 84, 89, 107, 109, 110, 133, 134, 136, 141, 150, 172, 174, 177, 187, 191, 193, 200, 206, 211, 212, 217
Lynn, Betty 213

M

M.G.M. Musical Comedy Theater 115
MacMurray, Fred 74
Magic Carpet Revue, New York-Paris-Paradise 158
Main, Marjorie 113, 120
Major Bowes 26
Major Bowes' Amateur Hour 24
Major Bowes' Amateur Theater of the Air 26
"Man Across the Hall, The" 169
Markett, Russell 33
Martin, Mary 31
Martin, Tony 77, 160, 162, 164, 166, 167, 172
Marx Brothers 89, 90, 91
Marx, Harpo 91
Masquerade Party 169, 172
Massine, Leonide 62, 63, 66

Mauer, Fred 8, 13, 131, 135, 141, 174, 181, 182, 184, 197, 199, 200, 201, 211, 212, 213, 214, 219, 220,
Maurer, Julia 64, 131, 211
Maurer, Mark 214, 215
Maurer, Mary 212, 215, 220
Maurer, Toddy 12, 64, 134, 214, 215, 216
Mayer, Louis B. 82,120
Mayo, Virginia 48, 54, 55, 56, 58
McCracken, Joan 43
McLeod, Norman Z. 54
McMahon, Jere 43
Meles, Jose 46
Mercer, Johnny 113
Merman, Ethel 33, 122, 123, 124
Miller, Ann 11, 12, 84, 89, 97, 110, 113, 133, 190, 204
Miller, Dean 136, 137, 138
Miller, Marilyn 73, 74, 77
Monroe, Marilyn 89, 90, 118, 160
Montalban, Ricardo 120, 121
Montgomery, George 59
Moore, Constance 37
Morgan, Diana 167
Morgan, Henry 168
Munshin, Jules 83, 84
Murphy, Paul 53, 182
Murray, John Anderson 29

N

Nelson, Miriam 37
Nesbitt, Robert 158
Niven, David 98, 99, 100
No, No, Nanette 180
Nutrilite Show 158

O

O'Connor, Donald 8, 11, 77, 89, 121-130, 142, 161, 172, 183, 200, 215
Oklahoma! 32, 43
On the Town 46, 79,-89, 120, 180, 199, 200, 203, 204, 219
On Your Toes 45, 67, 79
Osato, Sono 43

P

Pal Joey 37
Pan, Hermes 92, 101, 187
Panaieff, Michael 178, 184, 188, 211

Panama Hattie 33, 36, 39, 77
Pearce, Alice 84, 115, 120
Pearce, Bernard 55, 159
Perry Como Show, The 160, 171
Porter, Cole 31
Powell, Eleanor 12, 29, 49, 50, 57, 133, 187
Powell, Jane 142, 158
Powers, Stefanie 213

R

Rapf, Matthew 139
Ratoff, Gregory 67, 68, 75
Raye, Martha 48, 59, 94
Reynolds, Debbie 97, 121, 158, 198, 204, 205, 214
Richards, Jeff 139, 140, 141
Robbins, Jerome 84
Robinson, Bill 32, 55
Robinson, Edward G. 138, 141
Rockettes 33
Rodgers, Richard 31, 33, 38, 40, 41, 45
Rogers, Ginger 11, 12, 73, 86, 96, 112, 169, 219
Rohe, Alma 8, 14, 17, 23, 27, 34, 67, 72, 82, 134, 136, 155, 156, 173, 175, 178, 187, 200, 201
Rohe, Herman 13
Rohe, Martin 13, 14, 92
Rohe, Mary 64, 74
Romero, Cesar 62, 67, 69, 98, 99, 100, 213
Rooney, Mickey 42
Rose, Billy 28, 29
Rose, David 50
Rothschild, Victor 151, 152, 176, 189, 211, 213
Rothschild, Victoria-Ellen 173, 174
Ruby, Harry 62, 94
Russell, Betty 55

S

Sanders, George 124, 125
Schary, Dore 120
Schlader, Jim 46, 47
Schnee, Charles 139
Scott, Douglas 105
Secret Life of Walter Mitty, The 58
Segal, Vivienne 42
Severin, Russ 138
Sharaff, Irene 122, 123

The Magic and the Mystery

Shirley Temple 23, 32, 54, 60, 61, 78
Shore, Dinah 48, 172
Shoup, Howard 159
Sidney, George 34, 68, 77, 173, 178, 188, 212, 213
Sinatra, Frank 24, 50, 68, 89, 160
Singin' in the Rain 56, 64, 97, 123
Skelton, Red 94, 98
"Slaughter on Tenth Avenue" 30, 31, 78, 79, 103-105, 127, 130, 182
Slezak, Walter 125
Smith, Charles 59, 60
Smith, Grace 214
Stabile, Trudy 145
Stack, Robert 153
Stedman, Dale 65
Stewart, Carol 59
Stordahl, Axel 50
Stratton, Charles 43
Strickling, Howard 120
Stuart, Aimée 162
Styne, Jule 55

T

Temple, Shirley 23, 32, 54, 60, 61, 78
That's Dancing 96, 183
That's Entertainment, Part II 182
That's Entertainment! 182, 183
Thompson, Julian F 36
Three Little Girls in Blue 40, 58-62, 69, 71-73, 76, 146
Three Little Words 79, 92-97, 100, 103, 219
Too Many Girls 31
Twain, Mark 40

U

Up in Arms 48

V

Venuta, Benay 37
Very Warm for May 31

W

Walters, Charles 116, 120
Warren, Harry 113, 171
Warrior's Husband 36
Washington Square 116, 169

White Christmas 30, 94, 130, 142-158, 180, 206, 217, 219
Willson, Henry 134, 136
Wiman, Dwight 39
Winchell, Walter 39
Windsor, Marie 8, 134, 157, 173, 174, 175, 196, 197, 200, 202, 211, 213, 217
Wonder Man 19, 48, 49, 50, 51, 52, 58, 94, 99, 113
Words and Music 30, 36, 42, 77, 80, 204, 219
Wray, John 50
Wynn, Keenan 113, 120

Y

Yolanda and the Thief 36

Z

Zorina, Vera 32, 45, 67, 73, 79

Made in the USA
San Bernardino, CA
11 January 2013